April 2011

Portrait of Dōgen Viewing the Moon
(Hōkyō-ji, Fukui Prefecture)

Moon in a Dewdrop

WRITINGS OF

Zen Master Dōgen

EDITED BY KAZUAKI TANAHASHI

Translated by
Robert Aitken, Reb Anderson, Ed Brown,
Norman Fischer, Arnold Kotler, Daniel Leighton,
Lew Richmond, David Schneider, Kazuaki Tanahashi,
Katherine Thanas, Brian Unger, Mel Weitsman,
Dan Welch, and Philip Whalen

NORTH POINT PRESS
Farrar, Straus and Giroux
New York

North Point Press
A division of Farrar, Straus and Giroux
18 West 18th Street, New York 10011

Library of Congress catalog card number: 84-62309
Paperback ISBN-13: 978-0-86547-186-3
Paperback ISBN-10: 0-86547-186-X

Designed by David Eullen

www.fsgbooks.com

21   23   24   22

Preface and Acknowledgments

Twenty essays from Dōgen's lifework, *Treasury of the True Dharma Eye* (Shō-bōgenzō), constitute the main portion of this book. Four important texts originally written as independent works are also included, along with a selection of Dōgen's poems.

Japan's foremost religious thinker and prose writer, Dōgen has a unique and often paradoxical style. To clarify the sequence of thoughts and subjects, each essay is divided into numbered sections. The essays are grouped in parts with the following emphases: (One) practical instructions, (Two) works of philosophical interest, (Three) works rich in poetic imagery, and (Four) works that deal with transmission of the teaching. The poems are presented in Part Five.

A glossary of terms, names, and symbolism related to Dōgen's writings follows the Appendix. Since Dōgen was probably the most systematic elucidator of the Zen tradition, the glossary may be useful in reading other Buddhist texts as well as Dōgen's. The sources of Dōgen's quotations are indicated in the notes whenever possible.

The translation has been done in fortunate circumstances. All my collaborators have been practicing students at San Francisco Zen Center and its affiliates, Green Gulch Farm and Berkeley Zen Center. Many of them have experienced monastic practice in Tassajara with the late Shunryū Suzuki-roshi, founder of Zen Center, and have been teachers of Zen meditation.

As a guest scholar at Zen Center, I shared study and work with them, and this collaboration continuously deepened my understanding of Dōgen's texts and later commentaries.

This project was fully supported by the Zen Center community and Zentatsu Baker-roshi, who was abbot during the period when most of the work was done. I am especially grateful to Baker-roshi, who originally invited me to come to Zen Center in 1977, and whose vision and generosity made this undertaking possible.

I would like to express gratitude to Robert Aitken-roshi, leader of Diamond Sangha in Honolulu and Maui Zendo, for permitting us to revise and publish the text of "Genjō Kōan," which he and I originally translated in 1965. That translation was revised by Taizan Maezumi-roshi and Francis Dojun Cook, whose work has been a helpful guide for our new version, entitled "Actualizing the Fundamental Point." I thank Maezumi-roshi also for enriching Dōgen scholarship in the West by organizing the International Dōgen Conferences.

Some of the translations have been used as texts for classes in Mountain Gate Study Center. The discussions in these classes have greatly enriched the revised translations. It has been encouraging to my collaborators and myself that Dainin Katagiri-roshi used our translations for a series of lectures at Minnesota Zen Meditation Center. "Plum Blossoms" was revised at Zen Community of New York as a part of their Zen practice in the fall retreat of 1982; discussion with Tetsugen Bernard Glassman-sensei, Yuho Helen Glassman, Muryo Peter Matthiessen, Mitsunen Lou Nordstrom, and Kosho Ishikawa was extremely pleasant and instructive to me.

Although I worked with one partner on each essay, all parts of the text have gone through many stages and have been reviewed and worked on by the other collaborators. Norman Fischer and David Schneider worked intensely with me for some months in the last stages of revision. Mel Weitsman and Daniel Leighton helped with the definitions in the glossary.

Carl Bielefeldt, Peter Coyote, and Paul Hawken, along with many others, have given valuable suggestions for improvement of the earlier manuscript. Karl Ray and Tom Cabarga went through the Introduction in its final stage. My wife, Linda Hess, has been my joyful tutor in the English language.

Credit for the fine production of the book must be given to the North Point Press staff, including editor Thomas Christensen and designer David

Bullen. Kate Gross's copyediting improved the accuracy of the text. Kate and Carol Christensen proofread the galleys. At Zen Center, Michael Wenger and Elaine Maisner assisted throughout the production process. Michael, Elaine, and Richard Jaffe helped in proofreading. Katherine Haimson did the major work on the index, which was checked by Graham Leggat; Kate Moses at North Point provided considerable assistance. Peter Bailey designed the maps. Komazawa University Library in Tokyo provided photographs. Toshiatsu Miyazaki helped obtain reproductions of the pictures. Rev. Myo Lahey checked the Sanskrit words for correct transliteration. Corrections for the revised edition were coordinated by Taigen Daniel Leighton.

Finally I would like to thank Gary Snyder. His enthusiasm in supporting our work, and in suggesting to Jack Shoemaker that North Point Press might publish it, has brought the reader and all of us together here—in the presence of Dōgen.

Kazuaki Tanahashi

Contents

Abbreviations, Transliteration, Systems of Counting, and Capitalization

ABBREVIATIONS

*	See Glossary for terms with asterisks
ALZSME	*Arrayed Lamps of the Zen School Merged in Essence**
FLMS	*Five Lamps Merged into Source**
JRTL	*Jingde Record of Transmission of Lamps**
RSPR	*Recorded Sayings of Priest Rujing**
TTDE	*Treasury of the True Dharma Eye**

TRANSLITERATION

1. *Sanskrit*: A simplified form of standard Sanskrit transliteration is used.

Simplified form	Standard form
ch	c, ch
m	m, ṃ
n	ṃ, n, ṇ, ñ
ri	ri, ṛ
sh	ś, ṣ
t	t, ṭ
th	th, ṭh

2. *Chinese*: The Pinyin System, the most widely accepted system of transliteration, is used instead of the older Wade-Giles System. The comparative
table of the two systems is in Appendix B. Symbols that require particular
attention are as follows:

Pinyin	English approximations
c	ts
q	ch
x	sh

3. *Japanese*: The standard form is used. Macrons are omitted in the terms
commonly used in English.

SYSTEMS OF COUNTING

1. *Dates*: The lunar calendar was traditionally used in East Asia. According
   to this system, the first to third months correspond to spring, and the
   other seasons follow in three-month periods. The fifteenth day of the
   month is the day of the full moon.
2. *Ages*: This book follows the traditional way of counting age in East Asia,
   by which a person is one year old at birth and gains a year on every New
   Year's Day.
3. *Years*: In Dōgen's text, as was customary, a partial year is counted as a
   full year.

CAPITALIZATION

Any official titles or posthumous names of Zen masters are capitalized (for
example, Great Master Kuangzhen). Lower case is used otherwise (for example, Zen master Benji).

Moon in a Dewdrop

See Glossary for terms with asterisks

Introduction

The Age of Decline in Buddhism

Eihei Dōgen was born in A.D. 1200 in Kyoto, which had been Japan's imperial capital for over four hundred years. Although the aristocratic class in Kyoto, which preserved the elegant and colorful Japanese culture, retained much of its political and cultural power, the rising warrior class had recently established a feudal government in Kamakura. Values were shifting: from the courtier's refinement to the samurai's strength and discipline; from the sophistication of the city to the rough simplicity of the countryside.

Japanese Buddhism, which had been developing for more than six hundred years, had reached the point where magic prayers and ceremonies were sold to the upper classes, and major monasteries had armed monks who engaged in combat. Many Buddhists, seeing how distant these practices were from Shākyamuni's original teaching, called it the age of decline of the dharma. They attributed calamities such as famines, wars, and epidemics to the character of the times. In this desperate situation, belief in Amitābha, the Savior Buddha who promised to lead people to the heavenly Pure Land, was rapidly spreading. Recitation of Amitābha's name was advocated as an expedient practice suitable for the age.

Dōgen's father was probably Michichika Koga, the most influential minister in the imperial court at the turn of the century. His mother was prob-

3

ably a daughter of Motofusa Fujiwara, a former regent at the court. Dōgen lost his father when he was three years old and his mother when he was eight. Confronted as a small child with the stark reality of death, Dōgen began to seek Buddha's teaching, eschewing the high position at court to which he was entitled. At thirteen he went to Mt. Hiei, the great center of Buddhist studies, where he was ordained the following year by Kōen, head of the Tendai School of Buddhism.

After studying scripture extensively, Dōgen found himself confronted by a compelling question:

> Both exoteric and esoteric teachings explain that a person in essence has true dharma nature and is originally a body of "buddha nature." If so, why do all buddhas in the past, present, and future arouse the wish for and seek enlightenment?[1]

Dōgen could not find a satisfying answer on Mt. Hiei. He visited Kōin, abbot of Onjō Monastery, the other center of the Tendai School, and asked the same question. Instead of giving him an answer, Kōin said he should consider going to China to study with the Zen School. Kōin sent Dōgen to Eisai, a senior Tendai monk who had traveled to China in search of a way to restore the Tendai School to its former vitality. In China Eisai had seen the flourishing of Zen (in Chinese, Chan) Buddhism. Even Mt. Tiantai, the head monastery of the Tiantai (in Japanese, Tendai) School, had been turned into a Zen monastery. Among the so-called Five Schools of Zen, the Linji School, which had carried on the tradition of vigorous dialogues between master and student, was dominant. On a second visit to China Eisai studied the Linji tradition of Zen with Huaichang, and in 1191 Eisai brought this teaching to Japan, which was the beginning of the Rinzai (Linji) tradition in Japan. But pressure from the Tendai orthodoxy, who were opposed to his teaching Rinzai Zen, eventually influenced Eisai to present Zen as only one of the four principal practices of Tendai—*Lotus Sūtra* study, practice of Mahāyāna precepts, esoteric rituals, and Zen meditation.

In 1214 Dōgen returned to Kyoto to study with Eisai at Kennin Monastery. When Eisai died in 1215, Dōgen continued his studies with Eisai's disciple Myōzen. In 1221 Myōzen gave him dharma transmission, or full acknowledgment that the young monk had mastered the teaching, and in 1223 both Myōzen and Dōgen went to China. Dōgen reflected on this phase of his career in his *Record of the Baoqing Era*:

When I was a child I aroused the wish for enlightenment, pursued the way with various masters in our country, and learned a little about the meaning of causes and effects. However, I did not understand the true source of name and form. Later I entered Zen master Senkō's [Eisai's] room and for the first time heard the Rinzai teaching. Then I accompanied priest Myōzen and went to prosperous Song China. Through a voyage of countless miles, entrusting my transient body to the billowing waves, I finally reached Great Song.

Studies in China

Dōgen visited the major monasteries of southern China, which were located along the Zhe River in the region now known as Zhejiang Province. In most practice centers the masters followed a method of using enigmatic questions called *gongan* (kōans) to guide students. Dōgen studied these questions but was disappointed with the teachers' tendency to emphasize illogical phrases and behavior as the only expression of Zen teaching, ignoring the meaning of Buddhist scriptures. He was even offered dharma transmission by one of the masters but politely refused it.² Unable to find a suitable teacher after a two-year search, Dōgen considered going back to Japan. Then he remembered that a monk had spoken of Rujing as the only authentic practitioner of the way. So he went to meet Rujing, who was then sixty-two years old and abbot of Tiantong Mountain, in the summer of 1225. Later Dōgen reflected on this crucial meeting:

> I first offered incense and bowed formally to my late master, old buddha Tiantong, in his abbot's room on the first day, fifth month, of the first year of Baoqing of Great Song. He also saw me for the first time. Upon this occasion, he transmitted dharma, finger to finger, face to face, and said to me, "The dharma gate of face-to-face transmission from buddha to buddha, ancestor to ancestor, is realized now."³

Rujing gave Dōgen permission to come to his quarters for instruction at any time of day or night, whether in formal or informal robe. Dōgen frequently asked him questions and recorded their dialogues in the *Record of the Baoqing Era*.

Rujing was a priest of the Caodong School of Zen. Although he had inherited the renowned master Daokai's brocade robe, he never wore it or any robe with woven patterns. He forbade his students to be intimate with kings and ministers. Rujing denied the view, conventional in his time, that each of the "Five Schools of Zen" had its own teaching. He called the teaching he was transmitting "the great way of all buddhas" and even disagreed with those who called it the Zen School. Rujing also denied the widely held definition of Zen teaching as "a separate transmission outside the scriptures." He said the great way is not concerned with inside or outside.

Soon after Dōgen arrived on Tiantong Mountain, his teacher and traveling companion, Myōzen, died. Dōgen continued to participate in the rigorous program of Zen training at Rujing's monastery. According to the *Record of the Baoqing Era*, Rujing taught that studying Zen is "dropping away body and mind" and that students should not engage in such other practices as reciting Buddha's name, chanting sūtras, or holding rites of repentance. He taught a method of meditation called *zhigan dazuo* (now better known in its Japanese transliteration, *shikan taza*)—a single-minded sitting meditation wherein one does not try to solve questions or attain realization.

In 1227, the same year he met Rujing, Dōgen received from him the document of heritage, which certifies "direct penetration of merged realization." Thus Dōgen, in his own words, completed his "life's study of the great matter."[4] In his extensive later writings there is only one terse reference to the moment of his realization: "I was able to enact this face-to-face transmission by dropping away body and mind, and I have established this transmission in Japan."[5]

Early Period of Teaching

Returning to Japan in 1227, Dōgen stayed at Kennin Monastery in Kyoto, where he had first encountered Zen. He then wrote a short, carefully prepared proclamation in Chinese called "The Broad Recommendation of Zazen." In this work he clarified his intention to concentrate on teaching Zen meditation rather than a mixed practice such as Eisai had taught.

The Tendai community continued in its efforts to suppress single-practice forms of Buddhism such as the Zen and Pure Land schools. This campaign led to the desecration of the tomb of Hōnen, the leading master of the Pure Land School, in 1227. It also forced Dōgen to move out of the city of Kyoto to one of its suburbs, Fukakusa, in 1230.

In the following year Dōgen wrote "On the Endeavor of the Way," his first attempt to elucidate Zen teaching in the Japanese language. In this text Dōgen expresses his determination to disseminate Zen teaching in Japan, though he realizes that the time may not yet be ripe.

I came back to Japan with the hope of spreading the teaching and saving sentient beings—a heavy burden on my shoulders. However, I will put aside the intention of having the teaching prevail everywhere until the occasion of a rising tide. I think of wandering about like a cloud or a water-weed, studying the wind of the ancient sages.

He further argues against the common view that Buddhism can be divided into the periods of the true dharma, the imitative dharma, and the decayed dharma. All people can attain the way, he affirms, regardless of the age they are born into. In 1233 Dōgen started writing his lifework, *Treasury of the True Dharma Eye* (Shōbōgenzō), the first fascicle being "Perfection of the Great Wisdom."

Also in 1233 Dōgen founded a small practice center in Fukakusa called Kannondōri Temple. Shortly thereafter he completed and gave to one of his lay students "Actualizing the Fundamental Point," one of the most beautiful and profound prose works in the Japanese language. In the following year he wrote "Guidelines for Studying the Way" in Chinese, the language Japanese Buddhists most frequently used for religious writings.

In 1234, when Dōgen was thirty-five, a monk named Ejō came to study with him. Two years older than Dōgen, he had already received the seal of realization in the Dahui line of Linji Zen. In 1235 a formal monks' hall was built at Kannondōri Temple and Ejō was appointed head monk. Two years later Dōgen wrote "Instruction for the Tenzo [Head Cook]" as part of an effort to establish monastic regulations for his temple, renamed Kōshō Hōrin Monastery. At the same time Ejō completed his *Treasury of the True Dharma Eye: Record of Things Heard*—transcriptions of Dōgen's informal lectures to his monks. In 1239 an annex to the monks' hall was constructed, and Dōgen wrote "Regulations for the Auxiliary Cloud Hall." Seven fascicles of *Treasury of the True Dharma Eye*, including "The Time-Being" and "Mountains and Waters Sūtra," were written in 1240. In the following year Ekan of Hōjaku Monastery, Echizen Province, who had been Ejō's fellow student, became Dōgen's disciple. Four other monks who had been studying with Ekan also joined Dōgen's community. The year 1242 was a prolific time for Dōgen: he wrote seventeen fascicles of *Treasury of the True Dharma Eye* and presented most of them to his community. One of the fascicles, "Undivided Activity," was taught in Kyoto at the residence of Lord Yoshishige Hatano of Shibi Manor, Echizen Province.

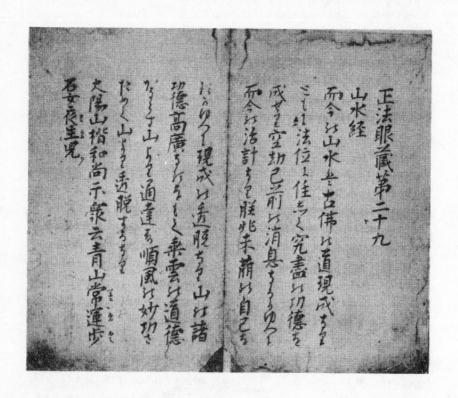

Dōgen's manuscript:
Opening of "Mountains and Waters Sūtra"
(Zenkyū-in, Aichi Prefecture)

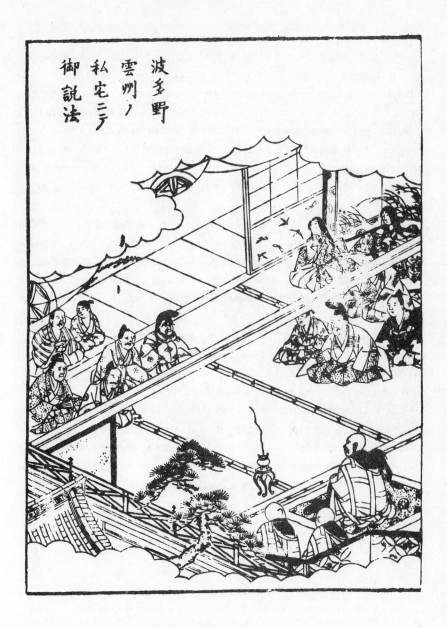

波多野
雲州ノ
私宅ニテ
御説法

Dōgen's Dharma Discourse at Lord Hatano's Residence
(From a revised and illustrated version of
Kenzei's Biography of Dōgen, *published in 1806)*

In the Mountains

Increasing criticism from the Tendai hierarchy on Mt. Hiei motivated Dōgen to accept the invitation of Lord Hatano in 1243 to move his community to Echizen Province, a place of severely cold winters situated northeast
of Kyoto on the Japan Sea. His students soon started building a full-scale
practice center, called Daibutsu Monastery, in a mountainous area of Shibi
County. In the meantime Dōgen gave discourses either in the hermitage at
the foot of Yamashi Peak or in Yoshimine Temple, an old monastery. Ejō
edited and copied those talks, which were to become fascicles in *Treasury of
the True Dharma Eye*.

The lecture hall of Daibutsu Monastery was completed in 1244, and
construction of the monks' hall began soon afterwards. In 1246 Dōgen renamed Daibutsu, calling it Eihei-ji. Collections of monastic regulations
and fascicles of *Treasury of the True Dharma Eye* continued to appear. The last
dated fascicle of the seventy-five-fascicle version of the *Treasury* was taught
in 1246.

Tokiyori Hōjō, who came to power as regent of the feudal government in
1246, invited Dōgen to lecture in Kamakura. Dōgen made the long jour-
ney east in the summer of 1247 and gave Tokiyori lay initiation. In the
spring of the following year he returned to Eihei-ji.

There remain no fascicles of *Treasury of the True Dharma Eye* dated between
1247 and 1253, the year of Dōgen's death. But most of the twelve-fascicle
version of the text, edited by Ejō from 1253 to 1255, were recent, according
to Ejō; we may therefore infer that they were written during that period. In
these fascicles Dōgen emphasizes monastic practice in a secluded environ-
ment and monkhood.

In 1249 Dōgen wrote a poem for his portrait, as is customary for a Zen
master. This painting is now known as the "Portrait of Dōgen Viewing the
Moon":[6]

> Fresh, clear spirit covers old mountain man this autumn.
> Donkey stares at the sky ceiling; glowing white moon floats.
> Nothing approaches. Nothing else included.
> Buoyant, I let myself go—filled with gruel, filled with rice.
> Lively flapping from head to tail,
> Sky above, sky beneath, cloud self, water origin.

FASCICLE = "SMALL BUNDLE"
A BOOK PUBLISHED IN SEPARATE
SECTIONS

Eihei-ji
Founded by Dōgen in 1244, rebuilt in the fifteenth century
(Photograph by Tetsuo Kurihara)

Dōgen became ill in the autumn of 1252. In the first month of 1253 he wrote the "Eightfold Awareness of Great People." Quoting the last words of Shākyamuni Buddha from the *Parinirvāna Brief Admonitions Sūtra* and explaining the meaning of the Buddha's admonitions, Dōgen ended his twenty-two-year work, *Treasury of the True Dharma Eye.*

In the seventh month of 1253 Dōgen was very ill. Appointing Ejō abbot of Eihei Monastery, Dōgen gave him a robe he had sewn with his own hands. In the eighth month, at Lord Hatano's request, he went to Kyoto to seek a cure for his disease. He wrote during the full-moon evening of the fifteenth:

53 yrs old.

> In autumn
> even though I may
> see it again,
> how can I sleep
> with the moon this evening?[7]

On the twenty-eighth day of the same month Dōgen passed away at the house of his lay student, Kakunen, in the city of his birth, Kyoto.

DŌGEN'S TEACHING

Concentration in Serenity

Dōgen uses the image of a dewdrop reflecting moonlight to describe the state of meditation. He suggests that just as the entire moon is reflected in a dewdrop, a complete awakening of truth can be experienced by the individual human being.

Zen meditation—sometimes described as mindfulness or concentration in serenity—is done sitting upright in a cross-legged position. Dōgen teaches that this practice, called zazen, is not merely a method by which one reaches awakening, but is itself awakening.

The model for awakening in Zen, as in other forms of Buddhism, is the understanding experienced by Shākyamuni Buddha in meditation. In Zen particularly, this understanding is regarded not as a step-by-step achievement but as an immediate and complete experience. One who experiences it is called a buddha—an awakened or enlightened person. The full moon illuminating the entire universe symbolizes this enlightenment:

The moon
abiding in the midst of
serene mind;
billows break
into light.[8]

This poem by Dōgen, titled "On Zazen Practice," illustrates the dynamic aspect of concentration in serenity. Moonlight, which appears to be still, shimmers on ocean waves that crash against rocks and burst into droplets. Millions of bits of light burst, spread, and merge with one another. For Dōgen, meditation practice implies this sort of mutual permeation between an individual's "light" and the activities of all things. Although one person's practice is part of the practice of all awakened beings, each individual practice is indispensable, as it actualizes and completes everyone's activity as a buddha.

This meditation is a source of creative engagement in life. While life is viewed as a continuation of birth, moment after moment, meditation is a total experience of this "birth" at each moment. Thus a person no longer lives a moment as a segment of life or takes life passively, but is fully engaged in an active and creative way. Dōgen explains this experience by using the metaphor of a boat:

Birth is just like riding in a boat. You raise the sails and row with the oar. . . .
You ride in the boat and your riding makes the boat what it is.[9]

Timelessness of a Moment

Awareness of each moment is indispensable to the way of mindfulness, because practice is complete only when a person focuses attention on the present moment: the very moment of one's existence. Time, according to Dōgen, is experienced from moment to moment; actual experience occurs only in the present. Past was experienced in the past as the present moment, and future will be experienced in the future as the present moment.

Time passes and things do not remain unchanged. A moment seems to be an extremely small segment of a long span of time. Yet past is remembered as past in the present moment and future is expected as future in the present moment. Each moment carries all of time. Thus a moment has an aspect of timelessness. In this respect, "now" is eternal.

This timeless moment is illustrated by reference to spring and summer.

A common view is that spring marks the beginning of summer and slowly
turns into summer. But to one who is awakened, spring is just spring; it is
not expected to turn into anything else.

> Spring with all its numerous aspects is called flowing. When spring flows
> there is nothing outside of spring. Study this in detail.

> Spring invariably flows through spring. Although flowing itself is not spring,
> flowing occurs throughout spring. Thus, flowing is completed at just this
> moment of spring.[10]

It is commonly understood that recognition of the impermanency of life
is the beginning of Buddhist studies. However, awareness of impermanency
is inseparable from recognition of the timelessness of a moment.

> As usual
> cherry blossoms bloom
> in my native place,
> their color unchanged—
> spring.[11]

This poem, called "Inconceivable Mind of Nirvāna," takes up the theme of
cherry blossoms, which in Japanese poetry typically symbolize the world's
transiency. But Dōgen, contrary to our expectations, suggests that something about the cherry blossoms goes beyond change.

In contrast with birth and death, which constantly appear and disappear,
the tranquility of nirvāna is timeless. Yet according to Mahāyāna Buddhist
teaching, nirvāna is experienced only in birth and death. Thus timelessness
is experienced in momentariness.

Realm of "All is Nonseparate"

Dōgen pointed out that time is inseparable from being, or existence—that
is, from space and matter. "Time itself is being," he says; "all being is
time."[12] His discussion of "the time-being" is based on this recognition.

To become familiar with Dōgen's concept of the time-being, we may need
to remind ourselves that all phenomena are in motion, and the motion is
perceived in relation to time. Every motion is relative. The impression of
speed is determined by a person's viewpoint. Fast for one person may be
slow for another. Motion for one person may be stillness for another. For
example, a person is observed riding in a boat. The observer on the shore

may see him moving quickly; the rider may experience himself as not moving at all. If two individuals are moving at the same speed, they may experience each other as motionless. Dōgen suggests that one who can "locate" himself in the timelessness of all moments will also discover the stillness of all movements.

Similarly, size is relative; an object is big or small according to one's viewpoint. If one becomes free of viewpoints, objects are no longer experienced in terms of comparisons. The timelessness of moments and the stillness of movements further translate to the sizelessness of objects. In this realm, there is no concept of whole or part. As Dōgen puts it:

> There are myriads of forms and hundreds of grasses throughout the entire earth, and yet each grass and each form itself is the entire earth.[13]

Here, the birth of a person at each moment is the birth of all phenomenal objects at each moment:

> Quietly think over whether birth and all things that arise together with birth are inseparable or not. There is neither a moment nor a thing that is apart from birth. There is neither an object nor a mind that is apart from birth.[14]

In this realm of nonduality, all things have buddha nature. It is also said that all things *are* buddha nature. In the same manner, all things are buddha-dharma; all buddhas are realization.

Breaking through Barriers

Dōgen emphasizes that the state of awakening is experienced immediately, even in the first moment of a beginner's meditation. But this awakening is not necessarily accompanied by intellectual recognition of it. Intellectual recognition is based on discriminatory concepts: self and other, large and small, good and bad. To discriminate is to create distinctions between things, whereas awakening is experience beyond discrimination. Dōgen explains:

> The boundary of realization is not distinct, for the realization comes forth simultaneously with the mastery of buddha-dharma. Do not suppose that what you realize becomes your knowledge and is grasped by your consciousness. Although actualized immediately, the inconceivable may not be distinctly apparent. Its appearance is beyond your knowledge.[15]

The truth realized by awakened ones, called dharma or buddha-dharma, is described as "endless, unremitting, unthinkable, unnameable." The experience of this nonduality is the source of all the understanding and teaching in Mahāyāna Buddhism. Buddhist wisdom (prajñā) is nothing but this realization. Such an experience of the world is often expressed by pairs of negative statements:

> The place, the way, is neither large nor small, neither yours nor others'. The place, the way, has not carried over from the past, and it is not merely arising now.[16]

The conventional, discriminating frame of mind is a barrier to entering this realm. In order to help students break through the barrier of intellectual thinking, Zen masters express themselves in all sorts of unconventional ways: enigmatic statements, non sequiturs, repetitions, tautologies, silence, eccentric behavior, even beating the students. Thus the Zen teaching is regarded as "not depending on letters," but as direct experience of truth itself.

Dōgen's writings follow this Zen tradition, in which a great number of paradoxical expressions and stories have been handed down as teaching devices. He comments on the words of older Zen masters, mostly Chinese. For him, these words are not illogical or incomprehensible. Though they cannot be understood by the ordinary mind, they make perfect sense to one who experiences truth in a nondualistic way. Their paradoxes have the logic of enlightenment.

The reason Dōgen's writing strikes many readers as difficult is that, although he gives detailed and acute explanations of the paradoxes, he does not necessarily try to explain them in a way that will satisfy the intellect. He develops his logic at the same level of insight as the Chinese Zen masters, who were trying to express a logic beyond normal logic. In fact, Dōgen's writings themselves are set up as barriers for the student to break through.

Anatomy of Nonduality

Typical of Dōgen's rhetoric is the following statement:

> An ancient buddha said, "Mountains are mountains, waters are waters." These words do not mean mountains are mountains; they mean mountains are mountains.[17]

To illuminate this statement, we may turn to the parallel rhetoric of another passage, the opening of "Actualizing the Fundamental Point":

As all things are buddha-dharma, there is delusion and realization, practice, birth and death, and there are buddhas and sentient beings.

Here Dōgen suggests that observing the different aspects of all things is the beginning of Buddhist study. At this stage, discriminatory observation is functional. Without noticing the difference between awakening and delusion or between those who are awakened and those who are not, a person cannot arouse the wish for enlightenment.

But according to traditional Buddhist teaching, there is no "self" as an unchanging entity. This teaching of "no-self" underlies the second sentence of "Actualizing the Fundamental Point":

As the myriad things are without an abiding self, there is no delusion, no realization, no buddha, no sentient being, no birth and death.

It is ironic that when one observes the tremendous difference between awakening and delusion and seeks awakening, one suddenly comes across the teaching, "There is no delusion, no awakening." A further irony is that only when a person is completely detached from himself does he find himself and realize what is common to himself and others. "Self" immediately opens into selflessness. This selflessness is called "true self" or "original face." It is also described as "something close" or "what is intimate." Thus, the teaching of no-self is not nihilism, not an assertion that nothing exists. Rather it is awareness of the interdependence of all things—the reality of things as they are. So the third sentence of "Actualizing the Fundamental Point" says:

The buddha way is, basically, leaping clear of the many and the one; thus there are birth and death, delusion and realization, sentient beings and buddhas.

Now we seem to be back to the first line, "There is delusion and realization." But we have actually reached a different point. Dōgen's demonstration starts with an affirmative statement, then negates that affirmation, and concludes with a negation of the negative, which is a positive statement. Thus the first step is discrimination, the second is denial of discrimination, and the third is beyond discrimination and denial of it.

When Dōgen quotes an ancient Zen master's words, "Mountains are mountains," and remarks, "These words do not mean mountains are mountains," he denies the conventional, dualistic understanding of the mountain as a symbol of enlightenment. When he says, "They mean mountains are mountains," he suggests that we should see the mountains as they are, beyond discrimination and denial of discrimination. This is the meaning of nonduality.

Here again we see a three-step demonstration: affirmative, negative, and affirmative. This tripartite elucidation of the fundamental Buddhist perspective, unlike Hegel's thesis, antithesis, and synthesis, does not develop from a lower to a higher level; rather, each step is given an absolute value, and each step is inclusive of the others.

Emancipation/Realization

Dōgen's writings are always grounded in practical methodology: how to concentrate body and mind, how to understand and follow monastic rules, how to view various aspects of life and regulate daily conduct. He repeatedly emphasizes the interpenetration of practice and enlightenment. "Practice" here means ongoing daily activity centered in zazen. "Enlightenment" is actualization of buddha nature through practice.

There is a tendency to view enlightenment as separate from practice and to seek some splendid insight as the goal of Zen practice. Dōgen teaches that this is an illusion. One must fully understand the wholeness of practice and enlightenment. Dōgen describes this understanding as mastery of Buddhism or the "true dharma eye." It is freedom from a dualistic frame of mind.

Enlightenment as actualization of buddha nature through practice is Dōgen's fundamental teaching. All his discourses are intended to help students "understand" the meaning of this practice-enlightenment. But understanding is not the final goal; continuous everyday practice is the ultimate goal:

> The buddha way is under everyone's heel. Immersed in the way, clearly understand right on the spot. Immersed in enlightenment, you yourself are complete. Therefore, even though you arrive at full understanding, still this is only a part of enlightenment. This is how it is with practice throughout the way.[18]

This is the practice of nonattachment, freedom from any aim, including "enlightenment." The fourth sentence of "Actualizing the Fundamental Point" goes:

> Yet in attachment flowers fall, and in aversion weeds spread.

Although this statement may seem unrelated to the previous three, flowers here represent awakening and weeds represent delusion. Dōgen indicates that even if one fully understands the previous three sentences, experience of the buddha way is not complete unless there is nonattachment to practice and enlightenment.

Dōgen calls this practice of nonattachment "emancipation"—Japanese *tōdatsu*—which means a fish slipping out of the net. This aspect of teaching is usually associated with "letting go," "dropping away," or "abandoning." One needs to give up everything in order to open oneself to the ultimate truth.

"Realization," "actualization," or "actualizing"—Japanese *genjō*, which means coming forth and completing—is another aspect of the same teaching. Though the feeling of dropping away is quite different from that of coming forth, the two movements are inseparable. Once a person is entirely free from attachment he experiences all things without any preconceptions. This experience is itself realization. Dōgen says:

> The great way of all buddhas, thoroughly practiced, is emancipation and realization.

> Emancipation means that in birth you are emancipated from birth, in death you are emancipated from death. Thus, there is detachment from birth-and-death and penetrating birth-and-death. Such is the complete practice of the great way. There is letting go of birth-and-death, and vitalizing birth-and-death. Such is the thorough practice of the great way.

> Realization is birth, birth is realization. At the time of realization there is nothing but birth totally actualized, nothing but death totally actualized.[19]

Unusual Expression

> Flowers in spring
> cuckoos in summer
> moon in autumn
> snow in winter
> serene and cool[20]

The Japanese novelist Yasunari Kawabata, in his acceptance speech for the Nobel Prize in 1968, commented on this poem:

> One can, if one chooses, see in Dōgen's poem about the beauty of the four seasons no more than a conventional, ordinary, mediocre stringing together,

in a most awkward form, of representative images from the four seasons. One can see it as a poem that is not really a poem at all. And yet very similar is the deathbed poem of the priest Ryokan [1758–1831]:

> What shall be my legacy?
> The blossoms of spring,
> The cuckoo in the hills,
> The leaves of autumn.

In this poem, as in Dōgen's, the commonest of figures and the commonest of words are strung together without hesitation—no, to particular effect, rather—and so they transmit the very essence of Japan. . . . Dōgen entitled his poem about the seasons "Innate Reality," and even as he sang of the beauty of the seasons he was deeply immersed in Zen.[21]

As Kawabata points out, Dōgen here uses the most ordinary images of Japanese poetry. But his intention is not to express gentle melancholy (*mono no aware*)—the traditional aesthetic mood. As the title of the poems, *Honrai no Memmoku* ("Innate Reality" or "Original Face"), suggests, Dōgen is presenting the experience of being free from the conventional attributes of things.

In this realm unusual insights arise. Dōgen quotes startling and paradoxical statements of earlier Zen masters: plum blossoms open early spring (instead of "plum blossoms open *in* early spring"); Bodhidharma did not come to the eastern land; the green mountains are always walking; a stone woman gives birth to a child; a bowl rolls over a pearl. These unusual images upset the conventional way of looking at things and remind us that there are always other points of view and that there is no absolute standard as to whether one view is correct or not.

Furthermore, distinctions between the general and the particular, oneness and differentiation, disappear, as Dōgen remarks in his poem called "The Point of Zazen":

> Realization, neither general nor particular,
> is effort without desire.
> Clear water all the way to the bottom;
> a fish swims like a fish.
> Vast sky transparent throughout;
> a bird flies like a bird.[22]

Dōgen also bends and subverts the usual meanings of words. He says, for example:

When you discuss "outside," skin, flesh, bones, and marrow are all outside. When you discuss "inside," skin, flesh, bones, and marrow are all inside.[23]

While giving essential and ultimate value equally to "skin," "flesh," "bones," and "marrow," Dōgen uses "inside" and "outside" as if each were entire and all-inclusive so that neither word retains its normal meaning.

Words that usually carry negative values are used in positive ways in Dōgen's rhetoric. "Lost," "missed," and "dead" can mean complete experience of selflessness, as can "hunger," "fatigue," and "sleep." "Delusion," "hindrance," and "twining," as well as "blind" and "darkness," can mean nonduality. Thus, words carry both their ordinary meanings and the reverse of those meanings.

Treasury of the True Dharma Eye

Although Dōgen concentrated on training a small number of monks, his community grew larger after his death and he came to be regarded as the founder of the Sōtō School, a Japanese form of the Chinese Caodong School. At present the Sōtō School is one of the largest Buddhist orders in Japan, with approximately fourteen thousand temples, fifteen thousand priests, and five million members. Sōtō and Rinzai are the major Zen Buddhist schools in Japan. This very fact is ironic, because Dōgen, following Rujing's precedent, did not permit his students to identify themselves with any school—not even the Zen School.

Dōgen is regarded as one of the reformers of Buddhism during the Kamakura Period (1185–1333). The pioneers of Kamakura Buddhism were not satisfied with the elaborate philosophy and the various practices that had been established during the Heian Period (792–1185). Each of these masters sought and eventually selected a single practice powerful enough to provide a complete experience of Buddhism. Thus, Hōnen and Shinran adopted a Chinese method of reciting Amitābha Buddha's name as their entire practice; Nichiren taught recitation of the title of the *Lotus Sūtra*; and Dōgen introduced wholehearted zazen practice. Unlike the other three masters, who tried to suit their practice to the needs of lay people in an age of decline in Buddhism, Dōgen showed no interest in compromising or simplifying the practice that had been handed down by monks of Zen monastic communities for centuries in China and finally transmitted to him by Rujing.

Dōgen's concern as a writer lay solely in transmitting the authentic principle and practice of Buddhism, which he called "true dharma," to his students as well as to later generations. His understanding of authenticity was based on the belief that the dharma, originally transmitted by Shākyamuni Buddha to his disciple Mahākāshyapa, was inherited by generations of Indian masters through Bodhidharma, and then by Chinese masters until it reached Dōgen himself. This belief is traced back to the legend that Shākyamuni Buddha, without uttering a word, took up a flower in his assembly and winked. When Mahākāshyapa alone responded by smiling, Buddha said, "I have the treasury of the true dharma eye, the inconceivable mind of nirvāna. This I entrust to Mahākāshyapa."[24] Although the story is not found in Indian texts, it was widely cited by Chinese Zen Buddhists to illustrate the nonscriptural nature of the Zen teaching.

Far from denying the validity of Buddhist scriptures, Dōgen understood them to be true expressions of Buddha's enlightenment. As one who thoroughly studied scripture in Japan and who inherited the teaching of the nonscriptural Zen tradition in China, Dōgen effected a unity of what had historically been rival traditions.

Dōgen calls this teaching "the treasury of the true dharma eye" and affirms that it is essentially the same through the entire lineage of Buddhist teachers since Shākyamuni, yet it is expressed in innumerable forms, according to circumstances. An awakened one is a person who breaks through intellectual or conventional ways of thinking and directly experiences this unchanging, universal truth. Because this experience is obscured by preconceived ideas and realized only in unique and creative expression, an awakened one cannot arrive at some stable state of consciousness and simply "stay there." Thus, the state of an awakened one is described as "going beyond buddha."

Dōgen is unique both as a thinker and as a Buddhist teacher. Like his predecessors, he presents paradoxical statements; but unlike them, he makes continuous and systematic efforts to verbalize the process of his thinking. He demonstrates the extraordinary quality of intuitive logic in Zen tradition.

Throughout his teaching career, Dōgen hardly changed the tone of his voice. He simply expanded the variety of topics bearing on the same theme—practice-enlightenment. His writings are an unfolding of the single truth that was transmitted to him through the buddha ancestors.

Rediscovery of Dōgen's Work

Although he is now considered one of the greatest thinkers Japan has produced, Dōgen was not read outside his own school for nearly seven hundred years after his death in 1253. Even the Sōtō monks largely forgot him during the centuries between 1400 and 1800. The *Treasury of the True Dharma Eye*, his major work, was published by the Sōtō School for the first time in 1816.

It was the Rinzai School that captured the imaginations and patronage of the ruling classes in the thirteenth century. During the Muromachi Period (1333–1568), Rinzai was supported by the imperial family as well as by the leaders of the warrior government in Kyoto, and Rinzai powerfully influenced the main expressions of Japanese culture: painting, landscape designs, noh drama, flower arrangement, and tea ceremony. Sōtō, on the other hand, had much less official recognition and little cultural influence. Some Sōtō masters responded to public demand by blending Dōgen's pure and strict teaching with esoteric Buddhist rituals and folk beliefs. In this way the Sōtō teaching gained popularity among farmers and low-class warriors of the rural districts.

No commentary to Dōgen's work was written during the Muromachi Period. Some of his writings were copied but kept secret and were scarcely available. Around 1690, during the Edo Period (1600–1868), the thirty-fifth abbot of Eihei-ji, Kōzen, collected all the available versions of the *Treasury of the True Dharma Eye*, rearranged the text in chronological order, and compiled the ninety-five-fascicle version.

In the eighteenth century an attempt was made to restore the Sōtō School. Manzan Dōhaku fought against the custom by which one student could receive dharma transmission from several teachers, and helped to reestablish the rite of face-to-face transmission by a single teacher as taught by Dōgen. Tenkei opposed Manzan's formalism and wrote a commentary on the sixty fascicles of the *Treasury* with daring textual criticism and arbitrary revision, which was soon regarded in the Sōtō School as heretical. Menzan Zuihō spent forty-four years searching for the sources of the terms and phrases found in the ninety-five-fascicle version of the *Treasury*. In the 1770s one of Menzan's dharma descendants, Fuzan, made a detailed explication of the text, which was transcribed by his students. At about the same time Honkō translated Dōgen's work into Chinese, since a text written in Japanese tended to be less respected than one in Chinese, and added his own commentary. Zōkai and Rōran also wrote commentaries on the *Treasury of the True Dharma Eye*.[25] In 1816 Kōzen's edition of the book was published by Eihei-ji.

Despite this sudden spurt of Sōtō sectarian scholarship, Dōgen's writings remained obscure for most Sōtō monks. The great poet-monk Ryōkan (1758–1831) wrote a poem about reading the *Record of Eihei Dōgen*, an abridged collection of Dōgen's lectures, poems, and other writings:

Now when I take the *Record of Eihei Dōgen* and examine it,
the tone does not harmonize well with usual beliefs.
Nobody has asked whether it is a jewel or a pebble.
For five hundred years it's been covered with dust
just because no one has had an eye for recognizing dharma.
For whom was all his eloquence expounded?
Longing for ancient times and grieving for the present, my heart is
    exhausted.[26]

Dōgen as a thinker was first introduced to the public by the renowned philosopher Tetsurō Watsuji. In a series of essays under the title "Monk Dōgen" (1920–23),[27] Watsuji criticized earlier biographies by Sōtō priests as attempts to "murder" Dōgen by attributing to him worldly merits and miraculous feats. Seeing Dōgen as a thinker who belongs to humanity rather than to a school of Buddhism, Watsuji excluded legends and described Dōgen as a historical figure, discussing his thoughts in relation to the basic concepts of Western philosophy.

Another distinguished philosopher of modern Japan, Hajime Tanabe, asserted in 1939[28] that he regarded Dōgen as the first Japanese philosopher. He described the *Treasury of the True Dharma Eye* as a supreme achievement of dialectical thinking.

Dōgen was gradually recognized by scholars of Japanese literature as a remarkable prose writer. Consequently, the *Treasury of the True Dharma Eye*, along with the *Treasury of the True Dharma Eye: Record of Things Heard*, was included in several collections of classical literature in the 1960s and 1970s.[29] In response to growing public interest, four different versions of the entire *Treasury* in modern Japanese translation were published.[30]

Western interest in Zen has been growing since the 1930s. But it was not until 1958 that the first English translation of Dōgen's writings appeared, in Reihō Masunaga's *The Sōtō Approach to Zen*.[31] Since that time translated portions of the *Treasury* have been published in several other books, and in 1983 Kōsen Nishiyama, John Stevens, and their collaborators completed a four-volume, ninety-two-fascicle version (see Bibliography).

As one of the translators of Dōgen into modern Japanese, I first visited Zen groups in the United States in 1964. At the Zen Center of San Francisco, led by Shunryū Suzuki-roshi, zazen as taught by Dōgen was strictly practiced, but students were not yet ready to study Dōgen's texts. "Genjō Kōan," a portion of the *Treasury* translated by Robert Aitken and myself in 1965,[32] was used by Suzuki-roshi and studied in various Zen groups.

In the late 1960s, Dōgen's teaching started to spread in other countries as well as in the United States. Monastic practice was initiated in some centers. At present, a number of Western students are studying the original Dōgen texts. Translators are trying to find ways to make Dōgen accessible to Western readers, and scholarly work in the field is increasing. It seems that the time is ripe for Dōgen to be a part of the common human heritage.

Kazuaki Tanahashi

PART ONE

Practical Instructions

Rules for Zazen

ZAZEN-GI[1]

1

Practicing Zen is zazen. For zazen a quiet place is suitable. Lay out a thick mat. Do not let in drafts or smoke, rain or dew. Protect and maintain the place where you settle your body. There are examples from the past of sitting on a diamond seat* and sitting on a flat stone covered with a thick layer of grass.

Day or night the place of sitting should not be dark; it should be kept warm in winter and cool in summer.

2

Set aside all involvements and let the myriad things rest.[2] Zazen is not thinking of good, not thinking of bad. It is not conscious endeavor.* It is not introspection.*

Do not desire to become a buddha;[3] let sitting* or lying down drop away. Be moderate in eating and drinking. Be mindful of the passing of time, and engage yourself in zazen as though saving your head from fire.* On Mt. Huangmei the Fifth Ancestor practiced zazen to the exclusion of all other activities.

29

3

When sitting zazen, wear the kashāya* and use a round cushion. The cushion should not be placed all the way under the legs, but only under the buttocks. In this way the crossed legs rest on the mat and the backbone is supported with the round cushion. This is the method used by all buddha ancestors* for zazen.

Sit either in the half-lotus position or in the full-lotus position. For the full-lotus put the right foot on the left thigh and the left foot on the right thigh. The toes should lie along the thighs, not extending beyond. For the half-lotus position, simply put the left foot on the right thigh.

4

Loosen your robes and arrange them in an orderly way. Place the right hand on the left foot and the left hand on the right hand, lightly touching the ends of the thumbs together. With the hands in this position, place them next to the body so that the joined thumb-tips are at the navel.

Straighten your body and sit erect. Do not lean to the left or right; do not bend forward or backward. Your ears should be in line with your shoulders, and your nose in line with your navel.

Rest your tongue against the roof of your mouth, and breathe through your nose. Lips and teeth should be closed. Eyes should be open, neither too wide, nor too narrow. Having adjusted body and mind in this manner, take a breath and exhale fully.

Sit solidly in samādhi* and think not-thinking.* How do you think not-thinking? Nonthinking.* This is the art of zazen.

Zazen is not learning to do concentration. It is the dharma gate* of great ease and joy. It is undefiled practice-enlightenment.*

In the eleventh month, first year of Kangen [1243], this was taught to the assembly at Yoshimine Monastery, Yoshida County, Echizen Province.

Translated by Dan Welch and Kazuaki Tanahashi

Guidelines for Studying the Way

GAKUDŌ YŌJIN-SHŪ[1]

I

You should arouse the thought of enlightenment.

The thought of enlightenment has many names but they all refer to one and the same mind.

Ancestor Nāgārjuna said, "The mind that fully sees into the uncertain world of birth and death is called the thought of enlightenment."[2]

Thus if we maintain this mind, this mind can become the thought of enlightenment.

Indeed, when you understand discontinuity the notion of self does not come into being, ideas of name and gain do not arise. Fearing the swift passage of the sunlight, practice the way as though saving your head from fire. Reflecting on this ephemeral life, make endeavor in the manner of Buddha raising his foot.*

When you hear a song of praise sung by a kinnara god* or a kalavinka bird,* let it be as the evening breeze brushing against your ears. If you see the beautiful face of Maoqiang or Xishi,* let it be like the morning dew-drops coming into your sight. Freedom from the ties of sound and form naturally accords with the essence of the way-seeking mind.

If in the past or present, you hear about students of small learning or meet people with limited views, often they have fallen into the pit of fame

31

and profit and have forever missed the buddha way in their life. What a pity! How regrettable! You should not ignore this.

Even if you read the sūtras of the expedient or complete teaching,* or transmit the scriptures of the exoteric or esoteric schools, without throwing away name and gain it cannot be called arousing the thought of enlightenment.

Some of these people say, "The thought of enlightenment is the mind of supreme, perfect enlightenment. Do not be concerned with the cultivation of fame or profit."

Some of them say, "The thought of enlightenment is the insight that each thought contains three thousand realms."*

Some of them say, "The thought of enlightenment is the dharma gate, 'Each thought is unborn.'"*

Some of them say, "The thought of enlightenment is the mind of entering the buddha realm."

Such people do not yet know and mistakenly slander the thought of enlightenment. They are remote from the buddha way.

Try to reflect on the mind concerned only with your own gain. Does this one thought blend with the nature and attributes of the three thousand realms? Does this one thought realize the dharma gate of being unborn? There is only the deluded thought of greed for name and love of gain. There is nothing which could be taken as the thought of enlightenment.

From ancient times sages have attained the way and realized dharma. Although as an expedient teaching they lived ordinary lives, still they had no distorted thought of fame or profit. Not even attached to dharma, how could they have worldly attachment?

The thought of enlightenment, as was mentioned, is the mind which sees into impermanence. This is most fundamental, and not at all the same as the mind pointed to by confused people. The understanding that each thought is unborn or the insight that each thought contains three thousand realms is excellent practice after arousing the thought of enlightenment. This should not be mistaken.

Just forget yourself for now and practice inwardly—this is one with the thought of enlightenment. We see that the sixty-two views* are based on self. So when a notion of self arises, sit quietly and contemplate it. Is there a real basis inside or outside your body now? Your body with hair and skin is just inherited from your father and mother. From beginning to end a drop of blood or lymph is empty. So none of these are the self. What about mind, thought, awareness, and knowledge? Or the breath going in and out, which ties a lifetime together: what is it after all? None of these are the self either. How could you be attached to any of them? Deluded people are attached to them. Enlightened people are free of them.

You figure there is self where there is no self. You attach to birth where there is no birth. You do not practice the buddha way, which should be practiced. You do not cut off the worldly mind, which should be cut off. Avoiding the true teaching and pursuing the groundless teaching, how could you not be mistaken?

2

Once you see or hear the true teaching, you should practice it without fail. One phrase offered by a loyal servant can have the power to alter the course of the nation. One word given by a buddha ancestor cannot fail to turn people's minds. The unwise ruler does not adopt the servant's advice. One who does not step forward cannot accept the buddha's teaching. If you are unbending, you cannot stop floating along in birth and death. If appropriate advice is not heeded, governing with virtue cannot be realized.

3

In the buddha way, you should always enter enlightenment through practice. A worldly teacher says, "Through study one can gain wealth."³ Buddha says, "Within practice there is enlightenment."

It is unheard-of that without studying someone should earn wealth or that without practicing someone should attain enlightenment. Though practice varies—initiated by faith or dharma knowledge, with emphasis on sudden or gradual enlightenment*—you always depend on practice to go beyond enlightenment. Though study can be superficial or profound, and students can be sharp or dull, accumulated studying earns wealth. This does not necessarily depend on the king's excellence or inability, nor should it depend on one's having good or bad luck. If someone were to get wealth without studying, how could he transmit the way in which ancient kings, in times of either order or disorder, ruled the country? If you were to gain realization without practice, how could you comprehend the Tathāgata's teaching of delusion and enlightenment?

You should know that arousing practice in the midst of delusion, you attain realization before you recognize it. At this time you first know that the raft of discourse is like yesterday's dream, and you finally cut off your old understanding bound up in the vines and serpents of words. This is not made to happen by Buddha, but is accomplished by your all-encompassing effort.

Moreover, what practice calls forth is enlightenment; your treasure house does not come from outside. How enlightenment functions is through practice; how could actions of mind-ground* go astray? So if you turn the eye of enlightenment and reflect back on the realm of practice, nothing in particular hits the eye, and you just see white clouds for ten thousand miles.[4] If you arouse practice as though climbing the steps of enlightenment, not even a speck of dust will support your feet; you will be as far from true practice as heaven is from earth.[5] Now step back and leap beyond the buddha land.

This portion was written on the ninth day, third month, second year of Tempuku [1234].

4

You should not practice Buddha's teaching with the idea of gain.
The practice of Buddha's teaching is always done by receiving the essential instructions of a master, not by following your own ideas. In fact, Buddha's teaching cannot be attained by having ideas or not having ideas. Only when the mind of pure practice coincides with the way will body and mind be calm. If body and mind are not yet calm, they will not be at ease. When body and mind are not at ease, thorns grow on the path of realization.

So that pure practice and the way coincide, how should we proceed? Proceed with the mind which neither grasps nor rejects, the mind unconcerned with name or gain. Do not practice buddha-dharma* with the thought that it is to benefit others.

People in the present world, even those practicing the buddha-dharma, have a mind which is far apart from the way. They practice what others praise and admire, even though they know it does not accord with the way. They reject and do not practice what others fail to honor and praise, even though they know it is the true way. How painful! You should try to quiet your mind and investigate whether these attitudes are buddha-dharma or not. You may be completely ashamed. The eye of the sage illuminates this.

Clearly, buddha-dharma is not practiced for one's own sake, and even less for the sake of fame and profit. Just for the sake of buddha-dharma you should practice it.

All buddhas' compassion and sympathy for sentient beings* are neither for their own sake nor for others. It is just the nature of buddha-dharma. Isn't it apparent that insects and animals nurture their offspring, exhausting themselves with painful labors, yet in the end have no reward when their offspring are grown? In this way the compassion of small creatures for their offspring naturally resembles the thought of all buddhas for sentient beings.

The inconceivable dharma of all buddhas is not compassion alone, but compassion is the basis of the various teachings that appear universally. Already we are children of the buddhas. Why not follow their lead?

Students! Do not practice buddha-dharma for your own sake. Do not practice buddha-dharma for name and gain. Do not practice buddha-dharma to attain blissful reward. Do not practice buddha-dharma to attain miraculous effects. Practice buddha-dharma solely for the sake of buddha-dharma. This is the way.

5

You should seek a true teacher to practice Zen and study the way.

A teacher of old said, "If the beginning is not right, myriad practices will be useless."

How true these words are! Practice of the way depends on whether the guiding master is a true teacher or not.

The disciple is like wood, and the teacher resembles a craftsman. Even if the wood is good, without a skilled craftsman its extraordinary beauty is not revealed. Even if the wood is bent, placed in skilled hands its splendid merits immediately appear. By this you should know that realization is genuine or false depending on whether the teacher is true or incompetent.

But in our country from ancient times, there have not been any true teachers. How do we know this is so? We can guess by studying their sayings, just as we can scoop up stream water and find out about its source. In our country from ancient times, various teachers have written books and instructed their disciples, offering their teaching to human and heavenly beings. Their words are immature, their discourse has not yet ripened. They have not yet reached the peak of study; how could they have come close to the state of realization? They only transmitted words and phrases or taught the chanting of Buddha's name. They count other people's treasure day and night, not having half a penny themselves.

Previous teachers are responsible for this. They taught people to seek enlightenment outside mind,[6] or to seek rebirth in another land. Confusion starts from this. Mistaken ideas come from this.

Though you give good medicine, if you do not teach a method of controlling its use it will make one sicker than taking poison. In our country since ancient times it seems as though no one has given good medicine. There are as yet no masters who can control the poisonous effects of medicine. Because of this, it is difficult to penetrate birth and death. How can old age and death be overcome?

All this is the teachers' fault, not at all the fault of the disciples. The reason is that those who are teachers let people neglect the root* and go out on the limbs.* Before they establish true understanding, they are absorbed only in their own thinking, and they unwittingly cause others to enter a realm of confusion. What a pity! Those who are teachers do not yet understand this confusion. How could students realize what is right and wrong?

How sad! In this small, remote nation buddha-dharma has not yet spread widely. True masters have not yet appeared here. If you wish to study the unsurpassed buddha way, you have to travel a great distance to call on the masters in Song China, and you have to reflect deeply on the vital road outside thought. Until you have a true teacher, it is better not to study.

Regardless of his age or experience, a true teacher is simply one who has apprehended the true teaching and attained the authentic teacher's seal of realization. He does not put texts first or understanding first, but his capacity is outside any framework and his spirit freely penetrates the nodes in bamboo.* He is not concerned with self-views* and does not stagnate in emotional feelings. Thus, practice and understanding are in mutual accord. This is a true master.

6

What you should know for practicing Zen.

Practicing Zen, studying the way, is the great matter of a lifetime. You should not belittle it or be hasty with it. A master of old cut off his arm* and another cut off his fingers.* These are excellent models from China.

Long ago Shākyamuni Buddha abandoned his home and left his country. This is an excellent precedent for practicing the way.

People of the present say you should practice what is easy to practice. These words are quite mistaken. They are not at all in accord with the buddha way. If this alone is what you regard as practice, then even lying down will be wearisome. If you find one thing wearisome, you will find everything wearisome. It is obvious that people who are fond of easy practice are not capable of the way.

In fact, the dharma spread and is now present in the world because our great teacher Shākyamuni practiced with difficulty and pain for immeasurable eons and finally attained this dharma. If the original source is like this, how could the later streams be easy?

Students who would like to study the way must not wish for easy practice. If you seek easy practice, you will for certain never reach the ground of truth or dig down to the place of treasure. Even teachers of old who had great capacity said that practice is difficult. You should know that the buddha way is vast and profound.

If the buddha way were originally easy to practice, then teachers of great capacity from olden times would not have said that practice is difficult and understanding is difficult. Compared with the people of old, those of today do not amount to even one hair from nine cows. With their small capacity and shallow knowledge, even if people of today strive diligently and regard this as difficult and excellent practice, still it does not amount to even the easiest practice and easiest understanding of the teachers of old.

What is this teaching of easy understanding and easy practice, which people nowadays like? It is neither a secular teaching nor Buddha's teaching. It does not come up to the practice of Pāpīyas,* the Demon King, nor does it come up to the practice of those outside the way or of the Two Lesser Vehicles.* We should regard it as the product of ordinary people's extreme delusion. Even though they try to attain liberation, they find nothing but endless rounds of suffering.

On the other hand, we can see that breaking bones or crushing marrow is not difficult, but to harmonize the mind* is most difficult. Again, the practice of prolonged austerities is not difficult, but to harmonize bodily activities* is most difficult.

Do you think crushing bones is of value? Although many endured such practice, few of them attained dharma. Do you think people practicing austerities are to be respected? Although there have been many, few of them have realized the way, for they still have difficulty in harmonizing the mind.

Brilliance is not primary, understanding is not primary, conscious endeavor* is not primary, introspection* is not primary. Without using any of these, harmonize body-and-mind and enter the buddha way.

Old man Shākyamuni said, "Avalokiteshvara* turns the stream inward and disregards knowing objects."[7]

That is the meaning. Separation between the two aspects of activity and stillness simply does not arise. This is harmonizing.

If anyone could enter the buddha way by means of brilliance or broad knowledge, then the senior monk Shenxiu would have been the one. If anyone of ordinary appearance or humble position were excluded from the buddha way, how could Huineng become the Sixth Ancestor? It is clear that the buddha way's transmission lies outside brilliance and broad knowledge. Search and find out. Reflect and practice.

Being old or decrepit does not exclude you. Being quite young or in your prime does not exclude you. Although Zhaozhou first studied when he was over sixty, he became a man of excellence in the ancestral lineage. Zheng's daughter had already studied long by the time she was thirteen, and she was outstanding in the monastery. The power of buddha-dharma is revealed depending on whether or not there is effort, and is distinguished depending on whether or not it is practiced.

Those who have studied sūtras a long time and those who are accomplished in secular texts, all should study at a Zen monastery. There have been many examples of this. Huisi of Nanyue was a very learned man, but still he practiced with Bodhidharma. Xuanjue of Yongjia was an excellent scholar, and still he practiced with Dajian.

To understand dharma and attain the way can only be the result of studying with a teacher. However, when practicing and inquiring of a teacher, listen to his words without matching them with your previous views. If you understand his words in terms of your own views, you will not be able to grasp his teaching.

When you practice with a teacher and inquire about dharma, clear body and mind, still the eyes and ears, and just listen and accept the teaching without mixing in any other thoughts. Your body and mind will be one, a receptacle ready to be filled with water. Then you will certainly receive the teaching.

Nowadays, there are foolish people who memorize the words of texts or accumulate sayings and try to match these words with the teacher's explanation. In this case they have only their own views and old words, and have not yet merged with the teacher's words.

For some people their own views are primary; they open a sūtra, memorize a word or two, and consider this to be buddha-dharma. Later when they visit with an awakened teacher or a skilled master and hear the teaching, if it agrees with their own view they consider the teaching right, and if it does not agree with their old fixed standards they consider his words wrong. They do not know how to abandon their mistaken tendencies, so how could they ascend and return to the true way? For ages numberless as particles of dust and sand, they will remain deluded. It is most pitiable. Is it not sad?

Students should know that the buddha way lies outside thinking, analysis, prophecy, introspection, knowledge, and wise explanation. If the buddha way were in these activities, why would you not have realized the buddha way by now, since from birth you have perpetually been in the midst of these activities?

Students of the way should not employ thinking, analysis, or any such thing. Though thinking and other activities perpetually beset you, if you examine them as you go your clarity will be like a mirror. The way to enter the gate is mastered only by a teacher who has attained dharma; it cannot be reached by priests who have studied letters.

This portion was written on the "clear and bright" day,[8] third month, second year of Tempuku {1234}.

7

Those who long to leave the world and
practice buddha-dharma should study Zen.

The buddha-dharma excels among various ways. For that reason people seek it.

When the Tathāgata dwelt in the world there were neither two teachers nor two masters. The great master Shākyamuni guided sentient beings solely by means of his unsurpassed enlightenment. Ever since Mahākāshyapa transmitted the treasury of the true dharma eye,* the twenty-eight generations in India, the six early generations in China, and all the ancestors in the Five Schools* have in direct succession inherited it without any interruption. Consequently, ever since the Putong Era [520–27] of Liang, all those who were outstanding—from monks to kings and retainers—never failed to pay homage to buddha-dharma. Indeed, those who are able to love excellence should love excellence. It should not be like Minister She's love for a dragon.*

In the countries east of China the net of scriptural teaching covers the oceans and pervades the mountains. Although it pervades the mountains it lacks the heart of the clouds.* Although it covers the oceans it dries out the heart of the waves.* Foolish people are fond of this kind of teaching, just like taking a fish eye and holding it to be a jewel. Deluded people take pleasure in this kind of teaching, just like treasuring a pebble from Mt. Yan* as an honored jewel. Many fall into a demon's pit, often destroying themselves. How pitiable!

In a distant country a mistaken teaching easily spreads, and the correct teaching has difficulty prevailing. Although China has already taken refuge in Buddha's correct teaching, in our country and Korea Buddha's correct teaching has not yet spread widely. Why is that? What is the reason? In Korea the name of the correct teaching has at least been heard. But in our country not even this has happened. The reason is that teachers in the past who went to China were all caught in the net of scriptural teachings. Although they transmitted the Buddhist scriptures it seems they forgot the buddha-dharma. What is the benefit of that? In the end it is of no use. This is simply because they did not have the key to studying the way. It is a pity that they spent a lifetime as human beings in useless effort.

When you first enter the gate to study the buddha way, listen to the teacher's instruction and practice as instructed. When you do that there is something you should know: Dharma turns you, and you turn dharma.* When you turn dharma, you are leading and dharma is following. On the other hand when dharma turns you, dharma is leading and you are following. Buddha-dharma originally has these two modes, but those who are not true heirs have never understood it; unless they are patch-robed monks they scarcely have heard of it. Without knowing this key, you cannot yet judge how to study the way. How could you determine the correct from the mistaken?

On the other hand, those practicing Zen and studying the way are always given this key, so they do not make mistakes. Other schools do not do this.

Without studying Zen those who seek the way cannot know the true way.

8
The conduct of Zen monks.

The conduct of Zen monks has been directly and uniquely transmitted by buddha ancestors throughout twenty-eight generations in India and six early generations in China, without the addition of a single hair and without the destruction of a single particle. Thus the robe was transmitted to Caoxi and dharma has spread in boundless worlds. Presently the Tathāgata's treasury of the true dharma eye is flourishing in Great China.

This dharma is such that it cannot be attained by groping or searching about. In the realm of seeing, knowledge perishes. At the moment of attaining, mind is surpassed.

Once a face was lost at Mt. Huangmei.[9] Once an arm was cut off* at Shaolin. By attaining the marrow* and turning around mind, you acquire genuine life. By bowing formally and stepping inward* you stumble into the realm of great ease. However, in mind and body there is no abiding, no attaching, no standing still, and no stagnating.

A monk asked Zhaozhou, "Does a dog have buddha nature or not?"

Zhaozhou replied, "Mu."*

Beyond this word *mu* can you measure anything or grasp anything? There is entirely nothing to hold on to.

Please try releasing your hold, and releasing your hold, observe: What is body-and-mind? What is conduct? What is birth-and-death? What is buddha-dharma? What are the laws of the world? What, in the end, are mountains, rivers, earth, human beings, animals, and houses? When you observe thoroughly, it follows that the two aspects of motion and stillness do not arise at all. Though motion and stillness do not arise, things are not fixed. People do not realize this; those who lose track of it are many. You who study the way will come to awakening in the course of study. Even when you complete the way, you should not stop. This is my prayer indeed.

9
You should practice throughout the way.

Courageous people who study the way should first know what is correct and what is incorrect in practice throughout the way.

The great tamer of beings, Shākyamuni, sat under the bodhi tree and was immediately awakened to the way, the unsurpassed vehicle, when he saw the morning star. This way of enlightenment cannot be reached by shrāvakas,* pratyekabuddhas,* or beings such as this. Buddhas alone can be enlightened and buddhas have transmitted to buddhas, ceaselessly. How can those who have attained enlightenment not be buddhas?

To practice throughout the way is to actualize the limitless realm of the buddha way and to illuminate all aspects of the buddha way. The buddha way is under everyone's heel. Immersed in the way, clearly understand right on the spot. Immersed in enlightenment, you yourself are complete. Therefore, even though you arrive at full understanding, still this is only a part of enlightenment. This is how it is with practice throughout the way.

People nowadays who study the way do not understand where the way leads or ends, so they strongly desire to gain visible results. Who would not make this mistake? It is like someone who runs away from his father, leaving a treasure behind and wandering about. Though he is the only child of a wealthy family, he endlessly wanders as a menial in foreign lands. Indeed it is just like this.

Those who study the way seek to be immersed in the way. For those who are immersed in the way, all traces of enlightenment perish. Those who practice the buddha way should first of all trust in the buddha way. Those who trust in the buddha way should trust that they are in essence within the buddha way, where there is no delusion, no false thinking, no confusion, no increase or decrease, and no mistake. To arouse such trust and illuminate the way in this manner, and to practice accordingly, are fundamental in studying the way.

You do this by sitting, which severs the root of thinking and blocks access to the road of intellectual understanding.[10] This is an excellent means to arouse true beginner's mind. Then you let body and mind drop away and let go of delusion and enlightenment. This is the second aspect of studying the way.

Generally speaking, those who trust that they are within the buddha way are most rare. If you have correct trust that you are within the buddha way, you understand where the great way leads or ends, and you know the original source of delusion and enlightenment. If once, in sitting, you sever the root of thinking, in eight or nine cases out of ten you will immediately attain understanding of the way.

10
Immediately hitting the mark.

There are two ways to penetrate body and mind: studying with a master to hear the teaching, and devotedly sitting zazen. Listening to the teaching opens up your conscious mind, while sitting zazen is concerned with practice-enlightenment. Therefore, if you neglect either of these when entering the buddha way, you cannot hit the mark.

Everyone has a body-and-mind. In activity and appearance its function is either leading or following, courageous or cowardly. To realize buddha immediately with this body-and-mind is to hit the mark. Without changing your usual body-and-mind, just to follow buddha's realization is called "immediate," is called "hitting the mark."

To follow buddha completely means you do not have your old views. To hit the mark completely means you have no new nest* in which to settle.

Translated by Ed Brown and Kazuaki Tanahashi

Bodhisattva's Four Methods of Guidance

BODAISATTA SHISHŌ-HŌ[1]

The bodhisattva's four methods of guidance are giving, kind speech, beneficial action, and identity-action.[2]

I

"Giving" means nongreed. Nongreed means not to covet. Not to covet means not to curry favor. Even if you govern the Four Continents,* you should always convey the correct teaching with nongreed. It is to give away unneeded belongings to someone you don't know, to offer flowers blooming on a distant mountain to the Tathāgata, or, again, to offer treasures you had in your former life to sentient beings. Whether it is of teaching or of material, each gift has its value and is worth giving. Even if the gift is not your own, there is no reason to keep from giving. The question is not whether the gift is valuable, but whether there is merit.

When you leave the way to the way,* you attain the way. At the time of attaining the way, the way is always left to the way. When treasure is left just as treasure, treasure becomes giving. You give yourself to yourself and others to others. The power of the causal relations* of giving reaches to devas, human beings, and even enlightened sages. When giving becomes actual, such causal relations are immediately formed.

Buddha said, "When a person who practices giving goes to an assembly,

44

people take notice."³ You should know that the mind of such a person communicates subtly with others. Therefore, give even a phrase or verse of the truth; it will be a wholesome seed for this and other lifetimes. Give your valuables, even a penny or a blade of grass; it will be a wholesome root for this and other lifetimes. The truth can turn into valuables; valuables can turn into the truth. This is all because the giver is willing.

A king gave his beard as medicine to cure his retainer's disease;⁴ a child offered sand to Buddha and became King Ashoka in a later birth.⁵ They were not greedy for reward but only shared what they could. To launch a boat or build a bridge is an act of giving. If you study giving closely, you see that to accept a body and to give up the body are both giving. Making a living and producing things can be nothing other than giving. To leave flowers to the wind, to leave birds to the seasons, are also acts of giving.

King Ashoka was able to offer enough food for hundreds of monks with half a mango.* People who practice giving should understand that King Ashoka thus proved the greatness of giving. Not only should you make an effort to give, but also be mindful of every opportunity to give. You are born into this present life because of the merit of giving in the past.

Buddha said, "If you are to practice giving to yourself, how much more so to your parents, wife, and children." Therefore you should know that to give to yourself is a part of giving. To give to your family is also giving. Even when you give a particle of dust, you should rejoice in your own act, because you correctly transmit the merit of all buddhas, and for the first time practice an act of a bodhisattva. The mind of a sentient being is difficult to change. You should keep on changing the minds of sentient beings, from the first moment that they have one particle, to the moment that they attain the way. This should be started by giving. For this reason giving is the first of the six pāramitās.*

Mind is beyond measure. Things given are beyond measure. Moreover, in giving, mind transforms the gift and the gift transforms mind.

2

"Kind speech" means that when you see sentient beings you arouse the mind of compassion and offer words of loving care. It is contrary to cruel or violent speech.

In the secular world, there is the custom of asking after someone's health. In Buddhism there is the phrase "Please treasure yourself" and the respectful address to seniors, "May I ask how you are?" It is kind speech to speak to sentient beings as you would to a baby.

Praise those with virtue; pity those without it. If kind speech is offered, little by little virtue will grow. Thus even kind speech which is not ordinarily known or seen comes into being. You should be willing to practice it for this entire present life; do not give up, world after world, life after life. Kind speech is the basis for reconciling rulers and subduing enemies. Those who hear kind speech from you have a delighted expression and a joyful mind. Those who hear of your kind speech will be deeply touched—they will never forget it.

You should know that kind speech arises from kind mind, and kind mind from the seed of compassionate mind. You should ponder the fact that kind speech is not just praising the merit of others; it has the power to turn the destiny of the nation.

3

"Beneficial action" is skillfully to benefit all classes of sentient beings, that is, to care about their distant and near future, and to help them by using skillful means. In ancient times, someone helped a caged tortoise;[6] another took care of an injured sparrow.[7] They did not expect a reward; they were moved to do so only for the sake of beneficial action.

Foolish people think that if they help others first, their own benefit will be lost; but this is not so. Beneficial action is an act of oneness, benefiting self and others together.

To greet petitioners, a lord of old three times stopped in the middle of his bath and arranged his hair, and three times left his dinner table.[8] He did this solely with the intention of benefiting others. He did not mind instructing even subjects of other lords. Thus you should benefit friend and enemy equally. You should benefit self and others alike. If you have this mind, even beneficial action for the sake of grasses, trees, wind, and water is spontaneous and unremitting. This being so, make a wholehearted effort to help the ignorant.

4

"Identity-action" means nondifference. It is nondifference from self, nondifference from others. For example, in the human world the Tathāgata took the form of a human being. From this we know that he did the same in other realms. When we know identity-action, others and self are one. Lute, song, and wine are one with human being, deva, and spirit being.[9] Human being is one with lute, song, and wine. Lute, song, and wine are one with lute, song, and wine. Human being is one with human being; deva is one with deva; spirit being is one with spirit being. To understand this is to understand identity-action.

"Action" means right form, dignity, correct manner. This means that you cause yourself to be in identity with others after causing others to be in identity with you. However, the relationship of self and others varies limitlessly with circumstances.

The *Guanzi** says, "The ocean does not exclude water; that is why it is large. Mountain does not exclude earth; that is why it is high. A wise lord does not exclude people; that is why he has many subjects."[10]

That the ocean does not exclude water is identity-action. Water does not exclude the ocean either. This being so, water comes together to form the ocean. Earth piles up to form mountains. My understanding is that because the ocean itself does not exclude the ocean, it is the ocean, and it is large. Because mountains do not exclude mountains, they are mountains and they are high. Because a wise lord does not weary of people, his subjects assemble. "Subjects" means nation. "Wise lord" means ruler of the nation. A ruler is not supposed to weary of people. "Not to weary of people" does not mean to give no reward or punishment. Although a ruler gives reward and punishment, he does not weary of people. In ancient times when people were uncomplicated, there was neither legal reward nor punishment in the country. The concept of reward and punishment was different. Even at present, there should be some people who seek the way without expecting a reward. This is beyond the understanding of ignorant people. Because a wise lord understands this, he does not weary of people.

People form a nation and seek a wise lord, but as they do not know completely the reason why a wise lord is wise, they only hope to be supported by the wise lord. They do not notice that they are the ones who support the wise lord. In this way, the principle of identity-action is applied to both a wise lord and all the people. This being so, identity-action is a vow of bodhisattvas.

With a gentle expression, practice identity-action for all people.

Each of these four methods of guidance includes all four. Thus, there are sixteen methods of guiding sentient beings.

This was written on the fifth day, fifth month, fourth year of Ninji [1243] by Monk Dōgen, who transmitted dharma from China.

Translated by Lew Richmond and Kazuaki Tanahashi

Regulations for the Auxiliary Cloud Hall

JŪUNDŌ-SHIKI[1]

1

Those who have way-seeking mind and wish to abandon fame and profit should enter. Those who are half-hearted and lack sincerity should not enter. If the entry is a mistake, after some consideration one may be asked to leave.

When the way-seeking mind is aroused inwardly, there is immediately freedom from fame and profit. In the vastness of billions of worlds, true heirs of dharma are rare. In spite of the long history of our country you should make the present moment the true source, having compassion for later generations by giving emphasis to the present.

2

The assembly of students in the hall should blend, like milk and water, to support the activity of the way. Although now for some period you are guest or host,[2] later you will be buddha ancestors equally throughout time. Therefore you should not forget the feeling of gratitude. It is rare to meet one another and to practice what is rare to practice. This is called the body and mind of buddha-dharma; you will certainly become a buddha ancestor.

You have left your home and birthplace. You depend on clouds* and you depend on water.* The support of you and your practice given by this assembly of students surpasses that which was given by your father and

49

mother. Your father and mother are temporarily close to you in birth and death, but this assembly of students is your companion in the way of enlightenment for all time.

3

Do not look for a chance to go out. But if necessary, going out is permitted once a month. People in the past lived in the remote mountains and practiced far away in the forests. Not only were they free of nearly all worldly affairs, but they also abandoned all relationships. You should learn the heart of their covering brilliance and obscuring traces.* Now is the time for the fire on your head* to be wiped out. Is it not sad if you waste this time, concerning yourself with secular affairs? The impermanent is unreliable. No one knows where and when this dew-like existence will drop into the grass. Not recognizing impermanence is truly regrettable.

4

Do not read books in the hall, even Zen texts, and do not bring personal correspondence. In the hall you should endeavor in the way of realizing the principle. When facing the bright window,* you should illuminate the mind with the authentic teaching. Do not waste a moment. Concentrate in your effort.

5

You should always inform the director of the hall where you are going to be, day or night. Do not play around according to your own impulses; your actions affect the discipline of the entire assembly. No one can tell if this moment is not the end of this life. It would be truly regrettable to die while indulging in pleasures.

6

Do not be concerned with the faults of other persons. Do not see others' faults with a hateful mind. There is an old saying that if you stop seeing others' faults, then naturally seniors are venerated and juniors are revered. Do not imitate others' faults; just cultivate virtue. Buddha prohibited unwholesome actions, but did not tell us to hate those who practice unwholesome actions.

7

When carrying out either important matters or trifles, you should always consult with the director of the hall. Those who do things without consulting with the director of the hall should leave. If you neglect the formality of guest and host, you can understand neither the true nor the phenomenal.

8

Inside or near the hall, do not put your heads together and talk loudly. The director should prohibit this.

9

Do not do chanting circumambulation in the hall.

10

Do not hold or carry beads in the hall. Do not enter or leave with your hands hanging down.[3]

11

Do not chant the names of buddhas or sūtras in the hall. However, this is permitted when supporters request sūtra chanting on a particular occasion.

12

Do not spit, blow your nose, or laugh loudly. You should be sobered by the fact that the work of the way is not yet thoroughly mastered. You should regret the subtle passage of time which is eating away this opportunity for practice of the way. Then you may have the sense of being a fish in a small puddle.

13

Those assembled in the hall should not wear brocade but rather things like paper robes. Those who understood the way in the past were all like this.

14

Do not enter the hall intoxicated with wine. If you do so by accident you should make formal repentance. Do not have wine brought into the hall. Do not enter the hall smelling of onions.

15

Quarreling persons should go out of the hall, because it hinders not only their own work in the way but also that of others. Those who see such quarreling and do not stop it are equally at fault.

16

Those who do not follow the admonitions of the hall should be removed. Those who are amused by or in sympathy with such students are also at fault.

17

Do not show monks or lay people around the hall, as this may disturb the students. Do not speak loudly with guests near the hall. And do not talk about practice in a self-praising way, in order to get offerings. However, those who have a long-standing intention to practice or those who are on pilgrimage may be allowed inside. In such cases you should always consult the director of the hall beforehand.

18

You should practice zazen in this hall just as in the monks' hall.* Never neglect early morning zazen or the evening practice instruction period.*

19

At meal time, those who drop monk's bowls or utensils on the floor should be fined* according to the regulations of the monastery.

20

The admonitions of buddha ancestors should always be followed. The pure rules of the monastery are to be inscribed on your bones and mind.

21

You should wish to be serenely composed for your entire life and to practice the way nonintentionally.*

These regulations are body and mind of the ancient buddhas. Respect and follow them.

This was written on the twenty-fifth day, fourth month, first year of En'ō [1239].

Translated by Reb Anderson and Kazuaki Tanahashi

Instruction for the Tenzo

TENZO KYŌKUN[1]

Zen monasteries have traditionally had six officers* who are all Buddha's disciples and all share buddha activities. Among them, the tenzo* is responsible for preparing meals for the monks. *Regulations for Zen Monasteries** states, "In order to make reverential offerings to monks, there is a position called tenzo."

Since ancient times this position has been held by accomplished monks who have way-seeking mind, or by senior disciples with an aspiration for enlightenment. This is so because the position requires wholehearted practice. Those without way-seeking mind will not have good results, in spite of their efforts. *Regulations for Zen Monasteries* states, "Use your way-seeking mind carefully to vary the menus from time to time, and offer the great assembly ease and comfort." Long ago, Guishan Lingyou, Dongshan Shouchu, and other great teachers held this position. A tenzo is not the same as an ordinary cook or waiter.

During my stay in Song China, in spare moments I questioned senior monks who had held various positions, and they spoke to me from their experience. Their words are the bones and marrow of the buddha ancestors who have attained the way and have been passed on since olden times. We need to read *Regulations for Zen Monasteries* carefully to understand the tenzo's responsibilities, and then consider carefully the words of these senior monks.

2

The cycle of the tenzo's work begins after the noon meal.* First go to the director and assistant director to receive the ingredients for the next day's morning and noon meals—rice, vegetables, and so on. After you have received these materials, take care of them as your own eyes. Zen Master Baoning Renyong said, "Protect the property of the monastery; it is your eyeball." Respect the food as though it were for the emperor. Take the same care for all food, raw or cooked.

Next, in the kitchen, the officers carefully discuss the next day's meal, considering the tastes, the choice of vegetables, and the kinds of rice-gruel. *Regulations for Zen Monasteries* states, "The officers who oversee the kitchen should first discuss the menu-planning for the morning and noon meals." These officers are the director, assistant director, treasurer, ino,* tenzo, and work leader. Soon after the menu is decided, post it on the boards in front of the abbot's room and the study hall.* Then prepare the gruel for the next morning.

When you wash rice and prepare vegetables, you must do it with your own hands, and with your own eyes, making sincere effort. Do not be idle even for a moment. Do not be careful about one thing and careless about another. Do not give away your opportunity even if it is merely a drop in the ocean of merit; do not fail to place even a single particle of earth at the summit of the mountain of wholesome deeds.

Regulations for Zen Monasteries states, "If the six tastes* are not suitable and if the food lacks the three virtues,* the tenzo's offering to the assembly is not complete." Watch for sand when you examine the rice. Watch for rice when you throw away the sand. If you look carefully with your mind undistracted, naturally the three virtues will be fulfilled and the six tastes will be complete.

Xuefeng was once tenzo at the monastery of Dongshan Liangjie. One day when Xuefeng was washing rice, master Dongshan asked him, "Do you wash the sand away from the rice or the rice away from the sand?"

Xuefeng replied, "I wash both sand and rice away at the same time."

"What will the assembly eat?" said Dongshan. Xuefeng covered the rice-washing bowl.

Dongshan said, "You will probably meet a true person some day."[2]

This is how senior disciples with way-seeking mind practiced in olden times. How can we of later generations neglect this practice? A teacher in the past said, "For a tenzo, working with the sleeves tied back* is the activity of way-seeking mind."

Personally examine the rice and sand so that rice is not thrown away as sand. *Regulations for Zen Monasteries* states, "In preparing food, the tenzo should personally look at it to see that it is thoroughly clean." Do not waste rice when pouring away the rice water. Since olden times a bag has been used to strain the rice water. When the proper amount of rice and water is put into an iron pot, guard it with attention so that rats do not touch it or people who are curious do not look in at it.

After you cook the vegetables for the morning meal, before preparing the rice and soup for the noon meal, assemble the rice buckets and other utensils, and make sure they are thoroughly clean. Put what is suited to a high place in a high place, and what belongs in a low place in a low place. Those things that are in a high place will be settled there; those that are suited to be in a low place will be settled there.[3] Select chopsticks, spoons, and other utensils with equal care, examine them with sincerity, and handle them skillfully.

After that, work on the food for the next day's meals. If you find any grain weevils in the rice, remove them. Pick out lentils, bran, sand, and pebbles carefully. While you are preparing the rice and vegetables in this way, your assistant should chant a sūtra for the guardian spirit of the hearth.

When preparing the vegetables and the soup ingredients to be cooked, do not discuss the quantity or quality of these materials which have been obtained from the monastery officers; just prepare them with sincerity. Most of all you should avoid getting upset or complaining about the quantity of the food materials. You should practice in such a way that things come and abide in your mind, and your mind returns and abides in things, all through the day and night.

Organize the ingredients for the morning meal before midnight, and start cooking after midnight. After the morning meal, clean the pots for boiling rice and making soup for the next meal. As tenzo you should not be away from the sink when the rice for the noon meal is being washed. Watch closely with clear eyes; do not waste even one grain. Wash it in the proper way, put it in pots, make a fire, and boil it. An ancient master said, "When you boil rice, know that the water is your own life." Put the boiled rice into bamboo baskets or wooden buckets, and then set them onto trays. While the rice is boiling, cook the vegetables and soup. You should personally supervise the rice and soup being cooked. When you need utensils, ask the assistant, other helpers, or the oven attendant to get them. Recently in some large monasteries positions like the rice cook or soup cook have been created, but this should be the work of the tenzo. There was not a rice cook or a soup cook in olden days; the tenzo was completely responsible for all cooking.

3

When you prepare food, do not see with ordinary eyes and do not think with ordinary mind. Take up a blade of grass* and construct a treasure king's land;* enter into a particle of dust and turn the great dharma wheel.* Do not arouse disdainful mind when you prepare a broth of wild grasses; do not arouse joyful mind when you prepare a fine cream soup. Where there is no discrimination, how can there be distaste? Thus, do not be careless even when you work with poor materials, and sustain your efforts even when you have excellent materials. Never change your attitude according to the materials. If you do, it is like varying your truth when speaking with different people; then you are not a practitioner of the way.

If you encourage yourself with complete sincerity, you will want to exceed monks of old in wholeheartedness and ancient practitioners in thoroughness. The way for you to attain this is by trying to make a fine cream soup for three cents in the same way that monks of old could make a broth of wild grasses for that little. It is difficult because the present and olden times differ as greatly as the distance between heaven and earth; no one now can be compared with those of ancient times. However, if you practice thoroughly there will be a way to surpass them. If this is not yet clear to you it is because your thoughts run around like a wild horse and your feelings jump about like a monkey in the forest. When the monkey and horse step back and reflect upon themselves, freedom from all discrimination is realized naturally.

This is the way to turn things while being turned by things. Keep yourself harmonious and wholehearted in this way and do not lose one eye,* or two eyes. Taking up a green vegetable, turn it into a sixteen-foot golden body;[4] take a sixteen-foot golden body and turn it into a green vegetable leaf. This is a miraculous transformation—a work of buddha that benefits sentient beings.

4

When the food has been cooked, examine it, then carefully study the place where it should go and set it there. You should not miss even one activity from morning to evening. Each time the drum is hit or the bell struck, follow the assembly in the monastic schedule of morning zazen and evening practice instruction.*

When you return to the kitchen, you should shut your eyes and count the number of monks who are present in the monks' hall. Also count the number of monks who are in their own quarters, in the infirmary, in the aged monks' quarters, in the entry hall,* or out for the day, and then everyone else in the monastery. You must count them carefully. If you have the slightest question, ask the officers, the heads of the various halls or their assistants, or the head monk.

When this is settled, calculate the quantities of food you will need: for those who need one full serving of rice, plan for that much; for those who need half, plan for that much. In the same manner you can also plan for a serving of one-third, one-fourth, one-half, or two halves. In this way, serving a half portion to each of two people is the same as serving one average person. Or if you plan to serve nine-tenths of one portion, you should notice how much is not prepared; or if you keep nine-tenths, how much is prepared.

When the assembly eats even one grain of rice from Luling,* they will feel the monk Guishan in the tenzo, and when the tenzo serves a grain of this delicious rice, he will see Guishan's water buffalo[5] in the heart of the assembly. The water buffalo swallows Guishan, and Guishan herds the water buffalo.

Have you measured correctly or not? Have the others you consulted counted correctly or not? You should review this closely and clarify it, directing the kitchen according to the situation. This kind of practice—effort after effort, day after day—should never be neglected.

When a donor visits the monastery and makes a contribution for the noon meal, discuss this donation with the other officers. This is the traditional way of Zen monasteries. In the same manner, you should discuss how to share all offerings. Do not assume another person's functions or neglect your own duties.

When you have cooked the noon meal or morning meal according to the regulations, put the food on trays, put on your kashāya, spread your bowing cloth,* face the direction of the monks' hall, offer incense, and do nine full bows. When the bows are completed, begin sending out the food.

Prepare the meals day and night in this way without wasting time. If there is sincerity in your cooking and associated activities, whatever you do will be an act of nourishing the sacred body. This is also the way of ease and joy for the great assembly.

Although we have been studying Buddha's teaching in Japan for a long time, no one has yet recorded or taught about the regulations for preparing food for the monks' community, not to mention the nine bows facing the monks' hall, which people in this country have not even dreamed of. People in our country regard the cooking in monasteries as no more developed than the manners of animals and birds. If this were so it would be quite regrettable. How can this be?

5

During my stay at Mt. Tiantong, a priest named Yong from Qingyuan Prefecture held the position of tenzo. One day after the noon meal when I was walking along the eastern covered walkway to a sub-temple called Chaoran Hut, he was in front of the buddha hall drying some mushrooms in the sun. He had a bamboo stick in his hand and no hat on his head. The sun was very hot, scorching the pavement. It looked very painful; his backbone was bent like a bow and his eyebrows were as white as a crane.

I went up to the tenzo and asked, "How long have you been a monk?"

"Sixty-eight years," he replied.

"Why don't you let a helper do it?"

"Others are not myself."

"Reverend Sir, you follow regulations exactly, but as the sun is so hot why do you work so hard as this?"

"Until when should I wait?"

So I stopped talking. As I was walking further along the covered walkway, I thought about how important the tenzo's position is.

6

In the fifth month of the sixteenth year of Jiading {1223}, I was staying on a ship at Qingyuan. One time while I was talking with the captain, a monk about sixty years old came on board. He talked to a Japanese merchant and then bought some mushrooms from Japan. I invited him to have tea and asked where he came from. He was the tenzo of Mt. Ayuwang.

"I am from Shu in western China," he said, "and have been away from my native place for forty years. Now I am sixty-one years old. I have visited monasteries in various places. Some years ago, priest Daoquan became abbot of Guyun Temple at Mt. Ayuwang, so I went to Mt. Ayuwang and entered the community and have been there ever since. Last year when the summer practice period was over, I was appointed tenzo of the monastery. Tomorrow is the fifth day of the fifth month,* but I have nothing good to offer the community. I wanted to make a noodle soup, but we did not have mushrooms, so I made a special trip here to get some mushrooms to offer to the monks from the ten directions."

I asked him, "When did you leave there?"

"After the noon meal."

"How far is Mt. Ayuwang?"

"Thirty-four or thirty-five *li** [about twelve miles]."

"When are you going back to your monastery?"

"I will go back as soon as I have bought mushrooms."

I said, "Today we met unexpectedly and had a conversation on this ship. Is it not a good causal relationship? Please let me offer you a meal, Reverend Tenzo."

"It is not possible. If I don't oversee tomorrow's offering, it will not be good."

"Is there not someone else in the monastery who understands cooking? Even if one tenzo is missing, will something be lacking?"

"I have taken this position in my old age. This is the fulfillment of many years of practice. How can I delegate my responsibility to others? Besides, I did not ask for permission to stay out."

I again asked the tenzo, "Honorable Tenzo, why don't you concentrate on zazen practice and on the study of the ancient masters' words rather than troubling yourself by holding the position of tenzo and just working? Is there anything good about it?"

The tenzo laughed a lot and replied, "Good man from a foreign country, you do not yet understand practice or know the meaning of the words of ancient masters."

Hearing him respond this way, I suddenly felt ashamed and surprised, so I asked him, "What are words? What is practice?"

The tenzo said, "If you penetrate this question, how can you fail to become a person of understanding?"

But I did not understand. Then the tenzo said, "If you do not understand this, please come and see me at Mt. Ayuwang some time. We will discuss the meaning of words." He spoke in this way, and then he stood up and said, "The sun will soon be down. I must hurry." And he left.

7

In the seventh month of the same year, I was staying at Mt. Tiantong when the tenzo of Ayuwang came to see me and said, "After the summer practice period is over, I am going to retire as tenzo and return to my native place. I heard from a fellow monk that you were staying here, so I thought I should come to see you."

I was moved with joy. I served him tea and we talked. When I referred to the discussion of words and practice which had taken place on the ship, the tenzo said, "To study words you must know the origin of words. To endeavor in practice you must know the origin of practice."

I asked, "What are words?"

The tenzo said, "One, two, three, four, five."

I asked again, "What is practice?"

"Nothing in the entire universe is hidden."

We talked about many other things, which I will not introduce now. If I know a little about words or understand practice, it is because of the great help of the tenzo. I told my late master Myōzen about this in detail, and he was extremely pleased.

I later found a verse which Xuedou wrote for a monk:

> Through one word, or seven words, or three times five,
> even if you thoroughly investigate myriad forms
> nothing can be depended upon.
> Night advances, the moon glows and falls into the ocean.
> The black dragon jewel* you have been searching for is everywhere.[6]

What the tenzo had told me corresponded with Xuedou's poem. So I knew all the more that the tenzo was truly a person of the way.

By studying this poem we know that the words we saw before were one, two, three, four, five; the words we see now are six, seven, eight, nine, ten.[7] Fellow monks of later generations, from this you should understand practice and from that you should understand words. If you make effort in this way, you will understand pure one-taste Zen* beyond words. If you do not make such an effort, you will be troubled with the poison of five-taste Zen.* Then you will not be able to prepare the monks' food properly.

8

We can hear ancient stories and see present examples of monks in the position of tenzo. Much has been written and explained about this. It is the heart of the practice of the way.

Even if you become the abbot of a monastery, you should have this same mind. *Regulations for Zen Monasteries* states, "Prepare both meals of the day attentively and plentifully. Make certain that the four types of offering* are not lacking, just as the World-honored One offered his descendants the gift of the twenty remaining years of his life.[8] The merit of the light from even the smallest portion of the white hair tuft* between his eyes is inexhaustible." In this regard, it also states, "Just think about how best to serve the assembly, and do not worry about limitations. If you have unlimited mind, you will have limitless happiness." This is the way the abbot attentively serves the assembly.

9

In the art of cooking, the essential consideration is to have a deeply sincere and respectful mind regardless of the fineness or coarseness of the materials. Isn't it so, that by offering to the Tathāgata a bowl of water with which she had washed rice, a woman obtained inconceivable merit throughout her various lives?[9] By offering half a mango* to a monastery, King Ashoka created wholesome roots as the last act of his life. As a result, he received from Buddha prediction of attaining the way and realized the great fruit. Even a large offering to Buddha, if insincere, is not as good as a small one which is sincere. This is the right practice for people.

A refined cream soup is not necessarily better than a broth of wild grasses. When you gather and prepare wild grasses, make it equal to a fine cream soup with your true mind, sincere mind, and pure mind. This is because when you serve the assembly—the undefiled ocean of buddha-dharma—you do not notice the taste of fine cream or the taste of wild grasses. The great ocean has only one taste. How much more so when you bring forth the buds of the way and nourish the sacred body. Fine cream and wild grasses are equal and not two. There is an ancient saying that monks' mouths are like a furnace. You should be aware of this. Know that even wild grasses can nourish the sacred body and bring forth the buds of the way. Do not regard them as low or take this lightly. A guiding master of humans and devas should be able to benefit others with wild grasses.

Again, do not consider the merits or faults of the monks in the community, and do not consider whether they are old or young. If you cannot even know what categories you fall into, how can you know about others? If you judge others from your own limited point of view, how can you avoid being mistaken? Although the seniors and those who came after differ in appearance, all members of the community are equal. Furthermore, those who had shortcomings yesterday can act correctly today. Who can know what is sacred and what is ordinary? *Regulations for Zen Monasteries* states, "A monk whether ordinary or sacred can pass freely through the ten directions."

If you have the spirit of "not dwelling in the realm of right and wrong," how can this not be the practice of directly entering unsurpassable wisdom? However, if you do not have this spirit, you will miss it even though you are facing it. The bones-and-marrow of the ancient masters is to be found in this kind of effort. The monks who will hold the position of tenzo in the future can attain the bones-and-marrow only by making such an effort. How can the rules of reverend ancestor Baizhang* be in vain?

10

After I came back to Japan I stayed for a few years at Kennin Monastery, where they had the tenzo's position but did not understand its meaning. Although they used the name tenzo, those who held the position did not have the proper spirit. They did not even know that this is a buddha's practice, so how could they endeavor in the way? Indeed it is a pity that they have not met a real master and are passing time in vain, violating the practice of the way. When I saw the monk who held the tenzo's position in Kennin Monastery, he did not personally manage all of the preparations for the morning and noon meals. He used an ignorant, insensitive servant, and he had him do everything—both the important and the unimportant tasks. He never checked whether the servant's work was done correctly or not, as though it would be shameful or inappropriate to do so—like watching a woman living next door. He stayed in his own room, where he would lie down, chat, read sūtras, or chant. For days and months he did not come close to a pan, buy cooking equipment, or think about menus. How could he have known that these are buddha activities? Furthermore, he would not even have dreamed of nine bows before sending the meals out. When it comes time to train a young monk, he still will not know anything. How regrettable it is that he is a man without way-seeking mind and that he has not met someone who has the virtue of the way. It is just like returning empty-handed after entering a treasure mountain or coming back unadorned after reaching the ocean of jewels.

Even if you have not aroused the thought of enlightenment, if you have seen a person manifesting original self* you can still practice and attain the way. Or if you have not seen a person manifesting original self, but have deeply aroused the aspiration for enlightenment, you can be one with the way. If you lack both of these, how can you receive even the slightest benefit?

When you see those who hold positions as officers and staff in the monasteries of Great Song China, although they serve for a one-year term, each of them abides by three guidelines, practicing these in every moment, following them at every opportunity: (1) Benefit others—this simultaneously benefits yourself. (2) Contribute to the growth and elevation of the monastery. (3) Emulate masters of old, following and respecting their excellent examples.

You should understand that there are foolish people who do not take care of themselves because they do not take care of others, and there are wise people who care for others just as they care for themselves.

A teacher of old said:

> Two-thirds of your life has passed,
> not polishing even a spot of your source of sacredness.
> You devour your life, your days are busy with this and that.
> If you don't turn around at my shout, what can I do?[10]

You should know that if you have not met a true master, you will be swept away by human desire. What a pity! It is like the foolish son of the wealthy man who carries a treasure from his father's house and discards it like dung. You should not waste your time as that man did.

People of the way who held this position in the past kept equally high standards of responsibility and virtue. Great Guishan had his awakening as tenzo.[11] Dongshan Shouchu said, "Three jin [about one and a half pounds] of hemp,"* when he was tenzo.

If anything should be revered, it is enlightenment. If any time should be honored, it is the time of enlightenment. When you long for enlightenment and follow the way, even taking sand and offering it to Buddha is beneficial; drawing a figure of Buddha and paying homage also has an effect. How much more so to be in the position of tenzo. If you act in harmony with the minds and actions of our ancient predecessors, how can you fail to bring forth their virtue and practice?

II

In performing your duties along with the other officers and staff, you should maintain joyful mind, kind mind, and great mind.

"Joyful mind" is the mind that rejoices. You should think: "If I were born in the realm of gods, I would be attached to pleasure and would not arouse the aspiration for enlightenment nor have the opportunity to practice. Then how could I cook food to offer to the three treasures*?" The most excellent of all things are the three treasures. Even Indra's virtue cannot be compared to them, nor can that of a wheel-turning king.*

Regulations for Zen Monasteries states, "Respected in the world, quiet and secluded from daily affairs, pure and unconditioned—these qualities belong most of all to the community of monks." We are fortunate to be born in the human realm and even beyond this we have the good fortune of cooking meals to be offered to the three treasures. Is this not a great causal relationship*? We should be most grateful for this.

You should also think, "If I were born in hell, in the realms of hungry ghosts, beasts, or demons, or if I were born in the eight difficult situations,* I could not with my own hands cook pure meals to offer to the three treasures, even if I were to use a monk's miraculous power. This is so because it would be my destiny to be a vessel of suffering, with body and mind bound up."

But since you are cooking pure meals in this lifetime, this is a life of rejoicing and a body of rejoicing. It is a wholesome cause from limitless eons, it is merit that does not erode. I hope you will do your work and cook the meal this very day, at this very moment, with this body, the fruit of myriad births and thousands of lifetimes, thereby creating merit for myriad beings. To penetrate this is joyful mind. Even if you become a wheel-turning king, there will be no merit if the meal you cook is not an offering to the three treasures; your effort will be like bubbles or vanishing flames.

"Kind mind" is parental mind. Just as parents care for their children, you should bear in mind the three treasures. Even poor or suffering people raise their children with deep love. Their hearts cannot be understood by others. This can be known only when you become a father or a mother. They do not care whether they themselves are poor or rich; their only concern is that their children will grow up. They pay no attention to whether they themselves are cold or hot, but cover their children to protect them from the cold or shield them from the hot sun. This is extreme kindness. Only those who have aroused this mind can know it, and only those who practice this mind can understand it. Therefore, you should look after water and grain with compassionate care, as though tending your own children.

The great master Shākyamuni Buddha gave the final twenty years of his life to protect us in this age of the decline of learning. What was his intention? He offered his parental mind to us, without expecting any result or gain.

"Great mind" is a mind like a great mountain or a great ocean. It does not have any partiality or exclusivity. You should not regard a pound as light or a ton as heavy. Do not be attracted by the sounds of spring or take pleasure in seeing a spring garden. When you see autumn colors, do not be partial to them. You should allow the four seasons to advance in one viewing, and see an ounce and a pound with an equal eye. In this way, you should study and understand the meaning of *great*.

If the tenzo of Mt. Jia had not studied the word *great*, he would not have awakened senior Fu by laughing at him.[12] If Zen master Guishan had not understood the word *great*, he would not have blown the unlit firewood three times.[13] If priest Dongshan had not known the word *great*, he would not have taught a monk by saying, "Three jin of hemp." You should know that these great masters all studied the word *great* over hundreds of matters. Thus they brought forth the great shout of freedom, expounded the great principle, penetrated the great question, trained a great student, and in this way completed the single great matter.

The abbot, officers, staff, and other monks should never forget about these three kinds of mind.

In the spring of the third year of Katei {1237}, this was written for the students of later generations who will study the way, by Dōgen, dharma-transmitting monk, abbot of Kannondōri Kōshō Hōrin Zen Monastery.

Translated by Arnold Kotler and Kazuaki Tanahashi

PART TWO

Philosophical Works

Actualizing the Fundamental Point*

GENJŌ KŌAN[1]

I

As all things are buddha-dharma,[2] there is delusion and realization, practice, and birth and death, and there are buddhas and sentient beings.

As the myriad things are without an abiding self,[3] there is no delusion, no realization, no buddha, no sentient being, no birth and death.

The buddha way is, basically, leaping clear of the many and the one*; thus there are birth and death, delusion and realization, sentient beings and buddhas.

Yet in attachment blossoms fall, and in aversion weeds spread.[4]

2

To carry yourself forward and experience myriad things is delusion. That myriad things come forth and experience themselves is awakening.

Those who have great realization of delusion are buddhas; those who are greatly deluded about realization are sentient beings. Further, there are those who continue realizing beyond realization, who are in delusion throughout delusion.[5]

When buddhas are truly buddhas they do not necessarily notice that they are buddhas. However, they are actualized buddhas, who go on actualizing buddhas.

3

When you see forms or hear sounds fully engaging body-and-mind, you grasp things directly. Unlike things and their reflections in the mirror, and unlike the moon and its reflection in the water, when one side is illuminated the other side is dark.[6]

4

To study the buddha way is to study the self. To study the self is to forget the self. To forget the self is to be actualized by myriad things. When actualized by myriad things, your body and mind as well as the bodies and minds of others drop away. No trace of realization remains, and this no-trace continues endlessly.

5

When you first seek dharma, you imagine you are far away from its environs. But dharma is already correctly transmitted; you are immediately your original self.

6

When you ride in a boat and watch the shore, you might assume that the shore is moving. But when you keep your eyes closely on the boat, you can see that the boat moves. Similarly, if you examine myriad things with a confused body and mind you might suppose that your mind and nature are permanent. When you practice intimately and return to where you are,* it will be clear that nothing at all has unchanging self.[7]

7

Firewood becomes ash, and it does not become firewood again.[8] Yet, do not suppose that the ash is future and the firewood past. You should understand that firewood abides in the phenomenal expression* of firewood, which fully includes past and future and is independent of past and future. Ash abides in the phenomenal expression of ash, which fully includes future and past. Just as firewood does not become firewood again after it is ash, you do not return to birth after death.

This being so, it is an established way in buddha-dharma to deny that birth turns into death. Accordingly, birth is understood as no-birth.* It is an unshakeable teaching in Buddha's discourse that death does not turn into birth. Accordingly, death is understood as no-death.*

Birth is an expression complete this moment. Death is an expression complete this moment. They are like winter and spring. You do not call winter the beginning of spring, nor summer the end of spring.

8

Enlightenment is like the moon reflected on the water. The moon does not get wet, nor is the water broken.[9] Although its light is wide and great, the moon is reflected even in a puddle an inch wide. The whole moon and the entire sky are reflected in dewdrops on the grass, or even in one drop of water.

Enlightenment does not divide you, just as the moon does not break the water. You cannot hinder enlightenment, just as a drop of water does not hinder the moon in the sky.

The depth of the drop is the height of the moon. Each reflection, however long or short its duration, manifests the vastness of the dewdrop, and realizes the limitlessness of the moonlight in the sky.[10]

9

When dharma does not fill your whole body and mind, you think it is already sufficient. When dharma fills your body and mind, you understand that something is missing.

For example, when you sail out in a boat to the middle of an ocean where no land is in sight, and view the four directions, the ocean looks circular, and does not look any other way. But the ocean is neither round nor square; its features are infinite in variety. It is like a palace. It is like a jewel.[11] It only looks circular as far as you can see at that time. All things are like this.

Though there are many features in the dusty world and the world beyond conditions,[12] you see and understand only what your eye of practice can reach. In order to learn the nature of the myriad things, you must know that although they may look round or square, the other features of oceans and mountains are infinite in variety; whole worlds are there. It is so not only around you, but also directly beneath your feet, or in a drop of water.

10

A fish swims in the ocean, and no matter how far it swims there is no end to the water.[13] A bird flies in the sky, and no matter how far it flies there is no end to the air. However, the fish and the bird have never left their elements. When their activity is large their field is large. When their need is small their field is small. Thus, each of them totally covers its full range, and each of them totally experiences its realm. If the bird leaves the air it will die at once. If the fish leaves the water it will die at once.

Know that water is life and air is life.[14] The bird is life and the fish is life.[15] Life must be the bird and life must be the fish.[16]

It is possible to illustrate this with more analogies. Practice, enlightenment, and people are like this.

11

Now if a bird or a fish tries to reach the end of its element before moving in it, this bird or this fish will not find its way or its place. When you find your place where you are, practice occurs, actualizing the fundamental point. When you find your way at this moment, practice occurs, actualizing the fundamental point; for the place, the way, is neither large nor small, neither yours nor others'. The place, the way, has not carried over from the past, and it is not merely arising now.

Accordingly, in the practice-enlightenment of the buddha way, meeting one thing is mastering it—doing one practice is practicing completely.

12

Here is the place; here the way unfolds. The boundary of realization is not distinct, for the realization comes forth simultaneously with the mastery of buddha-dharma.[17]

Do not suppose that what you realize becomes your knowledge and is grasped by your consciousness. Although actualized immediately, the inconceivable* may not be apparent. Its appearance is beyond your knowledge.

13

Zen master Baoche of Mt. Mayu was fanning himself. A monk approached and said, "Master, the nature of wind is permanent and there is no place it does not reach. Why, then, do you fan yourself?"[18]

"Although you understand that the nature of the wind is permanent," Baoche replied, "you do not understand the meaning of its reaching everywhere."[19]

"What is the meaning of its reaching everywhere?" asked the monk again. The master just kept fanning himself. The monk bowed deeply.[20]

The actualization of the buddha-dharma, the vital path of its correct transmission, is like this. If you say that you do not need to fan yourself because the nature of wind is permanent and you can have wind without fanning, you will understand neither permanence nor the nature of wind. The nature of wind is permanent; because of that, the wind of the buddha's house brings forth the gold of the earth and makes fragrant the cream of the long river.

Written in mid-autumn, the first year of Tempuku [1233], and given to my lay student Kōshū Yō of Kyūshū Island. [Revised in] the fourth year of Kenchō [1252].

Translated by Robert Aitken and Kazuaki Tanahashi
Revised at San Francisco Zen Center

Birth and Death

SHŌJI[1]

I

"Because a buddha is in birth and death, there is no birth and death."[2]

It is also said, "Because a buddha is not in birth and death, a buddha is not deluded by birth and death."[3]

These statements are the essence of the words of the two Zen masters, Jiashan and Dingshan. You should certainly not neglect them, because they are the words of those who attained the way.

2

Those who want to be free from birth and death should understand the meaning of these words. If you search for a buddha outside birth and death, it will be like trying to go to the southern country of Yue with your spear heading towards the north, or like trying to see the Big Dipper while you are facing south; you will cause yourself to remain all the more in birth and death and lose the way of emancipation.

Just understand that birth-and-death is itself nirvāna. There is nothing such as birth and death to be avoided; there is nothing such as nirvāna to be sought. Only when you realize this are you free from birth and death.

74

3

It is a mistake to suppose that birth turns into death. Birth is a phase that is an entire period of itself, with its own past and future. For this reason, in buddha-dharma birth is understood as no-birth.* Death is a phase that is an entire period of itself, with its own past and future. For this reason, death is understood as no-death.*

In birth there is nothing but birth and in death there is nothing but death. Accordingly, when birth comes, face and actualize birth, and when death comes, face and actualize death. Do not avoid them or desire them.

4

This birth and death is the life of buddha. If you try to exclude it you will lose the life of buddha. If you cling to it, trying to remain in it, you will also lose the life of buddha, and what remains will be the mere form of buddha. Only when you don't dislike birth and death or long for them, do you enter buddha's mind.

However, do not analyze or speak about it. Just set aside your body and mind, forget about them, and throw them into the house of buddha; then all is done by buddha. When you follow this, you are free from birth and death and become a buddha without effort or calculation. Who then continues to think?

5

There is a simple way to become a buddha: When you refrain from unwholesome actions, are not attached to birth and death, and are compassionate toward all sentient beings, respectful to seniors and kind to juniors, not excluding or desiring anything, with no designing thoughts or worries, you will be called a buddha. Do not seek anything else.

Translated by Arnold Kotler and Kazuaki Tanahashi

The Time-Being

UJI[1]

1

An ancient buddha said:

> For the time being stand on top of the highest peak.
> For the time being proceed along the bottom of the deepest ocean.
> For the time being three heads and eight arms.*
> For the time being an eight- or sixteen-foot body.*
> For the time being a staff* or whisk.*
> For the time being a pillar or lantern.
> For the time being the sons of Zhang and Li.*
> For the time being the earth and sky.[2]

"For the time being" here means time itself is being, and all being is time. A golden sixteen-foot body is time; because it is time, there is the radiant illumination of time. Study it as the twelve hours* of the present. "Three heads and eight arms" is time; because it is time, it is not separate from the twelve hours of the present.

2

Even though you do not measure the hours of the day as long or short, far or near, you still call it twelve hours. Because the signs of time's coming and going are obvious, people do not doubt it. Although they do not doubt it, they do not understand it. Or when sentient beings doubt what they do not understand, their doubt is not firmly fixed. Because of that, their past doubts do not necessarily coincide with the present doubt. Yet doubt itself is nothing but time.

3

The way the self arrays itself is the form of the entire world. See each thing in this entire world as a moment of time.

Things do not hinder one another, just as moments do not hinder one another. The way-seeking mind arises in this moment. A way-seeking moment arises in this mind. It is the same with practice and with attaining the way.

Thus the self setting itself out in array sees itself. This is the understanding that the self is time.

4

Know that in this way there are myriads of forms and hundreds of grasses* throughout the entire earth, and yet each grass and each form itself is the entire earth. The study of this is the beginning of practice.

When you are at this place, there is just one grass, there is just one form; there is understanding of form and no-understanding* of form; there is understanding of grass and no-understanding of grass. Since there is nothing but just this moment, the time-being is all the time there is. Grass-being, form-being are both time.

Each moment is all being, is the entire world. Reflect now whether any being or any world is left out of the present moment.

5

Yet an ordinary person who does not understand buddha-dharma may hear the words *the time-being* this way:

> For a while I was three heads and eight arms. For a while I was an eight- or sixteen-foot body. This is like having crossed over rivers and climbed mountains. Even though the mountains and rivers still exist, I have already passed them and now reside in the jeweled palace* and vermilion tower.* Those mountains and rivers are as distant from me as heaven is from earth.[3]

It is not that simple. At the time the mountains were climbed and the rivers crossed, you were present. Time is not separate from you, and as you are present, time does not go away.

As time is not marked by coming and going, the moment you climbed the mountains is the time-being right now. If time keeps coming and going, you are the time-being right now. This is the meaning of *the time-being*.

Does this time-being not swallow up the moment when you climbed the mountains and the moment when you resided in the jeweled palace and vermilion tower? Does it not spit them out?

6

Three heads and eight arms may be yesterday's time. The eight- or sixteen-foot body may be today's time. Yet yesterday and today are both in the moment when you directly enter the mountains and see thousands and myriads of peaks.⁴ Yesterday's time and today's time do not go away.

Three heads and eight arms move forward as your time-being. It looks as if they are far away, but they are here and now. The eight- or sixteen-foot body moves forward as your time-being. It looks as if it is nearby, but it is exactly here. Thus, a pine tree is time, bamboo is time.⁵

7

Do not think that time merely flies away. Do not see flying away as the only function of time. If time merely flies away, you would be separated from time.⁶ The reason you do not clearly understand the time-being is that you think of time only as passing.

In essence, all things in the entire world are linked with one another as moments. Because all moments are the time-being, they are your time-being.

8

The time-being has the quality of flowing. So-called today flows into tomorrow, today flows into yesterday, yesterday flows into today. And today flows into today, tomorrow flows into tomorrow.

Because flowing is a quality of time, moments of past and present do not overlap or line up side by side. Qingyuan is time, Huangbo is time, Jiangxi is time, Shitou is time, because self and other are already time. Practice-enlightenment is time. Being splattered with mud and getting wet with water* is also time.

9

Although the views of an ordinary person and the causes and conditions of those views are what the ordinary person sees, they are not necessarily the ordinary person's truth. The truth merely manifests itself for the time being as an ordinary person. Because you think your time or your being is not truth, you believe that the sixteen-foot golden body is not you.

However, your attempts to escape from being the sixteen-foot golden body are nothing but bits and pieces* of the time-being. Those who have not yet confirmed this should look into it deeply. The hours of Horse and Sheep,* which are arrayed in the world now, are actualized by ascendings and descendings of the time-being at each moment. The rat is time, the tiger is time, sentient beings are time, buddhas are time.[7]

10

At this time you enlighten the entire world with three heads and eight arms, you enlighten the entire world with the sixteen-foot golden body. To fully actualize the entire world with the entire world is called thorough practice.

To fully actualize the golden body—to arouse the way-seeking mind, practice, attain enlightenment, and enter nirvāna—is nothing but being, is nothing but time.

11

Just actualize all time as all being; there is nothing extra. A so-called "extra being" is thoroughly an extra being. Thus, the time-being half-actualized is half of the time-being completely actualized, and a moment that seems to be missed is also completely being. In the same way, even the moment before or after the moment that appears to be missed is also complete-in-itself the time-being. Vigorously abiding in each moment is the time-being. Do not mistakenly confuse it as nonbeing. Do not forcefully assert it as being.[8]

12

You may suppose that time is only passing away, and not understand that time never arrives. Although understanding itself is time, understanding does not depend on its own arrival.

People only see time's coming and going, and do not thoroughly under-

stand that the time-being abides in each moment. This being so, when can
they penetrate the barrier? Even if people recognized the time-being in each
moment, who could give expression to this recognition? Even if they could
give expression to this recognition for a long time, who could stop looking
for the realization of the original face?

According to ordinary people's view of the time-being, even enlightenment and nirvāna as the time-being would be merely aspects of coming and
going.

13

The time-being is entirely actualized without being caught up in nets or
cages. Deva kings and heavenly beings appearing right and left are the time-
being of your complete effort right now. The time-being of all beings
throughout the world in water and on land is just the actualization of your
complete effort right now. All beings of all kinds in the visible and invisible
realms are the time-being actualized by your complete effort, flowing due
to your complete effort.

Closely examine this flowing; without your complete effort right now,
nothing would be actualized, nothing would flow.

14

Do not think flowing is like wind and rain moving from east to west. The
entire world is not unchangeable, is not immovable. It flows.

Flowing is like spring. Spring with all its numerous aspects is called
flowing. When spring flows there is nothing outside of spring. Study this
in detail.

Spring invariably flows through spring. Although flowing itself is not
spring, flowing occurs throughout spring. Thus, flowing is completed at
just this moment of spring. Examine this thoroughly, coming and going.

In your study of flowing, if you imagine the objective to be outside yourself and that you flow and move through hundreds and thousands of worlds,
for hundreds, thousands, and myriads of eons, you have not devotedly studied the buddha way.

15

Great Master Hongdao of Mt. Yao [Yaoshan], instructed by Shitou, Great
Master Wuji, once went to study with Zen Master Daji of Jiangxi.

Yaoshan asked, "I am familiar with the teaching of the Three Vehicles* and twelve divisions.* But what is the meaning of Bodhidharma coming from the west?"

Zen Master Daji replied:

> For the time being have him raise his eyebrows and wink.
> For the time being do not have him raise his eyebrows and wink.
> For the time being to have him raise his eyebrows and wink is right.
> For the time being to have him raise his eyebrows and wink is not right.[9]

Hearing these words, Yaoshan experienced great enlightenment and said to Daji, "When I was studying with Shitou, it was like a mosquito trying to bite an iron bull."[10]

What Daji said is not the same as other people's words. The "eyebrows" and "eyes" are mountains and oceans, because mountains and oceans are eyebrows and eyes.[11] To "have him raise the eyebrows" is to see the mountains. To "have him wink" is to understand the oceans. The "right" answer belongs to him, and he is activated by your having him raise the eyebrows and wink. "Not right" does not mean not having him raise the eyebrows and wink. Not to have him raise the eyebrows and wink does not mean not right. These are all equally the time-being.

Mountains are time. Oceans are time. If they were not time, there would be no mountains or oceans. Do not think that mountains and oceans here and now are not time. If time is annihilated, mountains and oceans are annihilated. As time is not annihilated, mountains and oceans are not annihilated.

This being so, the morning star* appears, the Tathāgata appears, the eye appears, and raising a flower appears. Each is time. If it were not time, it could not be thus.

16

Zen master Guixing of She Prefecture is the heir of Shoushan, a dharma descendant of Linji. One day he taught the assembly:

> For the time being mind arrives, but words do not.
> For the time being words arrive, but mind does not.
> For the time being both mind and words arrive.
> For the time being neither mind nor words arrive.[12]

Both mind and words are the time-being. Both arriving* and not-arriving* are the time-being. When the moment of arriving has not appeared, the moment of not-arriving is here. Mind is a donkey, words are a horse.[13] Having-already-arrived is words and not-having-left is mind. Arriving is not "coming," not-arriving is not "not yet."

17

The time-being is like this. Arriving is overwhelmed* by arriving, but not by not-arriving. Not-arriving is overwhelmed by not-arriving, but not by arriving. Mind overwhelms mind and sees* mind, words overwhelm words and see words. Overwhelming overwhelms overwhelming and sees overwhelming. Overwhelming is nothing but overwhelming. This is time.

As overwhelming is caused by you, there is no overwhelming that is separate from you. Thus you go out and meet someone. Someone meets someone. You meet yourself. Going out meets going out. If these are not the actualization of time, they cannot be thus.

18

Mind is the moment of actualizing the fundamental point; words are the moment of going beyond, unlocking the barrier. Arriving is the moment of casting off the body; not-arriving is the moment of being one with just this, while being free from just this. In this way you must endeavor to actualize the time-being.

19

The old masters have thus uttered these words, but is there nothing further to say?

> Mind and words arriving "part-way" are the time-being.
> Mind and words not arriving "part-way" are the time-being.

In this manner, you should examine the time-being.

> To have him raise the eyebrows and wink is "half" the time-being.
> To have him raise the eyebrows and wink is the time-being "missed."

Not to have him raise the eyebrows and wink is "half" the time-being.
Not to have him raise the eyebrows and wink is the time-being "missed."[14]

Thus, to study thoroughly, coming and going, and to study thoroughly, arriving and not-arriving, is the time-being of this moment.

On the first day of winter, first year of Ninji {1240}, this was written at Kōshō Hōrin Monastery.

Translated by Dan Welch and Kazuaki Tanahashi

Undivided Activity*

ZENKI[1]

I

The great way of all buddhas, thoroughly practiced, is emancipation and realization.

"Emancipation" means that in birth you are emancipated from birth, in death you are emancipated from death. Thus, there is detachment from birth-and-death and penetrating birth-and-death. Such is the complete practice of the great way. There is letting go of birth-and-death and vitalizing birth-and-death. Such is the thorough practice of the great way.

"Realization" is birth, birth is realization. At the time of realization there is nothing but birth totally actualized, nothing but death totally actualized.[2]

2

Such activity makes birth wholly birth, death wholly death. Actualized just so at this moment, this activity is neither large nor small, neither immeasurable nor measurable, neither remote nor urgent.[3] Birth in its right-now-ness is undivided activity. Undivided activity is birth in its immediacy.

3

Birth neither comes nor goes. Birth neither appears nor is already existing.[4] Thus, birth is totally manifested, death is totally manifested.

84

4

Know that there are innumerable beings in yourself. Also there is birth, and there is death.

Quietly think over whether birth and all things that arise together with birth are inseparable or not. There is neither a moment nor a thing that is apart from birth. There is neither an object nor a mind that is apart from birth.

5

Birth is just like riding in a boat. You raise the sails and row with the oar. Although you row, the boat gives you a ride and without the boat no one could ride. But you ride in the boat and your riding makes the boat what it is. Investigate a moment such as this.

At just such a moment, there is nothing but the world of the boat. The sky, the water, and the shore all are the boat's world, which is not the same as a world that is not the boat's.

When you ride in a boat, your body and mind and the environs together are the undivided activity of the boat. The entire earth and the entire sky are both the undivided activity of the boat. Thus birth is nothing but you; you are nothing but birth.[5]

6

Zen Master Yuanwu, priest Keqin, said, "Birth is undivided activity. Death is undivided activity."[6]

Clarify and investigate these words. What you should investigate is: While the undivided activity of birth has no beginning or end and covers the entire earth and the entire sky, it hinders neither birth's undivided activity nor death's undivided activity. At the moment of death's undivided activity, while it covers the entire earth and the entire sky, it hinders neither death's undivided activity nor birth's undivided activity.[7] This being so, birth does not hinder death; death does not hinder birth.

7

Both the entire earth and the entire sky appear in birth as well as in death.

However, it is not that one and the same entire earth and sky are fully manifested in birth and also fully manifested in death: although not one,

not different; although not different, not the same; although not the same,
not many.[8]

Similarly, in birth there is undivided activity of all things, and in death
there is undivided activity of all things. There is undivided activity in what
is not birth and not death. There is birth and there is death in undivided
activity.

8

This being so, the undivided activity of birth and death is like a young man
bending and stretching his arm,[9] or it is like someone asleep searching with
his hand behind his back for the pillow.[10] This is realization in vast wondrous
light.

9

About just such a moment you may suppose that because realization is manifested in undivided activity, there was no realization prior to this. However,
prior to this realization, undivided activity was manifested.

But undivided activity manifested previously does not hinder the present
realization of undivided activity. Because of this your understanding can be
manifested moment after moment.[11]

Taught to the assembly at the residence of the former governor of Izumo
Province, next to Rokuharamitsu Temple, on the seventeenth day, twelfth
month, third year of Ninji [1242].

Translated by Ed Brown and Kazuaki Tanahashi

Body-and-Mind Study of the Way

SHINJIN GAKUDŌ[1]

I

The buddha way cannot be attained unless you practice, and without study it remains remote.

Zen Master Dahui of Nanyue said, "It is not that there is no practice and no realization, it is just that they cannot be defiled."[2]

Not to study the buddha way is to fall into the realm of shameless and erroneous ways. All preceding and succeeding buddhas always practice the buddha way.

2

For the time being let us say there are two approaches to studying the buddha way: to study with mind and to study with body.

To study with mind means to study with the various aspects of mind, such as consciousness, emotion, and intellect. After resonating with the way* and arousing the thought of enlightenment, take refuge in the great way of the buddha ancestors and devote yourself to the practice of way-seeking mind. Even if you have not yet aroused way-seeking mind, follow the examples of the buddha ancestors who did arouse way-seeking mind in former times.

There is the thought of enlightenment, bits and pieces* of straightfor-

ward mind,* the mind of the ancient buddhas, everyday mind, the triple
world which is one mind. Sometimes you study the way by casting off the
mind. Sometimes you study the way by taking up the mind. Either way,
study the way with thinking, and study the way not-thinking.

To correctly transmit and inherit the brocade robe,* to say, "You have
attained my marrow,"* to make three bows and return to the original place,
and to pound rice* and receive the robe—this is studying mind with mind.

Shaving the head and wearing the robe is itself turning the mind and
illuminating the mind. Leaving the castle and entering the mountains is
leaving one mind and entering one mind. To directly enter the mountains
is to think not-thinking. To leave the world behind is nonthinking.

Those who have rolled up this matter into wide-open eyeballs are two or
three bushels. Those who have tampered with it by karma-consciousness are
thousands and millions of pieces.[3]

When you study the way in this manner—having merit, the result comes
of itself; having the result, merit does not arrive—you will secretly borrow
the nostrils of the buddha ancestors and have them exhale; and taking up
the hoof of a donkey* you will have it imprint the seal of enlightenment.
These are authentic examples of the ancient tradition.

3

Now mountains, rivers, earth, the sun, the moon, and stars are mind. At
just this moment, what is it that appears directly in front of you? When we
say "mountains, rivers, and earth" we do not merely mean the mountains,
rivers, and earth where you are standing. There are various kinds of mountains such as Great Sumeru* and Small Sumeru; some mountains extend
widely, some rise up steeply. A billion worlds and innumerable lands can
be found in a mountain. There are mountains suspended in form; there are
mountains suspended in emptiness.

There are also many kinds of waters: heavenly rivers, earthly rivers, the
four great rivers. There are lakes without heat; in the Great Northern Con-
tinent the heatless lake Anavatapta is the source of the four great rivers.
There are oceans and there are pools.

Earth is not necessarily ground and ground is not necessarily earth. There
is earth-ground, there is mind-ground, there is treasure-ground. Although
the varieties are innumerable, it is not that there is no earth, but invariably
there is a world where emptiness is earth.

The sun, moon, and stars as seen by humans and by devas are not the same, and the views of various beings differ widely. Views about one mind differ as well. Yet these views are nothing but mind. Is it inside or outside? Does it come or go? Is there more of it at birth or not? Is there less of it at death or not? How do we understand this birth and death, and views of birth and death?

All this is merely a moment or two of mind. A moment or two of mind is a moment of mountains, rivers, and earth, or two moments of mountains, rivers, and earth. Because mountains, rivers, earth, and so forth neither exist nor do not exist, they are not large or small, not attainable or unattainable, not knowable or unknowable, not penetrable or impenetrable. They neither change with realization, nor change without realization. Just wholeheartedly accept and trust that to study the way with mind is this mountains-rivers-and-earth mind itself thoroughly engaged in studying the way.

This trust and acceptance is neither large nor small, neither existent nor nonexistent. To study in this manner—understanding that home is no-home, abandoning home, and entering the homeless life—this is not measurable as large or small, near or far. It is beyond beginning or end, beyond ascending or descending. Broaching the subject,* it is seven or eight feet.* Responding immediately, it benefits the self and others. All this is nothing but the study of the way.

4

Because the study of the way is like this, walls, tiles, and pebbles are mind. Other than this there is no triple-world-mind-only, and no phenomenal-universe-mind-only. Mind is walls, tiles, and pebbles, put together before the Xiantong Era* and taken apart after the Xiantong Era, splattered with mud and soaking wet. Binding the self with no-rope,* mind has the power to attract a pearl, and the ability to be a pearl in water. Some days the pearl is melted. Sometimes it is crushed. There are times when this pearl is reduced to extremely fine powder. Mind does not converse with bare pillars or rub shoulders with hanging lanterns. In this manner the mind studies the way running barefoot—who can get a glimpse of it? The mind studies the way turning somersaults—all things tumble over with it. At this time a wall crumbling away allows you to study the ten directions, and the gateless gate allows you to study the four quarters.

5

The thought of enlightenment can occur within birth-and-death, within nirvāna. It can also occur without concern for birth-and-death and nirvāna. It does not depend upon the place where it occurs, nor is it hindered by the place where it occurs.

Conditions do not arouse it, and knowledge does not arouse it. The thought of enlightenment arouses itself. This arousing is the thought of enlightenment. The thought of enlightenment is neither existent nor non-existent, neither good nor bad nor neutral. It is not the result of past suffering. Even beings in the blissful realms can arouse it. The thought of enlightenment arises just at the time of arising; it is not limited by conditions.

Just now the thought of enlightenment is aroused; the entire universe arouses the thought of enlightenment. Although the thought of enlightenment seems to create conditions, it actually does not encounter conditions. The thought of enlightenment and conditions together hold out a single hand—a single hand held out freely, a single hand held out in the midst of all being. Thus the thought of enlightenment is aroused even in the realm of hell, hungry ghosts, animals, and malevolent spirits.

6

"Bits and pieces of straightforward mind" means all the bits and pieces moment after moment are straightforward mind. Not only one or two pieces, but all bits and pieces.

> The lotus leaf is perfectly round,
>   round as a mirror.
> The tip of the water chestnut is extremely sharp,
>   sharp as a gimlet.[4]

Although straightforward mind resembles a mirror, it is bits and pieces. Though it resembles a gimlet, it is bits and pieces.

7

As for the mind of the ancient buddhas, a monk once asked National Teacher Dazheng, "What is the mind of the ancient buddhas?"

The master said, "Walls, tiles, pebbles."[5]

This being so, you should know that the mind of the ancient buddhas is not walls, tiles, and pebbles, and that walls, tiles, and pebbles are not called the mind of the ancient buddhas. The mind of the ancient buddhas is studied in this way.

8

"Everyday mind" means to maintain an everyday mind in this world or in any world. Yesterday goes forth from this moment, and today comes forth from this place. With going the boundless sky goes, with coming the entire earth comes. This is everyday mind.

Everyday mind opens the gate of the inner chamber.* Because thousands of gates and myriads of doors open and close all at once, it is everyday mind. Now this boundless sky and entire earth are like unrecognized words, a voice from the deep. Words are all-inclusive, mind is all-inclusive, things are all-inclusive.

Although there is birth and death in each moment of this life of birth and death, the body after the final body* is never known. Even though you do not know it, if you arouse the thought of enlightenment, you will move forward on the way of enlightenment. The moment is already here. Do not doubt it in the least. Even if you should doubt it, this is nothing but everyday mind.

9

To study the way with the body means to study the way with your own body. It is the study of the way using this lump of red flesh. The body comes forth from the study of the way. Everything which comes forth from the study of the way is the true human body.*

The entire world of the ten directions is nothing but the true human body. The coming and going of birth and death is the true human body.

To turn this body around, abandoning the ten unwholesome actions,* keeping the eight precepts,* taking refuge in the three treasures,* and leaving home and entering the homeless life, is the true study of the way. For this reason it is called the true human body. Those who follow this must not be like outsiders who hold the view of spontaneous enlightenment.*

10

Zen Master Dazhi of Baizhang said, "If you attach to the view that original purity and original emancipation are buddha, or Zen practice, you are a follower of the outsiders' way of spontaneous enlightenment."[6]

This teaching is not the broken furniture of an abandoned house, but the collected efforts and accumulated virtue of studying the way. The body suddenly leaps up, transparently clear in eight directions. It drops away, entwined around a tree like wisteria.*

Baizhang's words are nothing but manifesting this body, awakening beings, and expounding the dharma; manifesting another's body, awakening beings, and expounding the dharma; not manifesting this body, awakening beings, and expounding the dharma; not manifesting another's body, awakening beings, and expounding the dharma. Then again, his words are not expounding the dharma.

Thus, at the moment of dropping away of the body, there is a voice that stops all sound. At the moment of renouncing worldly life, the arm is cut off and the marrow is attained. Even if you begin to study the way before the eon of the King of Emptiness,* still your practice as a descendant of yourself is endless.

11

"The entire world of the ten directions" means the ten directions are the entire world. East, west, south, north, the four mid-points, up, and down are the ten directions. Consider the moment when front and back, vertical and horizontal are thoroughly mastered. To consider means to understand and to resolve that this human body, undivided by self and others, is the entire world of the ten directions. This is to hear what has never been heard, because directions are all-inclusive and all worlds are alike.

"The human body" means the four great elements* and the five skandhas.* However, none of these elements and skandhas is fully understood by ordinary people; only sages thoroughly master them. Now, penetrate the ten directions within one particle of dust, but do not confine them to one particle of dust. Construct a monks' hall and a buddha hall within a single particle of dust, and construct the entire world in the monks' hall and the buddha hall. In this way the human body is constructed, and such construction comes from the human body. This is the meaning of "The entire world of the ten directions is the true human body." Do not follow the mistaken views of spontaneous or natural enlightenment.

Because it is not in the realm of the measurable, the true human body is not broad or narrow. The entire world of the ten directions is eighty-four thousand dharma-expounding skandhas, eighty-four thousand samādhis, and eighty-four thousand dhāranīs.* Because the eighty-four thousand dharma-expounding skandhas are turning the dharma wheel, the moment the dharma wheel is turned, the true human body covers the whole universe and extends throughout all time. It is not that the true human body is unlimited; the true human body is just the true human body. At this moment it is you, at this moment it is I, who is the true human body, the entire world of the ten directions. Without missing these points we must study the way.

Even if you were to renounce the body or accept the body for three great eons, for thirteen great eons or for innumerable eons, invariably this is the moment to study the way, to study the way backwards and forwards.

To bow to the floor and to bow standing is dignified bearing* in motion and stillness. Painting a decayed tree* and polishing a brick* of dead ash* continues without stopping. Even though calendar days are short and urgent, study of the way in this manner is profound and deep.

Although the life of those who have abandoned home and entered the homeless realm may appear bleak and lonely, it should not be confused with that of woodcutters. Even if they are continually active, their life is not the same as that of farmers. Do not get caught up in discussions of delusion or enlightenment, good or bad. Do not stay in the realm of wrong or right, true or false.

12

"Coming and going of birth and death is the true human body" means that even though birth-and-death is where ordinary people drift about, it is where great sages are liberated. Merely going beyond the ordinary and surpassing the sage is not the true human body. Although there are two or seven kinds of birth and death, when they are thoroughly mastered they are not to be feared, as each one of them is nothing but birth and death. How is this so? Not abandoning birth, you see death. Not abandoning death, you see birth. Birth does not hinder death. Death does not hinder birth.

Neither birth nor death is known by ordinary people. Birth is like a

cypress tree.* Death is like an iron man.* Even if a cypress tree were to
hinder a cypress tree, birth is never hindered by death. Accordingly, birth
and death are the study of the way. Birth is not like one sheet of cloth; death
is not like two rolls of cloth. Death is not the opposite of birth; birth is not
the opposite of death.

13

Zen Master Yuanwu said, "Birth is undivided activity. Death is undivided
activity. Filling up the great empty sky, straightforward mind is always bits
and pieces."[7]

You should quietly pursue and examine these words. Although Zen Master Yuanwu once said this, he did not understand that birth-and-death further overflows undivided activity.

When you study coming and going, in coming there is birth-and-death,
in going there is birth-and-death. In birth there is coming and going, in
death there is coming and going. Coming and going is to fly in and fly out
with the entire world of the ten directions as two or three wings, and to
walk forward and backward with the entire world of the ten directions as
three or five feet.

With birth and death as its head and tail, the entire world of the ten
directions, the true human body, freely turns the body and flaps the brain.
When turning the body* and flapping the brain,* it is the size of a penny,
it is inside a particle of dust. It is the vast flat earth, it is a sheer eight-
thousand-foot cliff. Where there is a sheer eight-thousand-foot cliff, there
is the vast flat earth. In this way the true human body is manifested as the
Southern and Northern continents. To examine this is the study of the way.

The true human body is the bones and marrow of the realm beyond consciousness and unconsciousness.* Just raising this up is the study of the
way.

On the ninth day, ninth month, third year of Ninji [1242], this was taught
to the assembly at Hōrin Monastery.

                    Translated by Dan Welch and Kazuaki Tanahashi

PART THREE

Poetic Imagery

Mountains and Waters Sūtra

SANSUI-KYŌ[1]

I

Mountains and waters right now are the actualization of the ancient buddha way. Each, abiding in its phenomenal expression,* realizes completeness. Because mountains and waters have been active since before the Empty Eon,* they are alive at this moment. Because they have been the self* since before form arose they are emancipation-realization.

2

Because mountains are high and broad, the way of riding the clouds is always reached in the mountains; the inconceivable power of soaring in the wind comes freely from the mountains.[2]

3

Priest Daokai of Mt. Furong said to the assembly, "The green mountains are always walking; a stone woman gives birth to a child at night."[3]

Mountains do not lack the qualities of mountains. Therefore they always abide in ease and always walk. You should examine in detail this quality of the mountains' walking.

Mountains' walking is just like human walking.[4] Accordingly, do not

97

doubt mountains' walking even though it does not look the same as human walking. The buddha ancestors' words point to walking. This is fundamental understanding. You should penetrate these words.

4

Because green mountains walk, they are permanent.[5] Although they walk more swiftly than the wind, someone in the mountains does not realize or understand it. "In the mountains" means the blossoming of the entire world.* People outside the mountains do not realize or understand the mountains walking. Those without eyes to see mountains cannot realize, understand, see, or hear this as it is.

If you doubt mountains' walking, you do not know your own walking; it is not that you do not walk, but that you do not know or understand your own walking. Since you do know your own walking, you should fully know the green mountains' walking.

Green mountains are neither sentient nor insentient. You are neither sentient nor insentient.[6] At this moment, you cannot doubt the green mountains' walking.

5

You should study the green mountains, using numerous worlds as your standards. You should clearly examine the green mountains' walking and your own walking. You should also examine walking backward and backward walking* and investigate the fact that walking forward and backward has never stopped since the very moment before form arose, since the time of the King of the Empty Eon.*

If walking stops, buddha ancestors do not appear. If walking ends, the buddha-dharma cannot reach the present. Walking forward does not cease; walking backward does not cease. Walking forward does not obstruct walking backward. Walking backward does not obstruct walking forward. This is called the mountains' flow and the flowing mountains.

6

Green mountains master walking and eastern mountains master traveling on water.[7] Accordingly, these activities are a mountain's practice. Keeping its own form, without changing body and mind, a mountain always practices in every place.

Don't slander by saying that a green mountain cannot walk and an eastern mountain cannot travel on water. When your understanding is shallow, you doubt the phrase, "Green mountains are walking." When your learning is immature, you are shocked by the words "flowing mountains." Without fully understanding even the words "flowing water," you drown in small views and narrow understanding.

Yet the characteristics of mountains manifest their form[8] and life-force.* There is walking, there is flowing, and there is a moment when a mountain gives birth to a mountain child. Because mountains are buddha ancestors, buddha ancestors appear in this way.[9]

Even if you see mountains as grass, trees, earth, rocks, or walls, do not take this seriously or worry about it; it is not complete realization. Even if there is a moment when you view mountains as the seven treasures* shining, this is not returning to the source. Even if you understand mountains as the realm where all buddhas practice, this understanding is not something to be attached to. Even if you have the highest understanding of mountains as all buddhas' inconceivable qualities, the truth is not only this. These are conditioned views. This is not the understanding of buddha ancestors, but just looking through a bamboo tube at a corner of the sky.

Turning an object and turning the mind[10] is rejected by the great sage. Explaining the mind and explaining true nature[11] is not agreeable to buddha ancestors. Seeing into mind and seeing into true nature[12] is the activity of people outside the way. Set words and phrases are not the words of liberation. There is something free from all of these understandings: "Green mountains are always walking," and "Eastern mountains travel on water." You should study this in detail.

7

"A stone woman gives birth to a child at night" means that the moment when a barren woman gives birth to a child is called "night."*

There are male stones, female stones, and nonmale nonfemale stones.[13] They are placed in the sky and in the earth and are called heavenly stones and earthly stones. These are explained in the ordinary world, but not many people actually know about it.

You should understand the meaning of giving birth to a child. At the moment of giving birth to a child, is the mother separate from the child? You should study not only that you become a mother when your child is

born, but also that you become a child. [14] This is the actualization of giving
birth in practice-realization. You should study and investigate this thoroughly.

8

Great Master Kuangzhen of Yunmen said, "Eastern mountains travel on
water." [15]

The reason these words were brought forth is that all mountains are eastern mountains, and all eastern mountains travel on water. Because of this,
Nine Mountains,* Mt. Sumeru,* and other mountains appear and have
practice-realization. These are called "eastern mountains." But could Yunmen penetrate the skin, flesh, bones, and marrow of the eastern mountains
and their vital practice-realization?

9

Now in Great Song China there are careless fellows who form groups; they
cannot be set straight by the few true masters. They say that the statement,
"The eastern mountains travel on water," or Nanquan's story of a sickle,*
is illogical; what they mean is that any words having to do with logical
thought are not buddha ancestors' Zen stories, and that only illogical stories
are buddha ancestors' expressions. In this way they consider Huangbo's staff
and Linji's shout as beyond logic and unconcerned with thought; they regard
these as great enlightenments that precede the arising of form.

"Ancient masters used expedient phrases, which are beyond understanding, to slash entangled vines"*: People who say this have never seen a true
master and they have no eye of understanding. They are immature, foolish
fellows not even worth discussing. In China these last two or three hundred
years, there have been many groups of bald-headed rascals. What a pity!
The great road of buddha ancestors is crumbling. People who hold this view
are not even as good as listeners of the Small Vehicles* and are more foolish
than those outside the way. They are neither lay people nor monks, neither
human nor heavenly beings. They are more stupid than animals who learn
the buddha way.

The illogical stories mentioned by you bald-headed fellows are only illogical for you, not for buddha ancestors. Even though you do not understand, you should not neglect studying the buddha ancestors' path of un-

derstanding. Even if it is beyond understanding in the end, your present understanding is off the mark.

I have personally seen and heard many people like this in Song China. How sad that they do not know about the phrases of logical thought, or penetrating logical thought in the phrases and stories! When I laughed at them in China, they had no response and remained silent. Their idea about illogical words is only a distorted view. Even if there is no teacher to show you the original truth, your belief in spontaneous enlightenment is heretical.

10

You should know that "eastern mountains traveling on water" is the bones and marrow of the buddha ancestors. All waters appear at the foot of the eastern mountains. Accordingly, all mountains ride on clouds and walk in the sky. Above all waters are all mountains. Walking beyond and walking within are both done on water. All mountains walk with their toes on all waters and splash there. Thus in walking there are seven paths vertical and eight paths horizontal.* This is practice-realization.

11

Water is neither strong nor weak, neither wet nor dry, neither moving nor still, neither cold nor hot, neither existent nor nonexistent, neither deluded nor enlightened. When water solidifies, it is harder than a diamond. Who can crack it? When water melts, it is gentler than milk. Who can destroy it? Do not doubt that these are the characteristics water manifests. You should reflect on the moment when you see the water of the ten directions as the water of the ten directions. This is not just studying the moment when human and heavenly beings see water; this is studying the moment when water sees water. Because water has practice-realization of water, water speaks of water. This is a complete understanding. You should go forward and backward and leap beyond the vital path where other fathoms other.

12

All beings do not see mountains and waters in the same way.[16] Some beings see water as a jeweled ornament, but they do not regard jeweled ornaments as water. What in the human realm corresponds to their water? We only see their jeweled ornaments as water.

Some beings see water as wondrous blossoms, but they do not use blossoms as water. Hungry ghosts see water as raging fire or pus and blood. Dragons see water as a palace or a pavilion. Some beings see water as the seven treasures or a wish-granting jewel. Some beings see water as a forest or a wall. Some see it as the dharma nature of pure liberation, the true human body, or as the form of body and essence of mind. Human beings see water as water. Water is seen as dead or alive depending on causes and conditions.

Thus the views of all beings are not the same. You should question this matter now. Are there many ways to see one thing, or is it a mistake to see many forms as one thing? You should pursue this beyond the limit of pursuit. Accordingly, endeavors in practice-realization of the way are not limited to one or two kinds. The ultimate realm has one thousand kinds and ten thousand ways.

When we think about the meaning of this, it seems that there is water for various beings but there is no original water—there is no water common to all types of beings. But water for these various kinds of beings does not depend on mind or body, does not arise from actions, does not depend on self or other. Water's freedom depends only on water.

Therefore, water is not just earth, water, fire, wind, space, or consciousness. Water is not blue, yellow, red, white, or black. Water is not forms, sounds, smells, tastes, touchables, or mind-objects. But water as earth, water, fire, wind, and space realizes itself.

For this reason, it is difficult to say who is creating this land and palace right now or how such things are being created. To say that the world is resting on the wheel of space or on the wheel of wind is not the truth of the self or the truth of others. Such a statement is based only on a small view. People speak this way because they think that it must be impossible to exist without having a place on which to rest.

13

Buddha said, "All things are ultimately liberated. There is nowhere that they abide."[17]

You should know that even though all things are liberated and not tied to anything, they abide in their own phenomenal expression. However, when most human beings see water they only see that it flows unceasingly. This is a limited human view; there are actually many kinds of flowing. Water flows on the earth, in the sky, upward, and downward. It can flow around a single curve or into many bottomless abysses. When it rises it becomes clouds. When it descends it forms abysses.

14

Wenzi said, "The path of water is such that when it rises to the sky, it becomes raindrops; when it falls to the ground, it becomes rivers."[18]

Even a secular person can speak this way. You who call yourselves descendants of buddha ancestors should feel ashamed of being more ignorant than an ordinary person. The path of water is not noticed by water, but is realized by water. It is not unnoticed by water, but is realized by water.

"When it rises to the sky, it becomes raindrops" means that water rises to the heavens and skies everywhere and forms raindrops. Raindrops vary according to the different worlds. To say that there are places water does not reach is the teaching of the listeners of the Small Vehicles or the mistaken teaching of people outside the way. Water exists inside fire and inside mind, thought, and ideas. Water also exists within the wisdom of realizing buddha nature.

"When it falls to the ground, it becomes rivers" means that when water reaches the ground it turns into rivers. The essence of the rivers becomes wise people.

Now ordinary fools and mediocre people think that water is always in rivers or oceans, but this is not so. Rivers and oceans exist in water. Accordingly, even where there is not a river or an ocean, there is water. It is just that when water falls down to the ground, it manifests the characteristics of rivers and oceans.

Also do not think that where water forms rivers or oceans there is no world and there is no buddha land.* Even in a drop of water innumerable buddha lands appear. Therefore it is not a question of whether there is only water in the buddha land or a buddha land in water.

The existence of water is not concerned with past, future, present, or the phenomenal world. Yet water is actualization of the fundamental point. Where buddha ancestors reach, water never fails to appear. Because of this, buddha ancestors always take up water and make it their body and mind, make it their thought.

15

In this way, the words "Water does not rise" are not found in scriptures inside or outside of Buddhism. The path of water runs upward and downward and in all directions.

However, one Buddhist sūtra does say, "Fire and air go upward, earth and water go downward."[19] This "upward" and "downward" require examination. You should examine them from the Buddhist point of view. Although you use the word "downward" to describe the direction earth and water go, earth and water do not actually go downward. In the same way, the direction fire and air go is called "upward."

The phenomenal world does not actually exist in terms of up, down, or the cardinal directions. It is tentatively designated according to the directions in which the four great elements,* five great elements,* or six great elements* go. The Heaven of No Thought* should not be regarded as upward nor the Avīchi Hell* as downward. The Avīchi Hell is the entire phenomenal world; the Heaven of No Thought is the entire phenomenal world.

16

Now when dragons and fish see water as a palace, it is just like human beings seeing a palace. They do not think it flows. If an outsider tells them, "What you see as a palace is running water," the dragons and fish will be astonished, just as we are when we hear the words, "Mountains flow." Nevertheless, there may be some dragons and fish who understand that the columns and pillars of palaces and pavilions are flowing water.

You should reflect and consider the meaning of this. If you do not learn to be free from your superficial views, you will not be free from the body and mind of an ordinary person. Then you will not understand the land of buddha ancestors, or even the land or the palace of ordinary people.

Now human beings well know as water what is in the ocean and what is in the river, but they do not know what dragons and fish see as water and use as water. Do not foolishly suppose that what we see as water is used as water by all other beings. You who study with buddhas should not be limited to human views when you are studying water. You should study how you view the water used by buddha ancestors. You should study whether there is water or no water in the house of buddha ancestors.

17

Mountains have been the abode of great sages from the limitless past to the limitless present. Wise people and sages all have mountains as their inner chamber, as their body and mind. Because of wise people and sages, mountains appear.

You may think that in mountains many wise people and great sages are assembled. But after entering the mountains, not a single person meets another.[20] There is just the activity of the mountains. There is no trace of anyone having entered the mountains.

When you see mountains from the ordinary world, and when you meet mountains while in mountains, the mountains' head and eye are viewed quite differently. Your idea or view of mountains not flowing is not the same as the view of dragons and fish. Human and heavenly beings have attained a position concerning their own worlds which other beings either doubt or do not doubt.

You should not just remain bewildered and skeptical when you hear the words, "Mountains flow"; but together with buddha ancestors you should study these words. When you take one view you see mountains flowing, and when you take another view, mountains are not flowing. One time mountains are flowing, another time they are not flowing. If you do not fully understand this, you do not understand the true dharma wheel of the Tathāgata.

An ancient buddha said, "If you do not wish to incur the cause for Unceasing Hell,* do not slander the true dharma wheel of the Tathāgata."[21] You should carve these words on your skin, flesh, bones, and marrow; on your body, mind, and environs; on emptiness and on form. They are already carved on trees and rocks, on fields and villages.

18

Although mountains belong to the nation, mountains belong to people who love them. When mountains love their master, such a virtuous sage or wise person enters the mountains. Since mountains belong to the sages and wise people living there, trees and rocks become abundant and birds and animals are inspired. This is so because the sages and wise people extend their virtue.

You should know it as a fact that mountains are fond of wise people and sages. Many rulers have visited mountains to pay homage to wise people or to ask for instructions from great sages. These have been important events in the past and present. At such times these rulers treat the sages as teachers, disregarding the protocol of the usual world. The imperial power has no authority over the wise people in the mountains. Mountains are apart from the human world. At the time the Yellow Emperor visited Mt. Kongdong to pay homage to Guangcheng, he walked on his knees, touched his forehead to the ground, and asked for instruction.[22]

When Shākyamuni Buddha left his father's palace and entered the mountains, his father the king did not resent the mountains, nor was he suspicious of those who taught the prince in the mountains. The twelve years of Shākyamuni Buddha's practice of the way were mostly spent in the mountains, and his attainment of the way occurred in the mountains. Thus even his father, a wheel-turning king, did not wield authority in the mountains.

You should know that mountains are not the realm of human beings nor the realm of heavenly beings. Do not view mountains from the scale of human thought. If you do not judge mountains' flowing by the human understanding of flowing, you will not doubt mountains' flowing and not-flowing.

19

On the other hand, from ancient times wise people and sages have often lived near water. When they live near water they catch fish, catch human beings, and catch the way. For long these have been genuine activities in water. Furthermore there is catching the self, catching catching, being caught by catching, and being caught by the way.

Priest Decheng abruptly left Mt. Yao and lived on the river.[23] There he produced a successor, the wise sage of the Huating. Is this not catching a fish, catching a person, catching water, or catching the self? The disciple seeing Decheng is Decheng. Decheng guiding his disciple is his disciple.

20

It is not only that there is water in the world, but there is a world in water. It is not just in water. There is also a world of sentient beings in clouds. There is a world of sentient beings in the air. There is a world of sentient beings in fire. There is a world of sentient beings on earth. There is a world of sentient beings in the phenomenal world. There is a world of sentient beings in a blade of grass.* There is a world of sentient beings in one staff.*

Wherever there is a world of sentient beings, there is a world of buddha ancestors. You should thoroughly examine the meaning of this.

21

Therefore water is the true dragon's* palace. It is not flowing downward. To consider water as only flowing is to slander water with the word "flowing." This would be the same as insisting that water does not flow.

Water is only the true thusness* of water. Water is water's complete virtue; it is not flowing. When you investigate the flowing of a handful of water and the not-flowing of it, full mastery of all things is immediately present.

22

There are mountains hidden in treasures. There are mountains hidden in swamps. There are mountains hidden in the sky. There are mountains hidden in mountains. There are mountains hidden in hiddenness. This is complete understanding.

An ancient buddha said, "Mountains are mountains, waters are waters." These words do not mean mountains are mountains; they mean mountains are mountains.

Therefore investigate mountains thoroughly. When you investigate mountains thoroughly, this is the work of the mountains.

Such mountains and waters of themselves become wise persons and sages.

At the hour of the Rat, eighteenth day, tenth month, first year of Ninji [1240], this was taught to the assembly at Kannondōri Kōshō Hōrin Monastery.

Translated by Arnold Kotler and Kazuaki Tanahashi

Spring and Autumn*

SHUNJŪ[1]

I

Great Master Wuben of Dongshan was once asked by a monk, "When cold or heat* comes, how can we avoid it?"

The master said, "Why don't you go where there is no cold or heat?"

The monk said, "What do you mean by 'where there is no cold or heat'?"

The master said, "When it is cold, cold finishes the monk. When it is hot, heat totals the monk."[2]

This story has often been examined in the past. You should also pursue it now. Buddha ancestors have never failed to master this matter, and those who have mastered it are buddha ancestors. Many buddha ancestors in India and China, both past and present, made this issue the eye of their realization. To bring forth this eye is the fundamental point of buddha ancestors.

Therefore, examine in detail the monk's question "When cold or heat comes, how can we avoid it?" This is to study the moment when cold comes or the moment when heat comes. This cold or heat—complete cold or complete heat—is cold itself or heat itself. Accordingly, when either comes, it comes from the summit of cold or the summit of heat and manifests from the eye of cold itself or heat itself. This summit is where there is no cold or heat. This eye is where there is no cold or heat.

The venerable ancestor's words "When it is cold, cold finishes the monk.

When it is hot, heat totals the monk" are how it is when the moment arrives. Even if there is the phrase "When it is cold, cold finishes," it is not necessary that when it is hot heat cancels this phrase. Cold penetrates the root of cold; heat penetrates the root of heat. Even if you try millions of times to avoid cold or heat, it is like trying to put a tail where your head is.[3] Cold is the vital eye of the ancestor school. Heat is the warm skin and flesh of my late master.

2

Zen master Kumu of Jingyin is an heir of priest Furong. His initiatory name is Facheng. He said:

> Many of you examine this dialogue and say, "This monk's question already falls into oneness.* Dongshan's answer brings the matter to differentiation.* The monk understood the meaning of Dongshan's words and entered oneness. Dongshan then entered differentiation." To analyze in such a way is to denigrate the ancient sage and lower yourself. Can't you understand these words? When I hear your interpretations the meaning is decorated and seems beautiful, but if your interpretations accumulate over time, they become a disease. If you, advanced wanderers, want to master this matter, you should understand the treasury of the true dharma eye of this ancient ancestor Dongshan. Other buddha ancestors' words are just the play of water in a hot bowl. Now, let me ask you: In the end, what is the place of no cold or heat? Do you understand?
>
> > In the jade pavilion a kingfisher builds a nest.*
> > In the gold palace ducks are enclosed.[4]

Master Kumu is a descendant of Dongshan and a distinguished person in the ancestral seat. Here he criticizes many of those who pay homage to the venerable ancestor Great Master Dongshan in the narrow house of differentiation and oneness. If buddha-dharma had been transmitted merely through the investigation of differentiation and oneness, how could it have reached this day?

Peasants or stray cats who never understood the inner chamber of Dongshan, and have not passed the threshold of the buddha-dharma, mistakenly say that Dongshan guided students with his theory of five ranks* of differentiation and oneness. This is an inadequate view. You should not pay attention to it. You should just investigate that the ancient ancestor has the treasury of the true dharma eye.

3

Zen Master Hongzhi of Mt. Tiantong, Qingyuan Prefecture, is an heir of priest Danxia. His initiatory name is priest Zhenjue. He said:

> When you take up this dialogue it is like you and I playing *go*.[5] You do not respond to my move—I'll swallow you up.[6] Only when you penetrate this will you understand the meaning of Dongshan's words.
>   I cannot help adding a footnote to this:
>
>> In here you see there is no cold or heat.
>> The great ocean dries out now.
>> I would say a great tortoise can be picked up if you just lean down.
>> I laugh to see you playing with a fishing pole on the sand.[7]

Suppose there is a *go* game; who are the two players? If you say that you and I are playing *go*, it means you have a handicap of eight stones.[8] If you have a handicap of eight stones, it is no longer a game.

What is the meaning of this? When you answer, answer this way: You play *go* by yourself; the opponents become one. Thus steadying your mind and turning your body, you should examine Hongzhi's words, "You do not respond to my move." That means "you" are not yet "you." You should not neglect the words, "I'll swallow you up." Mud within mud.[9] Wash your feet, wash the tassel on your hat.[10] A jewel within a jewel. Illuminate other, illuminate the self.

4

Zen Master Yuanwu of Mt. Jia is an heir of Zen master Fayan of Wuzu. His initiatory name is Keqin. On this matter he said:

> A bowl rolls over a pearl and a pearl rolls over a bowl.
> Oneness within differentiation; differentiation within oneness.
> A mountain goat hangs by its horns on a branch and leaves no trace.
> A hunting dog runs around in the forest taking empty steps.[11]

The words "A bowl rolls over a pearl" appear before the light and after the future—they are rarely heard in the past and present. Until now it has only been said that things do not abide; there are pearls rolling in a bowl. Right now a mountain goat hangs by its horns in emptiness. The forest runs around the hunting dog.

5

Zen Master Mingjue of Zisheng Monastery on Mt. Xuedou, Qingyuan Prefecture, is an heir of Beita Guangzuo. His initiatory name is priest Zhongxian. Once he said:

> Reaching out with your arms* is climbing the ten-thousand-foot cliff.
> Oneness and differentiation are not necessarily fixed.
> The old lapis lazuli hall brightly illuminates the moon.
> A fierce dog tiptoes up the stairs for nothing.[12]

Xuedou is a third-generation dharma descendant of Yunmen. He should be called a skin bag* who has mastered his study. By saying "Reaching out with your arms is climbing the ten-thousand-foot cliff," he seems to show the extraordinary mark, but it is not necessarily so. The matter discussed between the monk and Dongshan is not necessarily limited to reaching down the arms or not reaching down the arms, or going into the world or not going into the world. Furthermore, how can it be connected with differentiation or oneness? It seems that Xuedou cannot deal with this matter without the view of differentiation and oneness. The reason he does not grasp this study by the nose is because he has not reached the neighborhood of the venerable ancestor Dongshan and does not see the great house of buddha-dharma. He should take up his sandals* and inquire further. Do not mistakenly say that the Dongshan's buddha-dharma is the five ranks of oneness and differentiation.

6

Zen Master Changling, priest Shouzhuo of Tianning Monastery in Dongjing, wrote a poem on this matter:

> Within differentiation there is oneness.
> Oneness is differentiation.
> Drifting in the human world hundreds and thousands of years again and
>   again you want to depart but cannot.
> In front of the gate just as before, weeds abound.[13]

Although he talks about differentiation and oneness, somehow he has touched it. Indeed there is something he has touched. What would you say?

7

Priest Fuxing of Dagui, Tan Region, is an heir of Yuanwu. His initiatory name is Fatai. He said:

> The place where there is no cold or heat leads to you.
> A decayed tree* brings forth blossoms once again.
> It's laughable to look for the sword where you marked the boat.[14]
> Even now you are in the midst of cold ash.[15]

These words have some power to crush the fundamental point underfoot while raising it overhead.

8

Zhantang, Zen Master Wenzhun, of Letan said:

> When it is hot, heat prevails; when it is cold, cold prevails.
> From the beginning cold and heat do not interfere with each other.[16]
> Moving through the heavens you become well versed in worldly affairs.
> On your honorable head you place the skin of a wild boar.[17]

Now I ask, "What is not-interfering?" Answer quick, quick.

9

Zen Master Fudeng of Mt. He, Hu Region, is an heir of Huiqin, Zen Master Fujian, of Taiping. His initiatory name is priest Shouxun. He said:

> "Where there is no cold or heat" is Dongshan's phrase.
> This place is where a number of Zen persons get lost.
> Go for fire when it is cold and cool yourself when it is hot.
> In this life you can avoid cold and heat.[18]

Although master Shouxun is a dharma descendant of Zen master Wuzu Fayan, his words seem like child's talk. However, "In this life you can avoid cold and heat" will bring forth the mature style of a great old master. "In this life" is your whole life; "avoiding cold and heat" is nothing other than dropping away body and mind.

10

Various masters of different generations made noise in presenting these cap-ping verses,* but they did not even come close to the neighborhood of venerable ancestor Dongshan. The reason is that they mistakenly talked about cooling off and warming up without understanding cold or heat in the everyday activities of buddha ancestors. This is most pitiable. What did you learn about cold or heat from the old master? How sad that the ancestor way has declined.

Only after you understand the meaning of cold and heat permeating the moment of cold and heat and activating cold and heat, should you add a capping verse to explain the words of the venerable ancestor. Otherwise, you are not as good as those who know nothing. Even in the secular world the understanding of sun and moon, and how to abide with all things, varies according to sages, learned people, virtuous people, and ignorant people. Don't think that cold and heat in the buddha way are the same as the cold or heat that ignorant people talk about. Investigate this directly.

Taught twice to the assembly in the deep mountains of Echizen in the second year of Kangen [1244]. At the moment of meeting Buddha, the Unicorn Sūtra[19] is expounded. An ancestor said, "Although there are many horns a single horn is sufficient."[20]

Translated by Katherine Thanas and Kazuaki Tanahashi

Plum Blossoms

BAIKA[1]

My late master Tiantong was the thirtieth abbot of Tiantong Jingde Monastery, renowned Mt. Taibo, Gingyuan Prefecture, Great Song. He ascended the seat and taught the assembly:

> Tiantong's first phrase of mid-winter:[2]
> Old plum tree bent and gnarled
> all at once opens one blossom, two blossoms,
> three, four, five blossoms, uncountable blossoms,
> not proud of purity,
> not proud of fragrance;
> spreading, becoming spring,
> blowing over grass and trees,
> balding the head of a patch-robed monk.
> Whirling, changing into wind, wild rain,
> falling, snow, all over the earth.
> The old plum tree is boundless.
> A hard cold rubs the nostrils.[3]

This old plum tree is boundless. All at once its blossoms open and of itself the fruit is born.

It forms spring; it forms winter. It arouses wind and wild rain. It is the head of a patch-robed monk; it is the eyeball of an ancient buddha. It becomes grass and trees; it becomes pure fragrance. Its whirling, miraculous transformation has no limit. Furthermore, the treeness of the great earth, high sky, bright sun, and clear moon derives from the treeness of the old plum tree. They have always been entangled, vine with vine.

When the old plum tree suddenly opens, the world of blossoming flowers* arises. At the moment when the world of blossoming flowers arises, spring arrives. There is a single blossom that opens five blossoms. At this moment of a single blossom, there are three, four, and five blossoms, hundreds, thousands, myriads, billions of blossoms—countless blossoms. These blossomings are not-being-proud-of one, two, or countless branches of the old plum tree. An udumbara flower* and blue lotus blossoms are also one or two branches of the old plum tree's blossoms. Blossoming is the old plum tree's offering.

The old plum tree is within the human world and the heavenly world. The old plum tree manifests both human and heavenly worlds in its treeness. Therefore hundreds and thousands of blossoms are called both human and heavenly blossoms. Myriads and billions of blossoms are buddha-ancestor blossoms. In such a moment, "All the buddhas have appeared in the world" is shouted; "The ancestor was originally in this land"[4] is shouted.

2

My late master, old buddha, ascended the seat and taught the assembly:

> When Gautama's eyeball vanishes,
> plum blossoms in snow, just one branch,
> become thorn bushes, here, everywhere, right now.
> Laughing, spring wind blowing madly.[5]

This is the time for all human and heavenly beings to turn towards attaining the way, as the old buddha's dharma wheel is turned to the extreme limit of the entire world. Even clouds, rain, wind, and water, as well as grass, trees, and insects, do not fail to receive the benefit of this teaching. Heaven, earth, and land are vigorously turned by this dharma wheel. To hear words never heard before is to hear these words. To attain what has never existed is to attain this teaching. This is the dharma wheel which one cannot see or hear without having some inconceivable good fortune.

Now in Song China, both inside and outside of its one hundred and eighty regions, there are uncountable mountain temples and city temples. Many monks abide there, but those who have not seen my late master, old buddha, are many, and those who have seen him are few. Further, even fewer have heard his words, not to mention those who have personally met with him face-to-face. Even fewer have been allowed to enter his chamber. Among these few, how many have been allowed to take refuge in the skin, flesh, bones, and marrow, the eyeball and face of my late master?

My late master, old buddha, did not easily allow monks to join his monastery. He would say, "Those who are accustomed to a lax way-seeking mind cannot stay in this place." He would chase them out and say, "What can we do with those who have not realized original self? Such dogs* stir people up. They should not be permitted to join the monastery." I have personally seen and heard this. I think to myself, "Which roots of unwholesome actions made it impossible for them to abide with my late master even though they were from the same country? With what fortune was I allowed not only to join the monastery, but to enter the chamber whenever I wished, to take refuge in his venerable form and to listen to the dharma words, even though I was someone from a remote country? Although I was foolish and ignorant, it is an excellent causal relationship* which is not hollow."

When my late master was giving guidance in Song China, there were those who could study with him and those who could not. Now that my late master, old buddha, has left Song China, it is darker than dark night. Why? Because there is no old buddha like my late master—before or after him. Therefore, you who study later should think about this upon hearing these words. Do not think that human and heavenly beings everywhere hear this dharma wheel.

3

The "plum blossoms in snow" is the appearance of an udumbara flower. Although we repeatedly see the eyeball of the true dharma of our Buddha Tathāgata, we do not wink, nor do we smile. Now we correctly transmit and accept that plum blossoms in snow are truly the Tathāgata's eyeball. We take them up and hold them as the eye at the top of the head,* as the pupil of the eye.

When we enter into plum blossoms and fully study them, there is no room for doubt to arise. They are already the eyeball of "Alone above and below the heavens, I am the honored one,"* and again, "most honored in the dharma-world."

Therefore, heavenly blossoms in heaven, heavenly blossoms in the human world, māndāra* blossoms raining from heaven, great māndāra blossoms, manjūshaka* blossoms, great manjūshaka blossoms, and all blossoms of inexhaustible lands in the ten directions are one family of plum blossoms in snow. Because they bloom through the virtue of plum blossoms, billions of blossoms are one family of plum blossoms. They should be called young plum blossoms. Furthermore, flowers in the sky,* flowers on the earth, and flowers of samādhi are all the large and small members of plum blossoms' family.

To form billions of lands within blossoms and to bloom in the land is the work of plum blossoms. Without the virtue of plum blossoms there is no virtue of rain or dew. Life streams issue from plum blossoms. Do not think that plum blossoms are merely snow all over Shaolin Monastery of Mt. Song. They are eyeballs of the Tathāgata illuminating overhead and underfoot. Do not think that plum blossoms are merely snow of Snow Mountain or Snow Palace.* They are the eyeballs of old Gautama's eye of true teaching. The eyeballs of the five eyes* are fully manifested in this place. The eyeballs of one thousand eyes* are completed in this eye.

4

Indeed, old Gautama's brilliance of body-mind contains not one unillumined particle of the true suchness* of all things. Even if there is a difference of views between human and heavenly beings, and the minds of ordinary and sacred are separate from one another, snow-all-over is earth, earth is snow-all-over. Without snow-all-over there is no earth in the entire world. The outside-inside of this snow-all-over is old Gautama's eyeball.

Know that blossoms and ground are entirely no-birth. Because blossoms are no-birth, ground is no-birth. Because blossoms and ground are entirely no-birth, eyeball is no-birth. "No-birth" means unsurpassed wisdom. To see it just this moment is "plum blossoms in snow, just one branch." Ground and blossoms, birth permeating birth. This snow-all-over means snow covers entirely outside and in.

The entire world is mind-ground; the entire world is blossom-heart. Because the entire world is blossom-heart, the entire world is plum blossoms.

Because the entire world is plum blossoms, the entire world is Gautama's eyeball.

"Here, everywhere, right now" is mountains, rivers, and earth. Everything and every moment is realization everywhere of "I am originally in this land, transmit dharma, and save deluded minds. One blossom opens five petals; the fruit matures of itself."[6] Although there is the coming from India and proceeding eastward, this is the everywhere of plum blossoms right now.

5

Realization of this right-now is nothing other than "become thorn bushes everywhere right now." A great branch is the right-now* of old branches and new branches; a small twig is the everywhere of old twigs and new twigs. Study this place as everywhere and study everywhere as now.

Being within three, four, five, or six blossoms is being within countless blossoms. Blossoms have deep, vast characteristics of inside and reveal high, vast characteristics of outside. This outside-inside is the blooming of one blossom. Because there is "just one branch" there are no other branches, no other trees. Every place reached by one branch is right-now. This is old man Gautama. Because it is just one branch, it is entrusting, heir to heir.

This being so, "I have the treasury of the true dharma eye;* this is entrusted to Mahākāshyapa" and "You have attained my marrow."* This realization everywhere leaves nothing that is not deeply honored. Five petals open; the five petals are plum blossoms.

Accordingly, there are Seven Buddha ancestors,* twenty-eight Indian ancestors, six early Chinese ancestors, and nineteen later Chinese ancestors.* They are all one stem opening five petals, five petals in one stem. Studying thoroughly one branch and studying thoroughly five petals is plum-blossoms-in-snow correctly transmitting, entrusting, and meeting. Turning body and mind* inside the ceaseless murmuring* of just one branch, clouds and moon are one, valleys and mountains are distinct.*

However, those who have no penetrating eye say, " 'One blossom opens five petals' means that Bodhidharma brings forth the five Chinese ancestors. Because this line of five ancestors cannot be equaled by those coming either before or after, they are called five petals." This statement is not worth criticizing. Those who say so are not those who study with buddhas and ancestors. What a pity! How can the road of five petals in one blossom be limited to the five ancestors? Are those who came after the Sixth Ancestor not to be mentioned? This does not even attain the level of childish talk! Never pay attention to such statements.

6

My late master, old buddha, ascended the seat at the beginning of the year and said:

> The first day of the year is auspicious.
> Myriad things are all new.
> In prostration the great assembly reflects.
> Plum blossoms open early spring.[7]

Reflecting quietly: Even if all the old gimlets* in the past, present, and future drop away the body in the ten directions, unless they can say "Plum blossoms open early spring," who can acknowledge them as those who have mastered the way? My late master, old buddha, is alone the old buddha of old buddhas.

It means that, accompanied by an opening of plum blossoms, the entire spring comes forth early. The entire spring is one or two characteristics within plum blossoms. One spring causes myriad things to be all new, and causes all things to be of the first day of the year. "Auspicious" means true eyeball. Myriad things do not merely belong to past, present, and future, but are both before and after the King of the Empty Eon.* Because immeasurable, inexhaustible past, present, and future are entirely new, this newness drops away newness. Therefore, in prostration the great assembly reflects, because the great assembly which reflects in prostration is just this.

7

My late master, old buddha Tiantong, ascended the seat and taught the assembly:

> One word—precisely!
> The long ages do not move.
> Willow eyes arouse new twigs.
> Plum blossoms fill old branches.[8]

It means that the endeavor of the way throughout a hundred great eons is, from beginning to end, "One word—precisely!" Practice in the moment of a thought is both before and after "The long ages do not move."

This causes the new twigs to grow thickly and makes the eyeballs clear and bright. Although they are new twigs, they are eyes. Although they are nothing but eyes, they are seen as new twigs. Penetrate this newness as "Myriad things are all new."

"Plum blossoms fill old branches" means that plum blossoms are old branches entire and pervade old branches: old branches are nothing but plum blossoms. In this way blossoms and branches merge. Blossoms and branches are born of the same moment. At once blossoms and branches are filled. Because blossoms and branches are filled as one, "I have the true dharma. This is entrusted to Mahākāshyapa." Each face is filled with taking up the flower; each blossom is filled with breaking into a smile.

8

My late master, old buddha, ascended the seat and taught the assembly:

> Willows flourish a sash
> Plum blossoms wear an armband.[9]

This armband is not a brocade or a jewel,[10] but is plum blossoms blooming. Plum blossoms blooming is "My marrow has attained you."[11]

9

When King Prasenajit invited venerable Pindola and offered a noon meal, the king said, "I have heard that you saw buddha in person. Is that so?"

Pindola answered by raising his eyebrow with his hand.

My late master, old buddha, said in his poem:

> Raising an eyebrow he answers the question.
> He saw buddha in person and does not deceive.
> He still receives offering from the world.
> Spring lies in plum twigs accompanied by snow and cold.[12]

The story is that King Prasenajit once asked Pindola whether he had seen buddha or not. To see buddha is to become buddha. To become buddha is to raise the eyebrow. Even if Pindola had realized the fruit of an arhat,* unless he was a true arhat he could not have seen buddha. Unless he saw buddha he could not have become buddha. Unless he became buddha he could not have raised the eyebrow.

Know that venerable Pindola was a face-to-face transmission disciple of

Shākyamuni Buddha and, having realized the four fruits* of the way, was awaiting the appearance of another buddha—how could he not have seen Shākyamuni Buddha? "Seeing Shākyamuni Buddha" is not just seeing buddha but seeing Shākyamuni Buddha as Shākyamuni Buddha seeing himself. It has been studied in this way. When King Prasenajit opened this eye of study, he met a skilled hand which raised the eyebrow.

Have the penetrating-buddha-eye which calmly looks into the meaning of "seeing buddha in person." This spring lies neither in the human world nor in a buddha land, but in plum twigs. How do we know this? It is raising eyebrows of snow and cold.

10

My late master, old buddha, said:

> The original face has no birth and death.
> Spring is in plum blossoms and enters into a painting.[13]

When you paint spring, do not paint willows, plums, peaches, or apricots—just paint spring. To paint willows, plums, peaches, or apricots is to paint willows, plums, peaches, or apricots. It is not yet painting spring.

It is not that spring cannot be painted, but aside from my late master, old buddha, there is no one in India or China who has painted spring. He alone was a sharp-pointed brush that painted spring.

This "spring" is spring-in-the-painting because it "enters into a painting." He does not use other means, but lets plum blossoms initiate spring. He lets spring enter into a painting and into a tree. This is skillful means.

Because my late master, old buddha, clarified the treasury of the true dharma eye, he correctly transmitted it to buddha ancestors who assemble in the ten directions of past, present, and future. In this way he thoroughly mastered the eyeball and opened up plum blossoms.

This was written on the sixth day, eleventh month, first year of Kangen [1243], at Yoshimine Monastery, Yoshida County, Echizen Province. Snow three feet deep, all over the earth.

Postscript
1

If a doubt arises and you think that plum blossoms are not Gautama's eyeballs, consider whether anything other than plum blossoms may be seen as eyeballs. If you seek the eyeballs elsewhere, you will not recognize them even though you are facing them, because meeting is not consummated. This day is not this day of an individual; it is this day of the great house.* Realize right now plum blossoms as eyeballs. Stop seeking any further!

2

My late master, old buddha, said:

> Bright, bright! Clear, clear!
> Do not seek within the shadow of plum blossoms.
> Throughout past and present rain is created and clouds are formed.
> Past and present, solitary and silent—where does it end?[14]

This being so, to form clouds and to create rain is the activity of plum blossoms. The movement of clouds and the movement of rain are a thousand shades and myriad forms, a thousand merits and myriad characteristics of plum blossoms. "Throughout past and present" is plum blossoms; plum blossoms are called past and present.

3

Once Zen master [Wuzu] Fayan said:

> North wind mixed with snow shakes the valley forest.
> Myriad things are hidden, but resentment is not deep.
> There are only mountain plums which are high-spirited,
> Spitting out winter's cold heart just before the end of the year.[15]

Therefore, without penetrating the activities of plum blossoms it is impossible to know winter's cold heart. Some characteristics of plum blossoms harmonize with north wind and snow is formed. Thus I know that to scatter wind, to form snow, to initiate the year, and to cause the valley forest and myriad things to be as they are, are all due to the power of plum blossoms.

4

Senior Fu of Taiyuan said, in praise of the way of enlightenment:

> O! In olden days when I was not yet awakened,
> the sound of a painted horn was the sound of sorrow.

Now on my pillow there is no idle dream.
Letting go, plum blossoms blow vast and small.[16]

Senior Fu had been a lecturer before. He was opened up by the tenzo of
Mt. Jia and experienced great realization, allowing the spring wind of plum
blossoms to blow vast and small.

Translated by Mel Weitsman and Kazuaki Tanahashi
Revised at Zen Community of New York

Everyday Activity*

KAJŌ[1]

1

In the domain of buddha ancestors, drinking tea and eating rice is everyday activity. This having tea and rice has been transmitted over many years and is present right now. Thus the buddha ancestors' vital activity of having tea and rice comes to us.

2

Priest Daokai of Mt. Dayang asked Touzi [Yiqing], "It is said that the thoughts and words of buddha ancestors are everyday tea and rice. Besides this, are there any words or phrases for teaching?"

Touzi said, "Tell me, when the emperor issues a decree in his territory, does he need Emperor Yu, Tang, Yao, or Shun?"*

As Dayang was about to open his mouth, Touzi covered it with his whisk. "While you were thinking, you've already received thirty blows."*

Dayang was then awakened. He bowed deeply and began to leave.

Touzi said, "Wait, reverend." Dayang did not turn around, and Touzi said, "Have you reached the ground of no doubt?"

Dayang covered his ears with his hands and left.[2]

From this you should clearly understand that the thoughts and words of buddha ancestors are their everyday tea and rice. Ordinary coarse tea and plain rice are buddhas' thoughts—ancestors' words. Because buddha ancestors prepare tea and rice, tea and rice maintain buddha ancestors. Accordingly, they need no powers other than this tea and rice, and they have no need to use powers as buddha ancestors.

You should investigate and study the expression "Does he need Emperor Yu, Tang, Yao, or Shun?" You should leap over the summit of the question "Besides tea and rice are there any words or phrases for teaching?" You should try to see whether leaping is possible or not.

3

Great Master Wuji of Shitou Hut, Mt. Nanyue, said:

> I have built a grass hut where no coins are kept.
> Having had rice, I am ready for a leisurely nap.[3]

"Having had rice"—words come, words go, words come and go—filled with buddha ancestors' thoughts and words. Not to have rice is not to be filled. Yet, the point of "having had rice" and "a leisurely nap" is actualized before having rice, while having rice, and after having rice. To understand that having rice lies only in the domain of "having had rice" is the mere study of four or five *shō** of rice.

4

My late master, old buddha, taught the assembly:

> I heard that a monk asked Baizhang, "What is an extraordinary thing?" Baizhang said, "Sitting alone on Daxiong Peak.* The assembly cannot move him. For now let him totally sit."[4]

> Today if someone were to ask me, "What is an extraordinary thing?" I would say, "Is anything extraordinary? Do you know what it means? The bowl of Jingci[5] has moved—I'm having rice in Tiantong."[6]

In the domain of buddha ancestors there is always something extraordinary: sitting alone on Daxiong Peak. Being allowed to totally sit is itself an extraordinary thing. Even more extraordinary is "The bowl of Jingci has moved—I'm having rice in Tiantong."

Each and every extraordinary activity is simply having rice. Thus, sitting alone on Daxiong Peak is just having rice. The monk's bowl* is used for having rice, and what is used for having rice is the monk's bowl. Therefore it is "the bowl of Jingci" and it is "having rice in Tiantong." Being filled is to know rice. Eating rice is to be filled. To know is to be filled with rice. To be filled is to continue eating.

Now what is the monk's bowl? I say it is not wood and it is not black lacquer. Is it an immovable rock? Is it an iron person?* It is bottomless. It has no nostrils. One mouth swallows the empty sky. The empty sky is received with palms together.

5

My late master, old buddha, once taught the assembly at the buddha hall of Ruiyan Jingtu Monastery of Tai Region:

> When hunger comes, have rice.
> When fatigue comes, sleep.
> Furnace and bellows,* each covers the entire sky.[7]

"When hunger comes" is the vital activity of a person who has had rice. A person who has not had rice cannot have hunger. Since this is so, a person who gets hungry every day is someone who has had rice. You should understand this completely.

"When fatigue comes" means that there is fatigue in the midst of fatigue; it springs forth complete from the summit of fatigue. Accordingly, the entire body is completely turned immediately by the activity of the entire body.

To "sleep" is to sleep using buddha eye, dharma eye, wisdom eye, ancestor eye, and pillar-and-lantern* eye.

6

My late master, old buddha, once accepted an invitation and went to Jingci Monastery of Linan Prefecture from Ruiyan Monastery of Tai Region, ascended the seat and said:

> Half a year—just having rice and sitting on Wan Peak.
> This sitting cuts through thousands of layers of misty clouds.
> One sudden clap of roaring thunder.
> Spring in the mystic village—apricot blossoms are red.[8]

The teaching of buddha ancestors who transmit the buddha's lifelong practice is entirely "having rice and sitting on Wan Peak." To study and practice the inheritance of the buddha's ancestral wisdom is to bring forth the vital activity of having rice. "Half a year . . . sitting on Wan Peak" is called having rice. You cannot tell how many layers of misty clouds this sitting cuts through. However sudden the roar of thunder, spring apricot blossoms are just red. "Mystic village" means red through and through right now. This is having rice. Wan Peak is the name of a peak that represents Ruiyan Monastery.

7

My late master, old buddha, once taught the assembly at the buddha hall of Ruiyan Monastery, Qingyuan Prefecture, Ming Region:

> Inconceivable golden form*
> wears a robe and has rice.
> So I bow to you;
> go to sleep early and wake up late. Hah!
> Discussing the profound, expounding the inconceivable—endless.
> What I completely avoid is the self-deception of holding up a flower.[9]

You should immediately penetrate this. "Inconceivable golden form" means wearing a robe and having rice. Wearing a robe and having rice is inconceivable golden form. Do not wonder who is wearing a robe and having rice. Do not say whose inconceivable golden form it is.

Speaking in this way is complete expression. This is the meaning of "So I bow to you" and "I have already had rice. You have just bowed to the rice." This is because "I completely avoid holding up a flower."

8

Priest Daan, Zen Master Yuanzhi, of Changqing Monastery, Fu Region, ascended the seat and taught the assembly:

> I have been at Mt. Gui for thirty years and have been eating Mt. Gui's rice and shitting Mt. Gui's shit. I have not studied Guishan's Zen but just see a single water buffalo.* When it wanders off the road and begins grazing, I yank it back. When it trespasses onto other people's rice fields, I whip it. In this way, I have been taming it for a long time. Such an adorable one! It understands human speech, and now has transformed into a white ox. All day long it is walking round and round in front of us. Even if we try to drive it away, it does not leave.[10]

Clearly you should accept this teaching. Thirty years of pursuit in the assembly of buddha ancestors is having rice. There are no other pursuits. If you bring forth this activity of having rice, invariably you will be able to see one buffalo.

9

Zhaozhou, Great Master Zhenji, asked a newly arrived monk, "Have you been here before?"

The monk said, "Yes, I have been here."

The master said, "Have some tea."

Again, he asked another monk, "Have you been here before?"

The monk said, "No, I haven't been here."

The master said, "Have some tea."

The temple director then asked the master, "Why do you say, 'Have some tea,' to someone who has been here, and 'Have some tea,' to someone who has not?"

The master said, "Director." When the director responded, the master said, "Have some tea."[11]

Zhaozhou's word "here" does not mean the top of the head, the nostrils, or Zhaozhou. Since "here" leaps off "here," a monk said, "I have been here," and another said, "I have not been here." It means, "What is now?" I only say, "I have been here, I have not been here."

Therefore my late master said:

> In your picture of the wineshop
> Who faces you, drinking Zhaozhou's tea?[12]

Thus, the everyday activity of buddha ancestors is nothing but having tea and rice.

On the seventeenth day, twelfth month, first year of Kangen [1243], this was taught to the assembly at the foot of Yamashi Peak, Echizen Province.

Translated by Arnold Kotler and Kazuaki Tanahashi

The Moon

TSUKI[1]

The full actualization of all moons is not limited to "before, three-three"*
or "after, three-three." All moons of full actualization are not limited to
"before, three-three" or "after, three-three."

Since this is so, Shākyamuni Buddha said, "Buddha's true dharma body
as it is, is empty sky. In response to things, forms appear. Thus is the moon
in water."[2]

Thusness* of "Thus is the moon in water" is the moon in water. It is
water thusness, moon thusness, thusness within, within thusness. "Thus"
does not mean "like something." "Thus" means "as it is."

Buddha's true dharma body is the "as it is" of empty sky. This empty sky
is the "as it is" of buddha's true dharma body. Because it is buddha's true
dharma body, the entire earth, the entire universe, all phenomena, and all
appearances are empty sky. Hundreds of grasses and myriad forms—each
appearing "as it is"—are nothing but buddha's true dharma body, thusness
of the moon in water.

The time when the moon appears is not necessarily night. Night is not
necessarily dark. Do not be limited to the narrow views held by human
beings. Even where there is no sun or moon, there is day and night. Sun
and moon are not day and night; each is as it is.

The moon is not one moon or two moons, not thousands of moons or myriads of moons. Even if the moon itself holds the view of one moon or two moons, that is merely the moon's view. It is not necessarily the words or understanding of the buddha way.

Even if you say, "There was a moon last night," the moon you see tonight is not last night's moon. You should thoroughly study that tonight's moon, from beginning to end, is tonight's moon. Although there is a moon, it is neither new nor old, because moon inherits moon.

2

Zen master Baoji of Panshan said, "The mind moon is alone and full. Its light swallows myriad forms. Moonlight does not illuminate objects. Objects do not exist. Light and objects both disappear. What is this?"[3]

What is said here is that buddha ancestors and buddha heirs always have the mind moon, because they make moon their mind. There is no mind which is not moon, and there is no moon which is not mind.

"Alone and full" means nothing lacking. Beyond two or three is called "myriad forms." Myriad forms are moonlight, not merely forms. Accordingly, "Its light swallows myriad forms." Myriad forms completely swallow moonlight. Here moonlight swallowing moonlight is called "Its light swallows myriad forms." That is to say, the moon swallows the moon, the moonlight swallows the moon. Therefore it is said, "Moonlight does not illuminate objects. Objects do not exist."[4]

Since this is so, at the moment of awakening others with a buddha body, a buddha body comes forth and expounds dharma; at the moment of awakening others with the boundless body, the boundless body manifests and expounds dharma. This is nothing but turning the dharma wheel within the moon. No matter whether the yin spirit or the yang spirit[5] illuminates—no matter whether the moon is a fire jewel or water jewel,[6] it is immediately actualized.

This mind is the moon. This moon is itself mind. This is penetrating and comprehending the mind of buddha ancestors and buddha heirs.

3

An ancient buddha said, "A single mind is all things. All things are a single mind."

Thus, mind is all things, all things are mind. Since mind is the moon, the moon is the moon. Since mind which is all things is completely moon, the all-inclusive world is the all-inclusive moon; entire body is entire moon. Amid the "before and after, three-three" in the myriad years of a moment—which of these is not the moon?

Sun-face Buddha, Moon-face Buddha*—our body, mind, and environs—are also within the moon. The coming and going of birth and death is also the moon. The entire world in the ten directions is the up and down, the left and right of the moon. Everyday activity at this moment is hundreds of grasses brilliant in the moon, the mind of ancestors brilliant in the moon.

4

Great Master Ciji of Mt. Touzi, Shu Region, was once asked by a monk, "When the moon is not yet full, what then?"

The master said, "Swallow three or four."

The monk said, "After it is full, what then?"

The master said, "Spit out seven or eight."[7]

What is studied here is "not yet full" and "after it is full." Both are the moon's activity. Each of the three or four moons is a complete moon that is "not yet full." Each of the seven or eight moons is a complete moon that is "after it is full."

To swallow is three or four. At this moment, the moon which is "not yet full" is actualized. To spit out is seven or eight. At this moment, "after it is full" is actualized.

When the moon swallows the moon, that is three or four. In swallowing, the moon is brought forth. The moon is swallowing actualized. When the moon spits out the moon, that is seven or eight. In spitting out, the moon is brought forth. The moon is spitting out actualized.

Thus there is total swallowing, total spitting out. The whole earth and whole sky are spit out. The whole sky and whole earth are swallowed. Swallow yourself and swallow others. Spit out yourself and spit out others.

5

Shākyamuni Buddha said to Vajragarbha Bodhisattva, "When you look at deep water and shift your eyes, the water sways. The eyes of samādhi can turn fire around. When the clouds fly the moon travels; when a boat goes the shore moves. It is just like this."[8]

You should understand and investigate thoroughly this discourse of Buddha, "When the clouds fly the moon travels; when a boat goes the shore moves." Do not study in haste. Do not follow ordinary thinking. But those who see and hear Buddha's discourse as Buddha's discourse are rare. If you study it as Buddha's discourse, round, full enlightenment is not limited to body and mind, or to bodhi and nirvāna. Bodhi and nirvāna are not necessarily round, full enlightenment, nor are they body and mind.

The Tathāgata says that when clouds fly the moon moves, and when a boat goes the shore moves. In this way the moon travels when the clouds move and the shore moves when the boat goes. The meaning of these words is that clouds and moon travel at the same time, walk together, with no beginning or end, no before or after. The boat and the shore travel at the same time, walk together, without starting or stopping, without floating or turning.[9]

When you study someone's movement, the movement is not merely starting or stopping. The movement that starts or stops is not that person's. Do not take up starting or stopping and regard it as the person's movement. The clouds' flying, the moon's traveling, the boat's going, and the shore's moving are all like this. Do not foolishly be limited by a narrow view.

The clouds' flying is not concerned with east, west, south, or north. The moon's traveling has not ceased day or night from ancient times to the present. Do not forget this. The boat's going and the shore's moving are not bound by past, present, or future, but actualize past, present, and future. This being so, "full and not hungry just now"[10] is possible.

Foolish people think that because clouds run we see the immovable moon as moving, and because a boat goes we see the immovable shore as moving. But if they are right, why did the Tathāgata speak as he did? The meaning of buddha-dharma cannot be measured by the narrow views of human or heavenly beings. Although it is immeasurable, buddha-dharma is practiced in accordance with one's capacity. Who is unable to take up the boat or shore over and over? Who is unable to see through the clouds or moon immediately?

You should know that the Tathāgata's words do not make a metaphor of clouds for dharma suchness,* of the moon for dharma suchness, of the boat for dharma suchness, of the shore for dharma suchness. You should quietly examine and penetrate this. One step of the moon is the Tathāgata's round, full enlightenment. The Tathāgata's round, full enlightenment is the motion of the moon. Not moving or stopping, not going forward or backward, the moon's motion is not a metaphor. It is the actualization of "alone and full."

You should know that even though the moon passes quickly it is beyond beginning, middle, or end.[11] Thus, there is first-month moon and second-month moon. The first and second are both the moon.[12] Right practice is the moon. Right offering is the moon. Snapping the sleeves* and walking away is the moon.

Round and crescent are not the cycle of coming and going. The moons do and do not use coming and going: go freely and grasp firmly coming and going. Creating wind and stream* the moons are as they are.

On the sixth day, first month, fourth year of Ninji [1243], written at Kannondōri Kōsho Hōrin Monastery by Monk Dōgen.

Translated by Mel Weitsman and Kazuaki Tanahashi

Painting of a Rice-cake*

GABYŌ[1]

1

All buddhas are realization;[2] thus all things are realization.[3] Yet no buddhas or things have the same characteristics; none have the same mind. Although there are no similar characteristics or minds, at the moment of your actualization numerous actualizations manifest without hindrance. At the moment of your manifestation, numerous manifestations come forth without opposing one another.[4] This is the straightforward teaching of the ancestors.

Do not use the measure of oneness or difference as the criterion of your study. Thus it is said, "To penetrate* one thing is to penetrate myriad things."

To penetrate one thing does not take away its inherent characteristics. Just as penetration does not limit one thing, it does not make one thing unlimited. To try to make it unlimited is a hindrance. When you allow penetration to be unhindered by penetration, one penetration is myriad penetrations. One penetration is one thing. Penetrating one thing is penetrating myriad things.

2

An ancient buddha said, "A painting of a rice-cake does not satisfy hunger."[5]

Those in cloud robes and mist sleeves* who study this statement, as well

134

as bodhisattvas and shrāvakas who come from the ten directions, differ in name and position; the skin and flesh of divine heads or of demon faces in the ten directions differ, sometimes thick, sometimes thin.

This statement has been studied by ancient buddhas and present buddhas; nevertheless, it has become the mere chatter of seekers in grass-roofed huts and under trees. When they transmit their teaching, they say, "This statement means that studying the sūtras and commentaries does not nourish true wisdom." Or they suppose it means that to study the sūtras of the Three Vehicles or the One Vehicle* is not the way of perfect enlightenment.

To think this statement means that expedient teachings are useless is a great mistake. This is not the correct transmission of the ancestors' teaching; it obscures the words of the buddha ancestors. If you do not understand this one buddha's phrase, who could acknowledge that you have thoroughly understood the words of other buddhas?

To say "A painting of a rice-cake does not satisfy hunger" is like saying "to refrain from all unwholesome actions and to respectfully practice wholesome actions."* It is like saying "What is it that thus comes?"* It is like saying "I am always intimate with this."* You should investigate it in this way.

There are few who have even seen this "painting of a rice-cake," and none of them has thoroughly understood it. How is this so? When I inquired of a few skin bags in the past, they had never questioned or investigated this matter. They were unconcerned with it, as if it were someone else's gossip.

3

Know that a painted rice-cake is your face after your parents were born,* your face before your parents were born.* Thus, a painted rice-cake, made of rice flour, is neither born nor unborn. Since this is so, it is the moment of realization of the way. This cannot be understood by the limited view that a painted rice-cake comes and goes.

The paints for painting rice-cakes are the same as those used for painting mountains and waters.[6] For painting mountains and waters, blue and red paints are used; for painting rice-cakes, rice flour is used. Thus they are painted in the same way, and they are examined in the same way.

Accordingly, "painted rice-cakes" spoken of here means that sesame rice-cakes, herb rice-cakes, milk rice-cakes, toasted rice-cakes, millet rice-cakes, and the like are all actualized in the painting.[7] Thus, you should understand that a painting is all-inclusive, a rice-cake is all-inclusive, the dharma is all-inclusive. In this way, all rice-cakes actualized right now are nothing but a painted rice-cake.

If you look for some other kind of painted rice-cake, you will never find it, you will never grasp it. A painted rice-cake at once appears and does not appear. This being so, it has no mark of old or young, and has no trace of coming or going. Just here, the land of painted rice-cakes is revealed and confirmed.

4

The phrase "does not satisfy hunger" means this hunger—not the ordinary matter of the twelve hours—never encounters a painted rice-cake. Even if you were to eat a painted rice-cake, it would never put an end to this hunger. Rice-cakes are not separate from hunger. Rice-cakes are not separate from rice-cakes. Thus, these activities and teaching cannot be given away. Hunger is a single staff* maneuvered horizontally and vertically through a thousand changes and myriad forms. A rice-cake is wholeness of body and mind actualized. A rice-cake is blue, yellow, red, and white as well as long, short, square, and round.

5

When mountains and waters are painted, blue, green, and red paints are used, strange rocks and wondrous stones are used, the four jewels and the seven treasures are used. Rice-cakes are painted in the same manner. When a person is painted, the four great elements and the five skandhas are used. When a buddha is painted, not only a clay altar or lump of earth is used, but the thirty-two marks,* a blade of grass,* and the cultivation of wisdom for incalculable eons are used. As a buddha has been painted on a single scroll in this way, all buddhas are painted buddhas, and all painted buddhas are actual buddhas.

You should examine a painted buddha, and examine a painted rice-cake. Which is the black stone tortoise,* which is the iron staff? Which is form and which is mind? Pursue and investigate this in detail. When you penetrate this matter, the coming and going of birth and death is a painting. Unsurpassed enlightenment is a painting. The entire phenomenal universe and the empty sky are nothing but a painting.

6

An ancient buddha said:

> Attaining the way—a thousand snowflakes disappear.
> Painting green mountains—several scrolls appear.

This is an utterance of great enlightenment, actualized practice in the endeavor of the way. Accordingly, at the moment of attaining the way green mountains and white snow are painted on countless scrolls. Motion and stillness are nothing but a painting. Our endeavor at this moment is brought forth entirely from a painting.

The ten names* and the three cognitions* are a painting on a scroll. The virtues, the powers, the methods, and the noble path are also a painting on a scroll. If you say a painting is not real, then the myriad things are not real. If the myriad things are not real, then buddha-dharma is not real. As buddha-dharma is real, a painted rice-cake is real.

7

Great Master Kuangzhen of Yunmen once was asked by a monk, "What is your statement about going beyond buddhas and surpassing the ancestors?"

The master said, "A sesame rice-cake."[8]

You should quietly examine these words. When this sesame rice-cake is actualized, an ancient teacher gives expression to going beyond buddhas and surpassing the ancestors. An iron man asks this question and students understand it. Thus this expression is complete. Opening the matter and hurling it back as a sesame rice-cake is itself two or three painted rice-cakes. Yunmen's is a statement that goes beyond buddhas and surpasses the ancestors, an activity that enters buddhas and enters demons.

8

My late master said, "A tall bamboo and a plantain appear in a painting."[9]

This phrase means that things beyond measure are actualized together in a painting. A tall bamboo is long. Although it is moved by yin and yang, the months and years of the tall bamboo move yin and yang. The months and years of yin and yang are beyond measure. Although the great sages understand yin and yang, they cannot measure it. Yin and yang are all-inclusive phenomena, all-inclusive scale, and the all-inclusive way.

Yin and yang have nothing to do with views held by those outside the way or those in the Two Vehicles. Yin and yang belong to the tall bamboo. They are the passage of time of the tall bamboo, and the world of the tall bamboo. All buddhas of the ten directions are the family of the tall bamboo.

Know that the entire heaven and earth are the roots, stem, branches, and leaves of the tall bamboo. This makes heaven and earth timeless; this makes the great oceans, Mt. Sumeru, and the worlds of the ten directions indestructible. A walking stick and an arched bamboo staff are both old and not old.

A plantain has earth, water, fire, wind, emptiness, mind, consciousness, and wisdom as its roots, stems, branches, leaves, flowers, fruits, colors, and forms. Accordingly, the plantain wears the autumn wind and is torn in the autumn wind. We know that it is pure and clear and that not a single particle is excluded.

There is no muscle in the eye. There is no pigment in the paints. This is emancipation right here. As emancipation is not a matter of time, it is not concerned with a discussion of a certain moment or instant. Taking up this understanding, make earth, water, wind, and fire your vital activity; make mind, consciousness, and wisdom your great death.* In this manner, the activities of the house have been passed on with spring, autumn, winter, and summer as furnishings.

Now, the fluctuations of the tall bamboo and the plantain are a painting. Those who experience great awakening upon hearing the sound of bamboo, whether they are snakes or dragons, are all paintings. Do not doubt it with the limited view that separates ordinary from sacred.

That bamboo pole is just long. This pole is just short. This pole is just long. That pole is just short. As these are all paintings, the painted forms of long and short always accord with each other. When you paint something long, it cannot be without painting something short. Thoroughly investigate the meaning of this. Because the entire world and all phenomena are a painting, human existence appears from a painting, and buddha ancestors are actualized from a painting.

9

Since this is so, there is no remedy for satisfying hunger other than a painted rice-cake. Without painted hunger you never become a true person. There is no understanding other than painted satisfaction. In fact, satisfying hunger, satisfying no-hunger, not satisfying hunger, and not satisfying no-hunger cannot be attained or spoken of without painted hunger. For some time study all of these as a painted rice-cake.

When you understand this meaning with your body and mind, you will thoroughly master the ability to turn things and be turned by things. If this is not done, the power of the study of the way is not yet realized. To enact this ability is to actualize the painting of enlightenment.

On the fifth day, eleventh month, third year of Ninji [1242], this was taught to the assembly at Kannondōri Kōshō Hōrin Monastery.

Translated by Dan Welch and Kazuaki Tanahashi

PART FOUR

Transmission of the Teaching

On the Endeavor of the Way

BENDŌ-WA[1]

I

All buddha tathāgatas, who directly transmit inconceivable dharma and actualize supreme, perfect enlightenment, have a wondrous way, unsurpassed and unconditioned.* Only buddhas transmit it to buddhas without veering off; self-fulfilling samādhi* is its standard. Sitting upright, practicing Zen, is the authentic gate to the unconfined realm of this samādhi.

Although this inconceivable dharma is abundant in each person, it is not actualized without practice, and it is not experienced without realization. When you release it, it fills your hand—how could it be limited to one or many? When you speak it, it fills your mouth—it is not bounded by length or width.

All buddhas continuously abide in it, but do not leave traces of consciousness in their illumination. Sentient beings continuously move about in it, but illumination is not manifest in their consciousness.[2]

The concentrated endeavor of the way I am speaking of allows all things to come forth in enlightenment and practice, all-inclusivenesss* with detachment. Passing through the barrier and dropping off limitations, how could you be hindered by nodes in bamboo or knots in wood?*

143

2

After the thought of enlightenment arose, I began to search for dharma, visiting teachers at various places in our country. Then I met priest Myōzen, of Kennin Monastery, by whom I was trained for nine years. Thus I learned a little about the teaching of the Rinzai School. Priest Myōzen alone, as a senior disciple of ancestor Eisai, correctly transmitted the unsurpassable buddha-dharma; no one can be compared with him.

Later I went to Great Song China, visited masters on both sides of the Zhe River, and heard the teaching of the Five Schools. Finally I studied with Zen master Rujing of Taibo Peak and completed my life's quest of the great matter.

Then at the beginning of Shaoding Era [1228–33] of Great Song, I came back to Japan with the hope of spreading the teaching and saving sentient beings—a heavy burden on my shoulders. However, I will put aside the intention of having the teaching prevail everywhere until the occasion of a rising tide. I think of wandering about like a cloud or a water-weed, studying the wind of the ancient sages.

Yet there may be true students who are not concerned with fame and gain and who allow their thought of enlightenment to guide them, and they may be confused by incapable teachers and obstructed from the correct understanding. Indulging in smug self-satisfaction, they may sink into the land of delusion for a long time. How can they nourish the correct seed of prajñā* and have the opportunity to attain the way? If I am wandering about, which mountain or river can they call on? Because I feel concerned for them, I would like to record the standards of Zen monasteries which I personally saw and heard in Great Song as well as the profound principle which has been transmitted by my master. I wish to leave for students of the way the teaching of the buddha's house. This is indeed the essence.

3

Now, the great master Shākyamuni entrusted dharma to Mahākāshyapa at the assembly on Vulture Peak; it was then correctly transmitted from ancestor to ancestor down to venerable Bodhidharma. Bodhidharma himself went to China and entrusted dharma to the great master Huike; this was the beginning of dharma transmission in the eastern country. In this way, by direct transmission, it reached the Sixth Ancestor, Zen Master Dajian. Then the true Buddhist teaching spread in China, and the teaching that is not concerned with theories took form.

At that time there were two outstanding disciples of the Sixth Ancestor, Nanyue Huairang and Qingyuan Xingsi. They both equally received the buddha's seal,* as masters of human beings and devas. Their two lineages spread, and later the Five Gates opened: the Fayan School, the Guiyang School, the Caodong School, the Yunmen School, and the Linji School. At present in Great Song China only the Linji School prospers throughout the country. But in spite of their different styles, each of the Five Houses holds the single seal of the buddha mind.

In China after the Later Han Dynasty, the teachings of Buddhist scriptures were introduced and spread all over the land, but there was no conclusive teaching as yet. When Bodhidharma came from India, the root of twining vines* was immediately cut off and the pure, single buddha-dharma spread. We should hope that it will be like this in our country.

4

Now, all ancestors and all buddhas who uphold buddha-dharma have made it the true path of enlightenment to sit upright practicing in the midst of self-fulfilling samādhi. Those who attained enlightenment in India and China followed this way. It was done so because teachers and disciples personally transmitted this excellent method as the essence of the teaching.

In the authentic tradition of our teaching, it is said that this directly transmitted, straightforward buddha-dharma is the unsurpassable of the unsurpassable. From the first time you meet a master, without engaging in incense offering, bowing, chanting Buddha's name, repentance, or reading scriptures, you should just wholeheartedly sit, and thus drop away body and mind.

5

When even for a moment you express the buddha's seal in the three actions* by sitting upright in samādhi, the whole phenomenal world becomes the buddha's seal and the entire sky turns into enlightenment. Because of this all buddha tathāgatas as the original source increase their dharma bliss and renew their magnificence in the awakening of the way. Furthermore, all beings in the ten directions, and the six realms,* including the three lower realms,* at once obtain pure body and mind, realize the state of great emancipation, and manifest the original face. At this time, all things realize correct awakening; myriad objects partake of the buddha body; and sitting upright, a king under the bodhi tree, you immediately leap beyond the boundary of awakening. At this moment you turn the unsurpassably great dharma wheel and expound the profound wisdom, ultimate and unconditioned.

Because such broad awakening resonates back to you and helps you inconceivably, you will in zazen unmistakably drop away body and mind, cutting off the various defiled thoughts from the past, and realize essential buddha-dharma. Thus you will raise up buddha activity at innumerable practice places of buddha tathāgatas everywhere, cause everyone to have the opportunity of ongoing buddhahood,* and vigorously uplift the ongoing buddha-dharma.

Because earth, grass, trees, walls, tiles, and pebbles all engage in buddha activity, those who receive the benefit of wind and water caused by them are inconceivably helped by the buddha's guidance, splendid and unthinkable, and awaken intimately to themselves. Those who receive these water and fire benefits spread the buddha's guidance based on original awakening. Because of this, all those who live with you and speak with you will obtain endless buddha virtue and will unroll widely inside and outside of the entire universe, the endless, unremitting, unthinkable, unnameable buddha-dharma.

6

All this, however, does not appear within perception, because it is unconstructedness* in stillness—it is immediate realization. If practice and realization were two things, as it appears to an ordinary person, each could be recognized separately. But what can be met with recognition is not realization itself, because realization is not reached by a deluded mind. In stillness, mind and object merge in realization and go beyond enlightenment; nevertheless, because you are in the state of self-fulfilling samādhi, without disturbing its quality or moving a particle you extend the buddha's great activity, the incomparably profound and subtle teaching.

Grass, trees, and lands which are embraced by this teaching together radiate a great light and endlessly expound the inconceivable, profound dharma. Grass, trees, and walls bring forth the teaching for all beings, common people as well as sages. And they in accord extend this dharma for the sake of grass, trees, and walls. Thus, the realm of self-awakening and awakening others invariably holds the mark of realization with nothing lacking, and realization itself is manifested without ceasing for a moment.

This being so, the zazen of even one person at one moment imperceptibly accords with all things and fully resonates through all time. Thus in the past, future, and present of the limitless universe this zazen carries on the buddha's teaching endlessly. Each moment of zazen is equally wholeness of practice, equally wholeness of realization.

This is not only practice while sitting, it is like a hammer striking emptiness: before and after, its exquisite peal permeates everywhere. How can it be limited to this moment? Hundreds of things all manifest original practice from the original face; it is impossible to measure. Know that even if all buddhas of the ten directions, as innumerable as the sands of the Ganges, exert their strength and with the buddhas' wisdom try to measure the merit of one person's zazen, they will not be able to fully comprehend it.

Question 1: We have now heard that the merit of zazen is lofty and great. But an ignorant person may be doubtful and say, "There are many gates for buddha-dharma. Why do you recommend zazen exclusively?"
Answer: Because this is the front gate for buddha-dharma.

Question 2: Why do you regard zazen alone as the front gate?
Answer: The great master Shākyamuni correctly transmitted this splendid method of attaining the way, and tathāgatas of the past, future, and present all attain the way by doing zazen. For this reason it has been transmitted as the front gate. Not only that, but also all ancestors in India and China have attained the way by doing zazen. Thus I now teach this front gate to human beings and devas.

Question 3: We understand that you have correctly transmitted the tathāgatas' excellent method and studied the tracks of the ancestors. It is beyond the reach of ordinary thoughts. However, reading sūtras or chanting Buddha's name of itself must be a cause of enlightenment. How can zazen, just sitting uselessly and doing nothing, be depended upon for attaining enlightenment?
Answer: If you think that the samādhi of all buddhas, their unsurpassable

great method, is just sitting uselessly and doing nothing, you will be one who slanders the Great Vehicle. Your delusion will be deep—like saying that there is no water when you are in the middle of the great ocean. Already all buddhas graciously sit at ease in self-fulfilling samādhi. Is this not producing great merit? What a pity that your eyes are not yet open, that your mind is still intoxicated!

Now, the realm of all buddhas is inconceivable. It cannot be reached by consciousnesss. Much less can those who have no trust, who lack wisdom, know it. Only those who have right trust and great capacity can enter this realm. Those who have no trust will not accept it however much they are taught. Even at the assembly on Vulture Peak, there were those who were told by Shākyamuni Buddha, "You may leave if you wish."[3]

When right trust arises, you can practice and study. If not, you may wait for a while and regret that you have not received the benefaction of dharma from the past.

Also, do you understand the merit attained by the act of reading sūtras, chanting Buddha's name, and so on? It is hopeless to think that just moving the tongue and making a sound is meritorious Buddhist activity. If you regard these as the buddha's teaching, the buddha's teaching will be further and further away.

Actually, the meaning of studying sūtras is that if you understand and follow the rules of practice for sudden or gradual realization taught by the buddha, you will unmistakably attain enlightenment. In studying sūtras you should not expend thoughts in the vain hope that they will be helpful for attaining wisdom.

To try foolishly to reach the buddha way by the practice of chanting myriad times is just like trying to go to the southern country of Yue with your spear heading towards the north, or to fit a square post into a round hole. To look at letters but be ignorant of the way of practice is just like a physician forgetting how to prescribe medicine; what use can it be? People who chant all the time are just like frogs croaking day and night in spring fields; their effort will be of no use whatsoever. Even worse off are those who, deluded by name and gain, cannot give up such practices, because their greed for gain is so deep. There were such people in the past. Are there not even more? What a pity, indeed!

Just understand that when a master who has attained the way with a clear mind correctly transmits to a student who has merged himself with realization, then the inconceivable dharma of the Seven Buddhas, in its essence, is actualized and maintained. This cannot be known by monks who study words. Therefore stop your doubt, practice zazen under a correct teacher, and actualize the self-fulfilling samādhi of all buddhas.

Question 4: The Lotus School and the Avatamsaka School, which have been transmitted to Japan, are both the ultimate of Mahāyāna teaching. Furthermore, the teaching of the Mantra School was directly transmitted by Vairochana Tathāgata to Vajrasattva, and its lineage from teacher to disciple has not been disturbed. This teaching explains that "mind itself is buddha; everyone's mind becomes buddha." They also advocate the Five Buddhas' correct enlightenment within one sitting, instead of practice through many eons. It should be regarded as the supreme buddha-dharma. So, which good aspect of the practice you mention makes you recommend it, ignoring the practice of other schools?

Answer: You should know that in the buddha's house we do not discuss superiority or inferiority of the teaching; nor do we concern ourselves with the depth or shallowness of the dharma, but only with the genuineness or falseness of practice.

There are those who, attracted by grass, flowers, mountains, and waters, flow into the buddha way. And there are those who, grasping earth, rocks, sand, and pebbles, manifest the buddha's seal. In fact, although the boundless words of the buddha overflow among myriad things, the turning of the great dharma wheel is contained inside a single particle. In this sense, the words "Mind itself is buddha" are like the moon reflected on water; the teaching "Sitting itself is becoming buddha" is like the reflection in the mirror. Do not be concerned with the splendor of the words. By showing the excellent way of direct transmission by buddha ancestors, I am just recommending the practice of the immediate realization of wisdom, hoping that you will become true practitioners of the way.

For the transmission of buddha-dharma, the teacher should be a person who has merged with realization. Scholars who count letters cannot do it; it would be like the blind leading the blind.

Those within the gate of the correct transmission of buddha ancestors venerate an accomplished artisan who has attained the way and merged with realization, and entrust him with the upholding of buddha-dharma. Because of this, when the spirit beings* of the visible and invisible realms come to pay homage, or when the arhats who have attained the fruits of realization come to inquire about the dharma, this master will not fail to give the means to clarify their mind-ground. This is not known in other teachings. So the buddha's disciples should study only the buddha's teaching.

You should also know that we do not originally lack unsurpassed enlightenment, and we are enriched with it always. But because we cannot accept it, and we tend to create groundless views, regarding them as actual things, we miss the great way; our efforts are fruitless. Because of these views, illusory flowers bloom in various ways.

You tend to imagine inexhaustibly the twelvefold causation of rebirth,* or twenty-five existences,* or such views as the Three Vehicles, Five Vehicles, buddha existing or not existing. But do not take up these views and regard them as the correct way of practicing buddha-dharma.

Instead, sit zazen wholeheartedly, forming the buddha's seal and letting all things go. Then you will go beyond the boundary of delusion and enlightenment, and being apart from the paths of ordinary and sacred, immediately wander freely outside ordinary thinking, enriched with great enlightenment. If you do this, how can those who are concerned with the fish trap or hunting net of words and letters be compared with you?

Question 5: Among the three learnings,* there is the learning of samādhi. Among the six perfections,* there is the perfection of meditation. Both of these have been studied by all the bodhisattvas from the moment of arousing the thought of enlightenment, and both are practiced by the clever and dull. The zazen you are speaking of seems to be something like this. Why do you say that the true teaching of the Tathāgata is contained in it?

Answer: Your question arises because the treasury of the true dharma eye, the single great matter of the Tathāgata, the unsurpassable great dharma, has been named the Zen School. You should know that the name "Zen School" appeared in China and spread eastwards. It was not heard of in India. When the great master Bodhidharma was sitting facing the wall at Shaolin Monastery, Mt. Song, for nine years, neither monks nor lay people knew the buddha's true teaching. So they called him the Brahman who concentrated on zazen. Later, all the ancestors of every generation always devoted themselves to zazen. Foolish lay people who saw them, without knowing the truth, informally called them the Zazen School. They have dropped the word za—sitting—and nowadays call it the Zen School.

The meaning of this teaching is clear through the discourses of various ancestors. You should not compare this with the meditation of the six perfections or the three learnings.

The authenticity of the transmission of this buddha-dharma is unhidden through all time. Long ago at the assembly on Vulture Peak the Tathāgata entrusted venerable Mahākāshyapa alone with the unsurpassable great teaching, the treasury of the true dharma eye, the inconceivable mind of nirvāna. This event was witnessed by devas still alive in the heavenly world; you should not doubt it. Now the buddha-dharma is to be protected forever by these devas. Its merit has not decreased.

You should know that this is the entire way of buddha-dharma and it cannot be compared with anything else.

Question 6: Why, from among the four postures* taught in the buddha's house, do you emphasize sitting, recommend Zen meditation, and expound entry into realization?
Answer: It is impossible to know completely the methods by which all buddhas from the past practiced and entered realization one after another. If you wonder about the methods of all buddhas, you should know that whatever was used in the buddha's house are their methods.

But an ancestor said admiringly, "Zazen is the dharma gate of ease and joy."[4] Among the four postures, sitting has these qualities. Also, it is not only the practice of one or two buddhas; all buddhas and ancestors follow this way.

Question 7: Those who have not realized buddha-dharma should practice zazen and attain realization. But what of those who have already understood the buddha's correct teaching? What do they expect from zazen?
Answer: Although we should not talk about dreams in front of ignorant people, or give an oar to a woodcutter, nevertheless I will give instruction about this.

To suppose that practice and realization are not one is nothing but a heretical view; in buddha-dharma they are inseparable. Because practice of the present moment is practice-realization,* the practice of beginner's mind is itself the entire original realization.

Therefore, when we give instructions for practicing, we say that you should not have any expectation for realization outside of practice, since this is the immediate original realization. Because this is the realization of practice, there is no boundary in the realization. Because this is the practice of realization, there is no beginning in practice.

In this way, Shākyamuni Tathāgata and venerable Mahākāshyapa were both enriched with practice on realization*; great master Bodhidharma and venerable ancestor Dajian also were turned by practice on realization. The tradition of abiding in buddha-dharma is like this.

Already there is practice which is not apart from realization; fortunately each of us has individually inherited the inconceivable practice.* Beginner's practice is individually to attain original realization on the ground of the unconstructed. You should know that in order not to defile realization, which is inseparable from practice, buddha ancestors always caution you not to be slack in your practice. If you release the inconceivable practice, the original realization fills your hands; if you become free from the original realization, the inconceivable practice is upheld with your whole body.

Again, as I personally saw in Great Song, the Zen monasteries in various places all had meditation halls, where there were five hundred, six hundred, one or two thousand monks, and where the practice of zazen day and night was encouraged. When I asked the abbots of these monasteries, masters who had inherited the seal of buddha mind, about the essential meaning of buddha-dharma, I was told that practice and realization are not two different things.

Therefore, I recommend to students who are already studying with a teacher, as well as all those distinguished people who wish for the truth of buddha-dharma, to do zazen and endeavor in the way, depending on the teaching of the buddha ancestors, under the guidance of a teacher, without distinguishing between beginning or advanced, and without being concerned with ordinary or sacred.

Have you not heard that an ancestor said, "It is not that there is no practice and no realization,* it is just that they cannot be defiled." It is also said, "Someone who understands the way practices the way."[5] You should know that practice is done in the midst of attaining the way.

Question 8: Various teachers who went to Tang China spread the scriptural teaching in Japan in the past, and they introduced the teaching here. Why did they ignore a practice such as you have described and introduce only scriptural teaching?
Answer: The reason why these ancient teachers did not introduce this practice is that the time was not yet ripe.

Question 9: Did those masters in ancient times understand this teaching?
Answer: If they had understood it, it would have spread.

Question 10: One master said:

> Do not grieve over birth and death. There is an immediate way to be free from birth and death, namely, to know the principle that the nature of mind is permanent.
>
> It means that because this body is already in birth, it is brought to death, but the mind-nature will not perish. You should recognize that you have in your body the mind-nature, which is not affected by birth and death. This is the inherent nature. The body is a temporary form; it dies here and is born there, and is not fixed. Mind is permanent; it does not change through past, future, or present.
>
> To understand this is to be free from birth and death. Those who recognize this principle end birth and death forever. So when your body ends, you enter into the ocean of nature. When you flow into the ocean of nature, you attain wondrous virtue just as all buddha tathāgatas. Even if you know this now, because your body is formed as a result of deluded actions from past lives, you are not the same as all sages. Those who do not recognize this principle will go around in birth and death forever.
>
> Therefore you should hasten to understand that mind-nature is permanent. If you just spend your whole life leisurely sitting, what can you expect?

Does such a statement as this accord with the path of all buddhas and ancestors?
Answer: The view you have mentioned is not at all the buddha's teaching, but rather the view of the heretic Senika. He said:

> There is a soul in one's body, and this soul, on encountering conditions, recognizes good and bad, right and wrong. To discern aching and itching, or to know pain and pleasure, is also this soul's capacity. However, when the body is destroyed the soul comes out and is born in another world. So it appears to be dead here, but since there is birth in another place, it is permanent without dying.

To follow this view and regard it as the buddha's teaching is more foolish than grasping a tile or pebble and regarding it as gold. Such shameful ignorance cannot be compared to anything. National Teacher Huizhong of Great Tang criticized this deeply.[6] To take up the wrong view that mind is permanent and forms perish, while regarding this as equal to the inconceivable teaching of all buddhas, or to create the causes of birth and death while wishing to be apart from birth and death—is this not foolish? It is most pitiable. Just understand it as the wrong view of heretics and do not listen to it.

I cannot refrain from being sympathetic; let me rescue you from your wrong view. You should know that in buddha-dharma it is always being said that body and mind are nonseparate, nature and characteristics are not two. This was known both in India and China. So there is no room for mistake. In fact, the teaching about permanence says that all things are permanent, without dividing body and mind. The teaching about cessation says that all things cease, without separating nature and characteristics. How can you say body perishes but mind is permanent? Is it not against the authentic principle? Not only that, you should understand that birth-and-death is itself nirvāna. Nirvāna is not explained outside of birth-and-death. Even if you understand that mind is permanent apart from the body, and mistakenly assume that the buddha's wisdom is separate from birth-and-death, this mind of understanding or recognizing still arises and perishes and is not permanent. Is it not ephemeral?

You should know that the teaching that body and mind are one is always being explained in the buddha-dharma. Then how can mind alone leave the body and not cease when the body ceases? If body and mind are nonseparate sometimes and not nonseparate some other times, the buddha's teaching would be false. Again, to think that birth-and-death has to be rejected is the mistake of ignoring buddha-dharma. You must refrain from this.

You should know that the so-called "dharma gate of the whole reality of mind-nature" in buddha-dharma includes the entire phenomenal world without dividing nature from characteristics or birth from death. Nothing, not even bodhi or nirvāna, is outside of mind-nature. All things and all phenomena are just one mind—nothing is excluded or unrelated. It is taught that all the dharma gates are equally one mind, and there is no differentiation. This is how Buddhists understand mind-nature. How can you differentiate this into body and mind, and divide birth-and-death and nirvāna? You are already the buddha's child. Do not listen to the tongues of madmen, who quote heretical views.

Question 11: Should those who are entirely engaged in zazen strictly follow the precepts?
Answer: Holding to the precepts and pure actions is the rule of the Zen Gate and the teaching of buddha ancestors. Even those who have not yet received the precepts or have broken the precepts can still receive the benefit of zazen.

Question 12: Is it all right for those who study zazen also to engage in chant-ing mantras* or in the practice of calm and introspection?

Answer: When I was in China and inquired of masters about the essence of the teaching, I was told that none of the ancestors who correctly transmitted the buddha's seal in India and China in the past or present had ever engaged in such a combination of practices. Indeed, without devoting yourself to one thing you cannot reach the one wisdom.

Question 13: Should zazen be practiced by lay men and women, or should it be practiced by home-leavers alone?

Answer: The ancestors say, "In understanding buddha-dharma, men and women, noble and common people, are not distinguished."

Question 14: Home-leavers are free from various involvements and do not have hindrances in zazen in pursuit of the way. How can the laity, who are variously occupied, practice single-mindedly and accord with buddha-dharma which is unconstructed?

Answer: Buddha ancestors, out of their kindness, have opened the wide gate of compassion in order to let all sentient beings enter realization. Who among humans and heavenly beings cannot enter?

If you investigate olden times the examples are many. To begin with, emperors Daizong and Shunzong had many obligations on the throne; nevertheless, they practiced zazen in pursuit of the way, and penetrated the great way of buddha ancestors. Ministers Li and Fang both closely served their emperors but they practiced zazen, pursued the way, and entered re-alization in the great way of buddha ancestors.

This just depends on whether you have the willingness or not. It does not matter whether you are a lay person or home-leaver. Those who can discern excellence invariably come to this practice. Those who regard worldly affairs as a hindrance to buddha-dharma only think that there is no buddha-dharma in the secular world, and do not understand that there is no secular world in buddha-dharma.

Recently, there was a high official of Great Song, Minister Feng, who was advanced in the ancestors' way. He once wrote a poem concerning him-self:

> I enjoy zazen between my official duties,
> and seldom sleep lying on a bed.

> Although I appear to be a minister,
> I'm known as a Buddhist elder throughout the country.

Although he was busy in his official duties, he attained the way because he had a deep intention towards the buddha way. Considering someone like him, you should reflect on yourself and illuminate the present with the past.

In Song China, kings and ministers, officials and common people, men and women, kept their intention on the ancestors' way. Both warriors and literary people aroused the intention to practice Zen and study the way. Among those who aroused their intention, many of them illuminated their mind-ground. From this you know that worldly duties do not hinder the buddha-dharma.

If the buddha's true teaching is spread widely in the nation, the rule of the king is peaceful because all buddhas and devas protect it unceasingly. If the rule is peaceful the buddha's teaching gains power.

When Shākyamuni Buddha was alive, even those who committed serious crimes or had mistaken views attained the way. In the assemblies of ancestors, hunters and woodcutters attained realization. If it is so for them, it is so for others. You should just seek the teaching of an authentic master.

Question 15: Can we attain realization if we practice, even in this last age of decline?

Answer: In the scriptural schools they explain various names and aspects, but in the true Mahāyāna teachings dharma is not divided into periods of truth, imitation, and decline.* Instead, it is taught that everyone attains the way by practice. Particularly in this correctly transmitted teaching of zazen, you are enriched with the treasure of yourself, entering dharma and leaving bondage behind. Those who practice know whether realization is attained or not, just as those who drink water know whether it is hot or cold.

Question 16: Someone says:

> In buddha-dharma, if you comprehend the meaning of "Mind itself is buddha" that will be sufficient without any chanting of sūtras or practicing the buddha way. To know that buddha-dharma originally lies in the self is the completion of attaining the way. Other than this, you need not seek from anyone else. Why should you be troubled with practicing zazen and pursuing the way?

Answer: This statement is entirely groundless. If what you say is true, then everyone who has a mind would immediately understand the meaning of buddha-dharma. You should know that buddha-dharma is to be studied by giving up the view of self and other.

If the understanding of "Self itself is buddha" were the attaining of the way, Shākyamuni Buddha would not have taken the trouble to explain the way. Now let me illuminate this explanation with an excellent case of an old master:

Once a monk called director Xuanze was in the assembly of Zen master Fayan. Fayan asked him, "Director Xuanze, how long have you been in my community?"

Xuanze said, "I have been studying with you for three years."

The master said, "You are a latecomer. Why don't you ask me about buddha-dharma?"

Xuanze said, "I cannot deceive you, sir. When I was studying with Zen master Qingfeng [Baizhao Zhiyuan], I mastered the place of ease and joy in buddha-dharma."

The master said, "With what words did you enter this understanding?"

Xuanze said, "When I asked Qingfeng, 'What is the self of a Zen student?', he said, 'The fire god is here to look for fire.'"

Fayan said, "That is a good statement. But I'm afraid you did not understand it."

Xuanze said, "The fire god belongs to fire. So I understood that fire looks for fire and self looks for self."

The master said, "Indeed, you did not understand. If buddha-dharma were like that, it would not have been transmitted until now."

Then Xuanze was distressed and went away. But on his way he said to himself, "The master is a renowned teacher in this country, a great leader of five hundred monks. His criticism of my fault ought to have some point." He went back to Fayan, apologized, and said, "What is the self of a Zen student?"

Fayan said, "The fire god is here to look for fire."

Upon hearing this statement, Xuanze had a great realization of buddha-dharma.[7]

In this way, we know that mere understanding of "Self itself is buddha" is not knowing buddha-dharma. If the understanding of "Self itself is buddha" were buddha-dharma, Fayan would not have given such criticism or guidance. You should just inquire about the rules of practice as soon as you meet the master, single-mindedly practice zazen, and pursue the way, without leaving a half-understanding in your mind. Then the excellent art of buddha-dharma will not be in vain.

Question 17: We have heard that in India and China there have been people in the past and present who realized the way on hearing the sound of bamboo being struck, or who understood the mind seeing the color of blossoms. Great Master Shākyamuni was awakened to the way when he saw the morning star, and venerable Ānanda understood the dharma when a banner-pole fell down. Not only that, but after the Sixth Ancestor, in China, among the Five Schools, there were many who understood the mind-ground with one word of speech or half a phrase. Not all of them necessarily did zazen in pursuit of the way, did they?

Answer: Of those who understood the way upon seeing a form, or who realized the way upon hearing a sound, not one had any intellectual thinking regarding the endeavor of the way or had any self besides their original self.

Question 18: People in India and China by nature are refined. Since they are in the center of civilization, when buddha-dharma is taught to them they can immediately enter it. People in our country from olden times have had less wisdom, and it is difficult for the right seed of prajnā to be nourished. This is because we are uncivilized. Is it not regrettable? Thus, the monks in our country are inferior to even the laity in those great countries. Our entire nation is foolish and narrow-minded, and we are deeply attached to visible merit and are fond of worldly excellence. If such people as we do zazen, can we immediately realize buddha-dharma?

Answer: What you say is correct. Among people in our own country wisdom does not prevail yet, and their nature is rather coarse. Even if the correct dharma is explained to them, its nectar becomes poisonous. You easily pursue name and gain, and it is difficult for you to be free from delusion.

However, entering into realization of buddha-dharma does not require the worldly wisdom of humans and devas, as a boat for fleeing the world. When Buddha was alive, someone realized the four fruits when he was hit by a ball;[8] someone else understood the great way by wearing a robe in fun.[9] They were both ignorant people, like beasts, but with the aid of right trust they were able to be free from delusion. A lay woman serving food to an ignorant old monk, who was sitting in silence, was enlightened.[10] This did not depend upon wisdom, scripture, words, or speech, but it was only brought about by right trust.

Now, Shākyamuni Buddha's teaching has been spread in the trichilio-cosm* for about two thousand years. Those countries are not necessarily the countries of wisdom, and the people are not necessarily sharp and intelligent. However, the Tathāgata's true dharma in essence has a great inconceivable meritorious power, and spreads in those countries when the time is ripe.

If you practice with right trust, you will attain the way, regardless of being sharp or dull. Do not think that buddha-dharma cannot be understood in this country because this is not a country of wisdom and the people are foolish. In fact, everyone has in abundance the correct seed of prajnā, but it rarely hits the mark and enriches us.

This exchange of questions and answers may have been rather confusing; a number of times sky-flowers were made to bloom. However, since the meaning of zazen in pursuit of the way has not been transmitted in this country, those who wish to know about it may be regretful. Therefore, for the sake of those who wish to study, I have recorded some of the essential teachings of the clear-eyed teachers, which I learned in China. Besides this, the rules in the practice places and the regulations in the monasteries are more than I can mention now. They should not be discussed hastily.

Now our country lies to the east of the dragon ocean, far from China. But the buddha's teaching was transmitted eastward, about the time of emperors Kimmei and Yomei.* This is the good fortune of our people. Yet the philosophy and rituals have been entangled, and real practice was missed. Now if you make torn robes and mended bowl your life, build a grass-roofed hut near a mossy cliff or white rock, and practice sitting upright, you immediately go beyond buddha and directly master the great matter of your life's study. This is the admonition of Dragon Fang,* the transmitted way of practice of Rooster-foot.* Concerning the method of zazen, I would refer you to the "Broad Recommendation of Zazen" which I wrote during the Karoku Era [1225–27].

Although the king's edict is needed for spreading dharma in the country, if we think of the Buddha entrusting the dharma to kings and ministers on Vulture Peak, all the kings and ministers who have appeared in the trichiliocosm are born because of their wish from a previous birth to protect and guard buddha-dharma. Nevertheless, spreading the way of buddha ancestors does not necessarily depend upon place or circumstances. Just think that today is the beginning.

Thus I have written this to leave for people of excellence who have a wish for buddha-dharma and for true students who, wandering like water-weed, seek the way.

Mid-autumn day, in the third year of Kanki [1231], by Dōgen, who has transmitted dharma from Song China.

Translated by Lew Richmond and Kazuaki Tanahashi

Only Buddha and Buddha

YUIBUTSU YOBUTSU[1]

Buddha-dharma cannot be known by a person. For this reason, since olden times no ordinary person has realized buddha-dharma; no practitioner of the Lesser Vehicles has mastered buddha-dharma. Because it is realized by buddhas alone, it is said, "Only a buddha and a buddha can thoroughly master it."[2]

When you realize buddha-dharma, you do not think, "This is realization just as I expected." Even if you think so, realization invariably differs from your expectation. Realization is not like your conception of it. Accordingly, realization cannot take place as previously conceived. When you realize buddha-dharma, you do not consider how realization came about. You should reflect on this: What you think one way or another before realization is not a help for realization.

Although realization is not like any of the thoughts preceding it, this is not because such thoughts were actually bad and could not be realization. Past thoughts in themselves were already realization. But since you were seeking elsewhere, you thought and said that thoughts cannot be realization.

However, it is worth noticing that what you think one way or another is not a help for realization. Then you are cautious not to be small-minded. If

161

realization came forth by the power of your prior thoughts, it would not be trustworthy. Realization does not depend on thoughts, but comes forth far beyond them; realization is helped only by the power of realization itself. Know that then there is no delusion, and there is no realization.

2

When you have unsurpassed wisdom, you are called buddha. When a buddha has unsurpassed wisdom, it is called unsurpassed wisdom. Not to know what it is like on this path is foolish. What it is like is to be unstained.* To be unstained does not mean that you try forcefully to exclude intention or discrimination, or that you establish a state of nonintention. Being unstained cannot be intended or discriminated at all.

Being unstained is like meeting a person and not considering what he looks like. Also it is like not wishing for more color or brightness when viewing flowers or the moon.

Spring has the tone of spring, and autumn has the scene of autumn; there is no escaping it. So when you want spring or autumn to be different from what it is, notice that it can only be as it is. Or when you want to keep spring or autumn as it is, reflect that it has no unchanging nature.

That which is accumulated is without self, and no mental activity has self. The reason is that not one of the four great elements or the five skandhas can be understood as self or identified as self. Therefore, the form of the flowers or moon in your mind should not be understood as being self, even though you think it is self.[3] Still, when you clarify that there is nothing to be disliked or longed for, then the original face is revealed by your practice of the way.

3

A teacher of old said:

> Although the entire universe is nothing but the dharma body* of the self, you should not be hindered by the dharma body. If you are hindered by the dharma body, you will not be able to turn freely, no matter how hard you may try. But there should be a way to be free from hindrance. What, then, is the way for all people to be free from hindrance? If you cannot say clearly how to free all people, you will soon lose even the life of the dharma body and sink in the ocean of suffering for a long time.

If you are asked in this way, how can you answer so as to keep the dharma body alive and avoid sinking in the ocean of suffering?

In that case, say, "The entire universe is the dharma body of the self." When you say that the entire universe is the dharma body of the self, words cannot express it. When words cannot express it, should we understand there is nothing to be said? Without words, ancient buddhas said something.

There is birth in death, and there is death in birth. Death is entirely death, and birth is entirely birth. This is so not because you make it so, but because dharma is like this. Therefore, when Buddha turns the dharma wheel, there is insight such as this and expression such as this. Know that it is also like this when Buddha manifests a body to awaken sentient beings. This is called "awareness of no-birth."

"Buddha manifests a body and awakens sentient beings" means that awakening sentient beings is itself the manifestation of the buddha body. In the midst of awakening sentient beings, do not pursue manifestation. Seeing manifestation, do not look about for awakening.

Understand that in the midst of awakening sentient beings, the buddha-dharma is totally experienced. Explain it and actualize it this way. Know that it is the same with manifestation and having the buddha body.

This is so because "Buddha manifests a body and awakens sentient beings." This principle is clarified in that from the morning of attaining the way until the evening of parinirvāna, Buddha discoursed freely, without words getting in the way.

4

An ancient buddha said:

> The entire universe is the true human body.
> The entire universe is the gate of liberation.
> The entire universe is the eye of Vairochana.
> The entire universe is the dharma body of the self.

"The true human body" means your own true body. Know that the entire universe is your own true body, which is not a temporary body.

If someone asks you why we do not usually notice this, say, "Just reflect within yourself that the entire universe is the true human body." Or say, "The entire universe is the true human body—already you know this."

Also, "The entire universe is the gate of liberation" means that you are not at all entangled or captivated. What is called "the entire universe" is undivided from the moment, the ages, mind, and words. This limitless and boundless experience is the "entire universe." Even if you seek to enter or go through this gate of liberation, it cannot be done. How is this so? Reflect on the question raised. If you intend to seek outside what it is, nothing will be attained.

"The entire universe is the eye of Vairochana" means that buddhas have a single eye.* Do not suppose that a buddha's eye is like those of human beings.

Human beings have two eyes, but when you say "a human eye," you don't say "two eyes" or "three eyes." Those who study the teaching should not understand that "the eye of a buddha," "the eye of dharma," or "the celestial eye" is like the two eyes of human beings. To believe that it is like human eyes is lamentable. Understand now that there is only a buddha's single eye, which is itself the entire universe.

A buddha may have one thousand eyes* or myriad eyes. But presently it is said that the entire universe is the one eye of Vairochana. Therefore, it is not mistaken to say that this eye is one of many eyes of a buddha, just as it is not mistaken to understand that a buddha has only one eye. A buddha indeed has many kinds of eyes—three eyes, one thousand eyes, or eighty-four thousand eyes. Do not be surprised to hear that there are eyes such as these.

Also learn that the entire universe is the dharma body of the self. To seek to know the self is invariably the wish of living beings. However, those who see the true self are rare. Only buddhas know the true self.

People outside the way regard what is not the self as the self. But what buddhas call the self is the entire universe. Therefore, there is never an entire universe that is not the self, with or without our knowing it. On this matter defer to the words of the ancient buddhas.

5

Long ago a monk asked an old master, "When hundreds, thousands, or myriads of objects come all at once, what should be done?"

The master replied, "Don't try to control them."[4]

What he means is that in whatever way objects come, do not try to change them. Whatever comes is the buddha-dharma, not objects at all. Do not understand the master's reply as merely a brilliant admonition, but realize that it is the truth. Even if you try to control what comes, it cannot be controlled.

6

An ancient buddha said, "The mountains, rivers, and earth are born at the same moment with each person. All buddhas of the three worlds* are practicing together with each person."

If we look at the mountains, rivers, and earth when a person is born, his birth does not seem to be bringing forth additional mountains, rivers, and earth on top of the existing ones. Yet the ancient buddha's word cannot be mistaken. How should we understand this? Even if you do not understand it, you should not ignore it. So, be determined to understand it. Since this word is already expounded, you should listen to it. Listen until you understand.

This is how to understand. Is there anyone who knows what his birth in its beginning or end is like? No one knows either birth's end or its beginning; nevertheless everyone is born. Similarly, no one knows the extremities of the mountains, rivers, and earth, but all see this place and walk here. Do not think with regret that the mountains, rivers, and earth are not born with you. Understand that the ancient buddha teaches that your birth is nonseparate from the mountains, rivers, and earth.

Again, all buddhas of the three worlds have already practiced, attained the way, and completed realization. How should we understand that those buddhas are practicing together with us? First of all, examine a buddha's practice. A buddha's practice is to practice in the same manner as the entire universe and all beings. If it is not practice with all beings, it is not a buddha's practice. This being so, all buddhas, from the moment of attaining realization, realize and practice the way together with the entire universe and all beings.

You may have doubts about this. But the ancient buddha's word was expounded in order to clarify your confused thinking. Do not think that buddhas are other than you. According to this teaching, when all buddhas of the three worlds arouse the thought of enlightenment and practice, they never exclude our body-and-mind. You should understand this. To doubt this is to slander the buddhas of the three worlds.

When we reflect quietly, it appears that our body-and-mind has practiced together with all buddhas of the three worlds and has together with them aroused the thought of enlightenment. When we reflect on the past and future of our body-and-mind, we cannot find the boundary of self or others. By what delusion do we believe our body-and-mind is apart from all buddhas of the three worlds? Such delusion is groundless. How then can delusion hinder the arousing of the thought of enlightenment and the practicing of the way by all buddhas of the three worlds? Thus, understand that the way is not a matter of your knowing or not knowing.

7

A teacher of old said, "Chopping down* is nothing other than chopping down; moving about is beyond discussion. Mountains, rivers, and earth are the entirely revealed body of the dharma king."⁵

A person of the present should study this phrase of the teacher of old. There is a dharma king who understands that the body of the dharma king is not different from chopping down, just as mountains are on earth, and the earth is holding up mountains.

When you understand, a moment of no-understanding* does not come and hinder understanding, and understanding does not break no-understanding. Instead, understanding and no-understanding are just like spring and autumn.

However, when you do not understand, the pervasive voice of dharma does not reach your ears; in the midst of the voice your ears dally about. But when you understand, the voice has already reached your ears; samādhi has emerged.

Know that no-understanding cannot be discerned by a self; the dharma king's understanding is just like this.

In the dharma king's body the eye is just like the body, and the mind is the same as the body. There is not the slightest gap between mind and body; everything is fully revealed. Similarly you should understand that in illumination and discourse the dharma king's body is revealed.

8

There has been a saying since olden times: "No one except a fish knows a fish's heart, no one except a bird follows a bird's trace."

Yet those who really understand this principle are rare. To think that no one knows a fish's heart or a bird's trace is mistaken. You should know that fish always know one another's heart, unlike people who do not know one another's heart. But when the fish try to go up through the Dragon Gate,* they know one another's intention and have the same heart. Or they share the heart of breaking through the Nine Great Bends.* Those who are not fish hardly know this.

Again, when a bird flies in the sky, beasts do not even dream of finding or following its trace. As they do not know that there is such a thing, they cannot even imagine this. However, a bird can see traces of hundreds and thousands of small birds having passed in flocks, or traces of so many lines of large birds having flown south or north. Those traces may be even more evident than the carriage tracks left on a road or the hoofprints of a horse seen in the grass. In this way, a bird sees birds' traces.

Buddhas are like this. You may wonder how many lifetimes buddhas have been practicing. Buddhas, large or small, although they are countless, all know their own traces. You never know a buddha's trace when you are not a buddha.

You may wonder why you do not know. The reason is that, while buddhas see these traces with a buddha's eye, those who are not buddhas do not have a buddha's eye, and just notice the buddha's attributes.

All who do not know should search out the trace of the buddha's path. If you find footprints, you should investigate whether they are the buddha's. On being investigated, the buddha's trace is known; and whether it is long or short, shallow or deep, is also known. To illuminate your trace is accomplished by studying the buddha's trace. Accomplishing this is buddhadharma.

Translated by Ed Brown and Kazuaki Tanahashi

Twining Vines*

KATTŌ[1]

At the assembly on Vulture Peak, only Mahākāshyapa, through realization, received Shākyamuni Buddha's treasury of the true dharma eye, unsurpassable wisdom. By a direct transmission of correct realization through twenty-eight generations, it reached venerable Bodhidharma.

Bodhidharma went to China and entrusted the treasury of the true dharma eye, unsurpassable wisdom, to Dazu, Great Master Zhengzong Pujue, and confirmed him as the Second Ancestor. Because the Twenty-eighth Ancestor in India went to China as the first teacher there, he is also called the First Ancestor in China. The Twenty-ninth Ancestor is called the Second Chinese Ancestor. This is the custom in China.

The First Chinese Ancestor once studied with venerable Prajnātāra and through realization directly received the admonitions of the buddha, the bones of the way. In realization he attained the source through the source and made it the root of branches and leaves.

Although there are a number of sages who try to study by cutting off the root of twining vines, they do not regard the cutting of twining vines with twining vines as "cutting." Also they do not know twining vines entangled with twining vines. Furthermore, how can they understand inheriting twining vines through twining vines? Those who notice that inheriting dharma is twining vines are rare. There is no one who has learned it, and there is no one who has spoken about it. How is it possible for many to have realized it?

2

My late master, old buddha, said, "Gourd vines entangle with gourd vines."[2]

This teaching has never been seen or heard in the various directions of past and present. My late master alone spoke it. "Gourd vines entangle with gourd vines" means that buddha ancestors master buddha ancestors; buddha ancestors merge with buddha ancestors in realization. This is transmitting mind by mind.

3

The Twenty-eighth Ancestor once said to his students, "The time has come. Can you express your understanding?"

Then one of the students, Daofu, said, "My present view is that we should neither be attached to letters nor be apart from letters, and allow the way to function freely."

The ancestor said, "You have attained my skin."

The nun Zongchi said, "My view is that it is like the joy of seeing Akshobhya Buddha's land just once and not again."[3]

The ancestor said, "You have attained my flesh."

Daoyu said, "The four great elements are originally empty and the five skandhas* do not exist. Therefore I see nothing to be attained."

The ancestor said, "You have attained my bones."

Finally Huike answered by bowing three times, stood up, and returned to where he was.

The ancestor said, "You have attained my marrow." Thus he confirmed Huike as the Second Ancestor and transmitted to him dharma and robe.[4]

You should investigate these words of Bodhidharma: "You have attained my skin, flesh, bones, and marrow." These are the ancestor's words. All four students had attainment and understanding. Each one's attainment and understanding is skin, flesh, bones, and marrow leaping out of body and mind: skin, flesh, bones, and marrow dropping away body and mind. You should not see or hear the ancestor with a limited understanding of these statements. Otherwise what was spoken and heard will not be fully grasped.

However, those who have not yet received correct transmission think that the ancestor's words "skin, flesh, bones, and marrow" are not equal in shallowness and depth, and because the views of the four students vary, one may seem to be closer than the others. They think that skin and flesh are not as close as bones and marrow. They think that the Second Ancestor was acknowledged as attaining the marrow because his view was better than those of the others. People who speak in this way have not yet studied with buddha ancestors and do not have transmission of the ancestor way.

4

You should know that the ancestor's words "skin, flesh, bones, and marrow" do not mean that one understanding is closer than another. Even if there are superior or inferior views, in the ancestor way there is only attaining the self. It means that neither the phrase "You have attained my marrow" nor the phrase "You have attained my bones" is more essential than the other for guiding a person in holding up grass, dropping grass.* It is like holding up a flower,* or it is like transmitting a robe. From the beginning, Bodhidharma's confirmation of each one was equal. Although the ancestor's confirmation was equal, the four views were not necessarily equal. However varied the four views are, the ancestor's words are just the ancestor's words. In fact, words and understanding do not necessarily match.

For example, Bodhidharma said to the four students, "You have attained my skin," and so forth. Had he hundreds or thousands of students after the Second Ancestor, he would have spoken hundreds or thousands of words. There should be no limit. Because he had only four students he spoke of "skin, flesh, bones, and marrow." But the words not spoken, and yet to be spoken, should be many.

You should know that even to the Second Ancestor he could have said, "You have attained my skin." Even saying, "You have attained my skin," he could have transmitted the treasury of the true dharma eye to Huike as the Second Ancestor. It does not go by the superiority or inferiority of attaining the flesh or attaining the marrow.

Even to Daofu, Daoyu, or Zongchi he could have said, "You have attained my marrow." Even though they attained the skin, he could have transmitted dharma to them. The ancestor's body-and-mind is the ancestor—skin, flesh, bones, and marrow. It is not that the marrow is close and the skin is far.

5

Now, to receive the seal of "You have attained my skin" by having the eye of studying is to fully attain the ancestor. There is an ancestor whose full body is skin, an ancestor whose full body is flesh, an ancestor whose full body is bones, and an ancestor whose full body is marrow. There is an ancestor whose full body is mind, an ancestor whose full body is body, an ancestor whose full mind is mind. There is an ancestor whose full ancestor is ancestor. And there is an ancestor whose full body is "attaining myself-yourself."

In this way, when these ancestors appear together and speak to hundreds and thousands of students they say, "You have attained my skin." Even if the ancestors in hundreds and thousands of words indicate skin, flesh, bones, and marrow in this way, people outside will think superficially about skin, flesh, bones, and marrow.

If there had been six or seven students in Bodhidharma's community he would have said, "You have attained my mind," "You have attained my body," "You have attained my buddhahood," "You have attained my eye," or "You have attained my realization." This is the moment when "you" are now an ancestor and this is the time when "you" are now Huike.

You should examine thoroughly the meaning of "attaining." You should know that there is "You have attained myself," "I have attained yourself," "attaining myself-yourself," and "attaining yourself-myself." Upon studying an ancestor's body-and-mind, if you say that inside and outside are not one or that the entire body is not the full body, you are not in the land where the buddha ancestors appear.

To attain skin is to attain bones, flesh, and marrow. To attain bones, flesh, and marrow is to attain skin, flesh, and face. It is to understand not only that all the worlds of the ten directions are the true body,* but that they are skin, flesh, bones, and marrow. In this way, you attain robe, you attain dharma.

Thus, words are bits and pieces of leaping out; teacher and disciple practice mutually. What is heard is bits and pieces leaping out; teacher and disciple practice mutually.

"Teacher and disciple practice mutually" is twining vines of buddha ancestors. "Twining vines of buddha ancestors" is the life stream of skin, flesh, bones, and marrow. "Taking up a flower and winking" is twining vines. "Breaking into a smile" is skin, flesh, bones, and marrow.

You should study further; the seeds of twining vines have the power of dropping away body. Branches, leaves, flowers, and fruit of twining vines do and do not interpenetrate one another.[5] Thus, buddha ancestors appear, and the fundamental point is actualized.

6

Great Master Zhenji of Zhaozhou taught his assembly, "Mahākāshyapa transmitted to Ānanda. Now say! To whom did Bodhidharma transmit?"

A monk said, "The Second Ancestor attained his marrow, how about that?"

The master said, "Do not slander the Second Ancestor." He also said, "If Bodhidharma means, 'Someone who has reached the outside attains the skin, someone who has reached the inside attains the bones,' then tell me: What does someone who has reached even deeper inside get?"

The monk said, "What does attaining the marrow mean?"

Zhaozhou said, "Just know about skin. There is no marrow to depend upon in my body."

The monk said, "What is marrow?"

The master said, "At that place you don't feel the skin."[6]

Then you should know: When you don't even feel the skin, how can you feel the marrow? When you feel the skin, you can attain the marrow.[7] Thus you should study the meaning of "At that place you don't feel the skin." When a monk asked, "What does attaining marrow mean?", Zhaozhou said, "Just know the skin. There is no marrow to depend upon in my body." Where you know the skin, there is no need to search for the marrow. This is truly attaining the marrow. Being so, the question "The Second Ancestor attained his marrow, how about that?" appeared.[8]

When we penetrate the occasion of Mahākāshyapa transmitting to Ānanda, Ānanda hides his body in Mahākāshyapa and Mahākāshyapa hides his body in Ānanda. Therefore, at the time of meeting for transmission, the practice of exchanging face, skin, flesh, bones, and marrow cannot be avoided. Because of this Zhaozhou said, "Now say! To whom did Bodhidharma transmit?"

When Bodhidharma gives transmission he is Bodhidharma. When the Second Ancestor attains the marrow he is Bodhidharma. By studying the meaning of this, buddha-dharma continues to be buddha-dharma to this day. If not, then buddha-dharma has not reached to this day. Quietly pursue and investigate the meaning of these words for yourself and for others.

Zhaozhou said, "If Bodhidharma means, 'Someone who has reached the outside attains the skin, someone who has reached the inside attains the bones,' then tell me: What does someone who has reached even deeper inside get?" You should directly understand the meaning of "outside" and "inside." When you discuss "outside," skin, flesh, bones, and marrow are all outside. When you discuss "inside," skin, flesh, bones, and marrow are all inside.

This being so, these four Bodhidharmas altogether mastered hundreds and thousands of myriad bits and pieces beyond skin, flesh, bones, and marrow. Do not suppose that you cannot go beyond the marrow. You can go beyond three pieces, five pieces.

This teaching of Zhaozhou, an ancient buddha, is a buddha's words. It is not what other masters like Linji, Deshan, Guishan, and Yunmen either reached or dreamed of. How could they talk about it? Some careless elders of recent times do not even know it exists. If you were to tell them about it, they would be shocked.

7

Zen Master Mingjue of Xuedou said, "Zhaozhou and Muzhou—both Zhous—are ancient buddhas."

The words of Zhaozhou, an ancient buddha, are realization of buddha-dharma, intimate words of himself.

Great Master Zhenjue of Xuefeng said, "Zhaozhou is an ancient buddha."

The former buddha ancestor admired Zhaozhou as an ancient buddha and the latter buddha ancestor admired Zhaozhou as an ancient buddha. Thus we know that he is an ancient buddha beyond buddhas of past and present who go beyond themselves. In this way the meaning of twining vines of skin, flesh, bones, and marrow is a standard of "You have attained myself," as taught by an ancient buddha. You should study and examine this standard thoroughly.

8

It is said that the First Ancestor returned to India. I have learned that this is wrong. What Songyun saw on the road as Bodhidharma could not have been actual.[9] How could Songyun have discovered Bodhidharma's destination? It is correct to learn and understand that his ashes were laid to rest in Mt. Xionger after he passed away.

On the seventh day, seventh month, first year of Kangen [1239], this was taught at Kannondōri Kōshō Hōrin Monastery, Uji County, Yamashiro Province.

Translated by Mel Weitsman and Kazuaki Tanahashi

Face-to-Face Transmission

MENJU[1]

I

Once Shākyamuni Buddha, on Vulture Peak in India, in the midst of a vast assembly of beings, held up an udumbara flower and winked. Venerable Mahākāshyapa smiled. Then Shākyamuni Buddha said, "I have the treasury of the true dharma eye, the inconceivable mind of nirvāna. This I entrust to Mahākāshyapa."

This is the meaning of transmitting the treasury of the true dharma eye face to face from buddha to buddha, from ancestor to ancestor. It was correctly transmitted by the Seven Buddhas to venerable Mahākāshyapa. From Mahākāshyapa there were twenty-eight transmissions up to and including venerable Bodhidharma. Venerable Bodhidharma himself went to China and gave face-to-face transmission to venerable Huike, Great Master Zhengzong Pujue. There were five transmissions through to Great Master Dajian Huineng of Mt. Caoxi. Then there were seventeen transmissions through to my late master, old buddha Tiantong of the renowned Mt. Taibo, Qingxuan Prefecture, Great Song.

2

I first offered incense and bowed formally to my late master, old buddha Tiantong, in the abbot's room on the first day, fifth month, of the first year of Baoqing of Great Song [1225]. He also saw me for the first time. Upon this occasion he transmitted dharma, finger to finger, face to face, and said to me, "The dharma gate of face-to-face transmission from buddha to buddha, ancestor to ancestor, is realized now."

This itself is holding up a flower on Vulture Peak, or attaining the marrow at Mt. Song. Or it is transmitting the robe at Mt. Huangmei, or the face-to-face transmission at Mt. Dong. This is buddha ancestors transmitting the treasury of the eye face to face. It occurs only in our teaching. Other people have not even dreamed of it.

3

Face-to-face transmission means between buddhas' and ancestors' faces; when Shākyamuni Buddha was in the assembly of Kāshyapa Buddha he received it from Kāshyapa Buddha and has continued this transmission. There are no buddhas without face-to-face transmission from the buddha face.

Shākyamuni Buddha, by seeing Mahākāshyapa, intimately entrusted him with it. Ānanda or Rāhula are not equal to Mahākāshyapa, who received the intimate entrustment. Nor are all the great bodhisattvas, who are unable to sit in Mahākāshyapa's seat.

The World-honored One and Mahākāshyapa sat together on the same seat and wore the same robe. This occurred only once in Buddha's life. Thus venerable Mahākāshyapa received the World-honored One's transmission directly face to face, mind to mind, body to body, and eye to eye. Mahākāshyapa respectfully regarded Shākyamuni Buddha while making offerings and bowing formally. Thousands of times Mahākāshyapa had pounded his bones and crushed his body. His face was no longer his own. Thus he received the Tathāgata's face by means of face-to-face transmission.

4

Shākyamuni Buddha saw venerable Mahākāshyapa in person. Venerable Mahākāshyapa saw venerable Ānanda in person, and venerable Ānanda bowed formally to venerable Mahākāshyapa's buddha face. This is face-to-face transmission. Venerable Ānanda maintained this face-to-face transmission, closely guided Shanavāsa and transmitted face to face. When venerable Shanavāsa respectfully saw venerable Ānanda, he was given face-to-face transmission and received face-to-face transmission, just face to face.

Thus, the authentic ancestors of all generations have continued face-to-face transmission, disciple seeing teacher, and teacher seeing disciple. An ancestor, a teacher, or disciple cannot be a buddha or an ancestor without having face-to-face transmission.

It is like pouring water into the ocean and spreading it endlessly, or like transmitting the lamp and allowing it to shine forever. In thousands of millions of transmissions, the trunk and branches are one, breaking an eggshell by pecking from the inside and outside at once.

5

In this way day and night venerable Mahākāshyapa closely attended Shākyamuni Buddha, and spent his whole life being intimately illuminated by the buddha face. How long this has been happening is beyond comprehension. You should quietly and joyously reflect on this.

Thus, venerable Mahākāshyapa bowed formally to Shākyamuni Buddha's face. Shākyamuni Buddha's eyes were reflected in his eyes, and his eyes were reflected in Shākyamuni Buddha's eyes. This is the buddha eye; this is the buddha face. It has been transmitted face to face without a generation's gap until now. This is face-to-face transmission.

All these authentic heirs are the buddha face; each of them has received face-to-face transmission from the original buddha face. Bowing formally to this right face-to-face transmission is bowing to the Seven Buddhas through Shākyamuni Buddha, and bowing and making offerings to venerable Mahākāshyapa and the rest of the twenty-eight Indian buddha ancestors.

The face and eyeball of buddha ancestors are like this. To see these buddha ancestors is to see Shākyamuni Buddha and the others of the Seven Buddhas. Exactly at this moment buddha ancestors are intimately transmitting to one another.

A face-to-face-transmitting buddha transmits to face-to-face-transmitting buddha. It is transmitted from vine to vine without being cut. It is transmitted from eye to eye, with the eye open. It is transmitted from face to face, with the face revealed.

Face-to-face transmission is given and received in the presence of the buddha face. Mind is taken up, transmitted to mind and received by mind. Body is manifested and transmitted to body. Even in other regions or in other countries this is regarded as the original ancestor. In China and eastward, there is face-to-face transmission only within the house of correctly transmitted buddha ancestors. Thus the correct eye that always sees the Tathāgata anew has been transmitted.

6

At the time of bowing formally to Shākyamuni Buddha's face, the fifty-one buddha ancestors and the Seven Buddhas are not present side by side or in one line. But it is face-to-face transmission among all the buddha ancestors at the same time. If you do not see in just one generation all the masters, you are not a disciple. If you do not see in just one generation all the disciples, you are not a master. Masters and disciples always see one another when transmitting and inheriting dharma. This is the realization of the way, face-to-face transmission of the ancestral source. Thus, masters and disciples bring forth the luminous face of the Tathāgata.

Accordingly, this face-to-face transmission is realizing the face and continuing the transmission of Shākyamuni Buddha through thousands and thousands of years or hundreds and billions of eons. When the World-honored One, Mahākāshyapa, and other members of the fifty-one buddha ancestors, and the Seven Buddhas, appear, their shadows appear, their light appears, their bodies appear, and their minds appear. An invisible leg appears, or a sharpened nose. Even without knowing one word or understanding half a phrase, the teacher sees the student within himself, and the student lowers the top of his head; this is correct face-to-face transmission.

You should venerate this face-to-face transmission. If the traces of mind were only projected in the field of mind, they would not be of great value. However, if you receive face-to-face transmission by exchanging your face,* and if you give face-to-face transmission by turning your head, the face skin* is three inches thick and ten feet thin.

This face skin is the great round mirror* of all buddhas. Because they have the great round mirror as their face skin, they are unmarred inside and outside. A great round mirror transmits to a great round mirror.

7

Those who rightly transmit the correct eye that directly sees Shākyamuni Buddha are more intimate with Shākyamuni Buddha than Shākyamuni Buddha with himself; with this eye they see and bring forth numerous past and future Shākyamuni Buddhas. Therefore, in order to express reverence for Shākyamuni Buddha, you should profoundly venerate correct face-to-face transmission and with formal bows acknowledge the extreme rarity of meeting with it. This is to bow formally to the Tathāgata and to be given face-to-face transmission by the Tathāgata. You may wonder if it is the self that now sees the unchanging practice of correct transmission of the face-to-face-transmitting tathāgatas. Whether it is the self or another that sees the transmission, you should treasure it and protect it.

8

It is taught in the buddha's house that those who bow formally to the Eight Pagodas* are liberated from the hindrances of unwholesome actions and perceive the fruit of the way. These pagodas are the actualization of Shākyamuni Buddha's way. They were built where he was born, where he turned the dharma wheel, attained the way, entered parinirvāna, at the city of Kanyākubja, and at Āmrapāli Grove, thus completing the earth and the sky. Or they are built by way of sounds, smells, tastes, tangibles, mental phenomena, and forms. The fruit of the way is realized by formally bowing to the Eight Pagodas. This is a common practice in India performed by lay people and monks, by devas and human beings who eagerly make offerings and prostrations. These pagodas are equal to one volume of the scriptures.

Buddhist scriptures are like this. Even beyond that, the practice of the thirty-seven bodhipākshikas* and attaining the fruit of the way in each and every birth is realized by allowing the trace of Shākyamuni Buddha's practice throughout all time to prevail as the authentic way everywhere and to be clearly expressed in past and present.

You should know that, although wind and rain wear them down, the Eight Pagodas, standing layer upon layer through numerous frosts and flowers, are not diminished in their merit, remaining in emptiness and form. Because of this, even if you have delusion and hindrance, when you practice the controlling power, the moral power, the limbs of enlightenment, and the noble path, the power of the Eight Pagodas is still vital in your practice and realization.

The merit of Shākyamuni Buddha is like this. Even so, face-to-face transmission is incomparably greater than the Eight Pagodas. The thirty-seven bodhipākshikas are rooted in the buddha face, the buddha mind, the buddha body, the buddha way, the buddha nose, and the buddha tongue. The merit of the Eight Pagodas is also based on the buddha face and so forth. While practicing the vital path of penetration, a person who studies dharma should day and night think deeply about this and rejoice in quietness.

9

Now, our country surpasses other countries and our way alone is unsurpassable. In other places there are not many people who are like us. The reason why I say so is this: Although the teaching of the assembly on the Vulture Peak has spread in the ten directions, still the Chinese masters are the only authentic heirs of the great master of Shaolin, and only the descendants of the great master of Mt. Caoxi have transmitted this dharma face to face up to the present.

This is a splendid opportunity for buddha-dharma to enter into mud and water.* If you do not realize the fruit at this moment, when will you realize it? If you do not cut off delusion at this moment, when will you cut it off? If you do not become a buddha at this moment, when will you? If you do not sit as a buddha at this moment, when will you practice as a buddha? Diligently examine this in detail.

10

Shākyamuni Buddha solemnly entrusted and transmitted dharma face to face to venerable Mahākāshyapa, saying, "I have the treasury of the true dharma eye. This is entrusted to Mahākāshyapa."

At the assembly of Mt. Song, venerable Bodhidharma said to the Second Ancestor, "You have attained my marrow."

From this we know that entrusting face to face the treasury of the true dharma eye and "You have attained my marrow" are this very face-to-face transmission. At the exact moment of jumping beyond your ordinary bones and marrow, there is transmission face to face of the buddha ancestors. The face-to-face transmission of great awakening along with the mind seal is extremely rare. Transmission is never exhausted; there is never a lack of awakening.

Now, the great way of buddha ancestors is only giving and receiving face to face, receiving and giving face to face; there is nothing excessive and there is nothing lacking. You should faithfully and joyously realize when your own face meets someone who has received this transmission face to face.

I first bowed formally to my late master, old buddha Tiantong, and received transmission face to face on the first day of the fifth month, the first year of Baoqing Era of Great Song [1225], and was thereby allowed to enter the inner chamber. I was able to enact this face-to-face transmission by dropping away body and mind, and I have established this transmission in Japan.

On the twentieth day, tenth month, first year of Kangen [1243], this was taught at Yoshimine Monastery, Yoshida County, Echizen Province.

Postscript

I

Among those who had not heard or learned about the meaning of such face-to-face transmission in the buddha way, there was someone called Zen master Chenggu of Jianfu Monastery in the Jingyou Era [1034–38] during the reign of Emperor Renzong of Great Song. He ascended the seat and said:

> Yunmen, Great Master Kuangzhen, is now present. Do you see him? If you do, you are the same as I. Do you see him? Do you see him? If you understand this immediately, you have got it; but do not boast.
>
> This is like Huangbo who, when he heard Baizhang present the story of great master Mazu's shout, experienced great understanding. Then Baizhang asked him, "Are you great master Mazu's heir or not?" Huangbo said, "I know the great master, but in a word, I haven't seen him. If I inherit from him, I fear I will lose my descendants."
>
> Attention, everyone! Since it was already five years after the death of great master Mazu, Huangbo said that he had not seen him. Thus we know that Huangbo's view was incomplete. That is to say, he had only one eye. But I am not like that. I know great master Yunmen, and I have seen great master Yunmen. Therefore I am great master Yunmen's heir.
>
> But more than one hundred years have passed since the death of Yunmen. Then how can we say that I have personally seen him? Do you understand this? Those who have reached this state, I will approve. But those who have dim eyes will produce doubt and slander in their mind, so they cannot see and explain it. Those of you who have not seen, can you get it now? Please take care of yourselves.[2]

Chenggu, admitting that you know great master Yunmen and have seen him, has great master Yunmen seen you or not? If great master Yunmen has not seen you, you cannot be great master Yunmen's heir. Because great master Yunmen has not seen you, you cannot say that great master Yunmen has seen you. Thus we know that you and great master Yunmen have not yet seen each other.

In the past, present, and future of the Seven Buddhas and all buddhas, which of the buddha ancestors have inherited dharma without teacher and disciple seeing each other? Chenggu, you should not say that Huangbo's view was incomplete. How can you evaluate Huangbo's practice, and how can you evaluate Huangbo's words? Huangbo is an authentic buddha; he thoroughly knew about inheriting dharma. But you have never dreamed of the meaning of inheriting dharma. Huangbo inherited dharma from his teacher; he was a re-enactment of the ancestor. Huangbo met and saw his teacher. But you have neither seen a teacher nor known an ancestor. You neither know the self nor see the self. No teacher has seen you, and your eye as a teacher has not yet opened. The truth is that your view is incomplete, your inheritance of dharma is incomplete.

Chenggu, do you understand that great master Yunmen is a dharma descendant of Huangbo? How can you evaluate the words of Baizhang and Huangbo? You cannot evaluate even the words of Yunmen. The words of Baizhang and Huangbo are presented by those who are able to study and are evaluated by those who have directly experienced dropping.* But you do not study and you do not experience dropping; you do not understand and you cannot evaluate it.

You say that Huangbo did not inherit dharma from great master Ma [Mazu] although it was less than five years since great master Ma's death. Your understanding is not worth a laugh. If you are to inherit dharma, you will inherit it even after innumerable eons. If not, you will not inherit it after half a day or even after a moment. You are a totally ignorant fool who has not yet seen the sun-face moon-face* of the buddha way.

You say that you are great master Yunmen's heir although more than one hundred years have passed since the death of Yunmen. Have you inherited from Yunmen because you have monumental power? You are as hopeless as a three-year-old child. Does this mean that someone who inherits dharma from Yunmen one thousand years later will have a power ten times as great as yours?

Let me rescue you now. Study these words: Baizhang said, "Are you great master Mazu's heir?" This does not mean that Huangbo was asked to inherit dharma from great master Mazu. You should now study the words of this attacking lion. By studying the story of a black tortoise climbing up a tree backward,* you should investigate the vital way of moving forward and moving backward. Upon inheriting dharma there is this kind of study. Huangbo's words "I fear I will lose my descendants" cannot be evaluated by you. Do you understand what he meant by "my" and "descendants"? You must examine this in detail; the meaning is already manifested, and nothing is hidden.

But someone called Weibo, Zen Master Fuguo, ignorant of the dharma heritage of buddha ancestors, listed Chenggu as the dharma heir of Yunmen. It is a mistake. Those who study the way later should not naively think that Chenggu had mastered the way.

On the seventh day, sixth month, second year of Kangen [1244], this was copied at the Attendant's Hall, Yoshimine Monastery, Echizen Province.

Ejō

2

Chenggu, if dharma heritage can be attained through literature as you imply, do all those who reach understanding by reading sūtras inherit dharma from Shākyamuni Buddha? It is never so. Understanding by sūtras always requires a correct master's seal of approval.

Your words show that you have not yet read the recorded sayings of Yunmen. Only those who have seen Yunmen's words have inherited from Yunmen. But you have not yet seen Yunmen with your own eyes; you have not yet seen the self with your own eyes. You have not seen Yunmen with Yunmen's eyes; you have not seen the self with Yunmen's eyes.

There are many people like you who have not thoroughly studied. You should continually buy straw sandals,* seeking a correct master to inherit dharma from.

You should not say that you have inherited dharma from great master Yunmen. If you do so, you will enter the stream of those outside the way. Even Baizhang would be mistaken if he talked like you.

Translated by Reb Anderson and Kazuaki Tanahashi

Buddha Ancestors

BUSSO[1]

Now, actualizing the buddha ancestors means to bring them forth and look at them respectfully. It is not limited to the buddhas of past, present and future, but it is going beyond buddhas who are going beyond themselves. It is taking up those who have maintained the face* and eye* of buddha ancestors, formally bowing and meeting them. They have manifested the virtue of the buddha ancestors, dwelt in it, and actualized it in the body. Their names are:

Vipashyin Buddha (*boundless discourse buddha*), Shikhin Buddha (*fire buddha*), Vishvabhū Buddha (*universal compassion buddha*), Krakucchanda Buddha (*gold wizard buddha*), Kanakamuni Buddha (*golden sage buddha*), Kāshyapa Buddha (*drinking light buddha*), Shākyamuni Buddha (*patience and silence buddha*), Mahākāshyapa, Ānanda, Shanavāsa, Upagupta, Dhritaka, Micchaka, Vasumitra, Buddhanandi, Buddhamitra, Pārshva, Punyayashas, Ashvaghosha, Kapimala, Nāgārjuna, Kānadeva, Rāhulata, Sanghānandi, Gayashāta, Kumārata, Jayata, Vasubandhu, Manorhita, Haklenayashas, Simhabhikshu, Basiasita, Punyamitra, Prajnātāra, Bodhidharma, Huike, Sengcan, Daoxin, Hongren, Huineng, Xingsi, Xiqian, Weiyan, Tansheng, Liangjie, Daoying, Daopi, Guanzhi, Yuanguan, Jingxuan, Yiqing, Daokai, Zichun, Qingliao, Zhongque, Zhijian, Rujing.

I saw my late master, old buddha Tiantong, at the time of summer practice period in the first year of Baoqing of Great Song {1227}, and with formal bow completed receiving these buddha ancestors.

This can only occur between a buddha and a buddha.

On the third day, first month, second year of Ninji {1241}, this was written and taught at Kannondōri Kōshō Hōrin Monastery, Uji County, Yamashiro Province, Japan.

Translated by Lew Richmond and Kazuaki Tanahashi

Document of Heritage*

SHISHO[1]

1

A buddha inherits dharma only from a buddha, an ancestor inherits dharma only from an ancestor—merging of realization, direct transmission. In this way, it is the unsurpassable bodhi. It is impossible to give the seal of realization without being a buddha, and it is impossible to become a buddha without receiving the seal of realization from a buddha. Who else, other than a buddha, can seal this realization as the most venerable, the most unsurpassable?

When you have the seal of realization from a buddha, you have realization without a teacher,* realization without self. This being so, it is said, "A buddha inherits realization from a buddha; an ancestor merges realization with an ancestor." The meaning of this principle cannot be understood by those who are not buddhas. How then can it be measured by bodhisattvas in the ten stages* or even in the stage of enlightenment equal to buddha's?* How, furthermore, can it be discerned by masters of sūtras or treatises? Even if they explain it, still they do not understand it.

2

Since a buddha inherits dharma from a buddha, the buddha way is mastered by a buddha and a buddha; there is no moment of the way without a buddha and a buddha. For example, rocks inherit from rocks, jewels inherit from jewels. When chrysanthemums inherit from chrysanthemums and a pine gives the seal of realization to a pine, the preceding chrysanthemum is one with the following chrysanthemum, and the preceding pine is one with the following pine. Those who do not understand this, even when they hear the words "correct transmission from buddha to buddha," have no idea what it means; they do not know heritage from buddha to buddha, merged realization of ancestor and ancestor. What a pity! They appear to be the buddha's family but they are not the buddha's heirs, nor are they heir-buddhas.*

3

The Sixth Ancestor once gave a discourse to the assembly. "There are forty ancestors from the Seven Buddhas to myself, and there are forty ancestors from myself to the Seven Buddhas."

This is clearly the principle of correct heritage of buddha ancestors. The Seven Buddhas include those who appeared in the last eon and those who appeared in the present eon. Nevertheless, the continuation of face-to-face transmission of the forty ancestors is the buddha way and the buddha heritage.

Thus, proceeding from the Sixth Ancestor to the Seven Buddhas is the buddha heritage of forty ancestors. And going up from the Seven Buddhas to the Sixth Ancestor is the buddha heritage of forty buddhas.

The buddha way, the ancestor way is like this. Without merging realization and without buddha ancestors, there is no buddha wisdom and there is no confidence in buddhas; without ancestors' mastery there is no merging of realization between ancestors.

4

The "forty ancestors" here represent only recent buddhas. Furthermore, the mutual heritage* between buddhas and buddhas is deep and vast, neither backing up nor turning away, neither cut off nor stopped.

This means that although Shākyamuni Buddha had realized the way before the Seven Buddhas,[2] he finally inherited dharma from Kāshyapa Buddha. Again, although he realized the way on the eighth day of the twelfth month in the thirtieth year since his birth, it is realization of the way before the Seven Buddhas. It is realization of the way simultaneously with all buddhas shoulder to shoulder, realization of the way before all buddhas, realization of the way after all buddhas.

In this way there is an understanding that Kāshyapa Buddha inherited dharma from Shākyamuni Buddha. If you do not know this you do not understand the buddha way. If you do not understand the buddha way you are not an heir of the buddha. The buddha's heir means the buddha's child.

5

Shākyamuni Buddha once caused Ānanda to ask, "Whose disciples were all buddhas of the past?"

Shākyamuni Buddha answered, "All buddhas of the past are disciples of myself, Shākyamuni Buddha."

The right form of all buddhas is like this. To see all buddhas, to inherit from all buddhas, to fulfill the way, is the buddha way of all buddhas. In this buddha way, at the time of inheriting dharma the document of heritage is always transmitted. Those without dharma heritage are heretics believing in spontaneous enlightenment. If the buddha way had not clearly established dharma heritage, how could it have come down to the present?

For this reason, when a buddha becomes a buddha, a document of heritage is given to a buddha-inheriting buddha and this document of heritage is received from a buddha-inheriting buddha.

The meaning of the document of heritage is this: you understand sun, moon, and stars, and inherit dharma; you attain skin, flesh, bones, and marrow, and inherit dharma; you inherit robe or staff, pine branch or whisk, udumbara flower or brocade robe; you inherit straw sandals or a bamboo staff.

At the time of dharma heritage, the document is handwritten with blood of the finger or of the tongue. Or it is handwritten with oil or milk. Every one of these is a document of heritage.

Those who entrust and those who receive this heritage are both the buddha's heirs. Indeed, whenever buddha ancestors are manifested, dharma heritage is manifested. At the time of manifestation innumerable buddha ancestors arrive without expectation and inherit dharma without seeking. Those who inherit dharma are all buddha ancestors.

6

In China, from the time the Twenty-eighth Ancestor came from India, the principle that there is dharma heritage in the buddha way was correctly understood. Before that time it had never been spoken of. This is something that was not known in India by teachers of scriptures or treatises. This is a state not reached by the ten stages or three classes of bodhisattvas; even the teachers of dhāranī* who study the meaning of the tripitaka* cannot understand it. What a pity! Although they have received a human body as a vessel of the way, they are uselessly entangled by the net of scriptures; they do not understand the method of breaking through, cannot realize the moment of leaping out. Because of this you must study the way in detail, and wholeheartedly determine to master it.

7

When I was in China, I had the opportunity to look at some documents of heritage. There were various kinds.

One of those who showed me documents of heritage was Visiting Abbot Weiyi at Mt. Tiantong, a former abbot of Guangfu Monastery. He was a man from Yue, like my late master. So my late master would say, "Ask Abbot Weiyi about the customs of my region."

One day the visiting abbot said, "Old writings worth seeing are treasures of mankind. How many of them have you seen?"

I said, "I have seen just a few."

Then he said, "I have a scroll of old writing. I will show it to you at your convenience." He brought it to me. It was a document of heritage of the Fayan lineage which he had obtained from the articles left behind by an old master. So it was not what elder Weiyi himself had received.

The document said, "The First Ancestor Mahākāshyapa was awakened with Shākyamuni Buddha. Shākyamuni Buddha was awakened with Kāshyapa Buddha."

Upon seeing this, I was firmly convinced that there is dharma heritage between a correct heir and a correct heir. That was a teaching I had never seen before. At that moment the buddha ancestors had inconceivably responded to my wish and helped me, a descendant of theirs. I had never been moved so much.

8

When elder Zongyue was filling the position of head monk on Mt. Tiantong, he showed me a document of heritage of the Yunmen lineage. The name of the teacher of the person receiving the document of heritage and the names of some Indian and all Chinese ancestors were written side by side, and below that the name of the person receiving the document. The name of the new ancestor was directly connected to those of the buddha ancestors. Therefore all the names of the more than forty ancestors from the Tathāgata are joined together with the name of the new heir. It was as though each of them had given heritage to the new ancestor. Mahākāshyapa, Ānanda, and others were lined up just as in other lineages.

I asked Zongyue, the head monk, "Reverend, there is some difference among the Five Schools in the arrangement of names on the document of heritage. Why is that so? If it came directly from India, why is there such a difference?"

Zongyue said, "Even if there is a vast difference, just understand that buddhas of Mt. Yunmen are like this. For what is the venerable Shākyamuni revered? He is revered for his way of awakening. For what is great master Yunmen revered? He is revered for his way of awakening."

Upon hearing these words, I understood his meaning.

9

Those who are heads of the large monasteries in Jiangsu and Zhenjiang now are mostly heirs of the Linji, Yunmen, and Dongshan lineages.

But among students, particularly among those who call themselves descendants of Linji, some intend wrongdoing. Usually those studying in the community of a master request a scroll of the master's portrait and a scroll of his dharma words in order to prepare to meet the standard requirement of dharma heritage. But these fellows ask the attendants of masters for dharma words and portraits, and collect and hide many of them. When they are old they bribe public officials to get a temple and hold the abbot's seat without having inherited dharma from the masters whose dharma words and portraits they obtained. Instead, they inherit dharma from the famous masters of the time or from the masters who have given dharma heritage to retainers of the king. They covet fame without regard to attaining dharma.

What a pity that there are such crooked habits at this wicked time of decayed teaching! Not even one of those fellows has ever dreamed of the way of buddha ancestors.

10

In fact, the masters' dharma words or portraits are also given to lecturers of scripture schools as well as lay men and women. They are even given to workers in the monasteries or to merchants. This is evident by the records of various masters.

In many cases, monks who are not qualified eagerly desire proof of dharma heritage and ask for a scroll of calligraphy. Although their teachers are distressed by this, they reluctantly take up the brush. In such cases the teacher does not follow the traditional format, but writes only that the person has studied with him.

The recent way is that when a person gains accomplishment under a master, he inherits dharma from that master as his dharma teacher. Some monks sitting on a long platform,* who have not received a seal from a master but have only received guidance in the abbot's room or listened to the formal lectures, constantly refer to what was given by their master after they become abbots of temples. But most students accept the master as dharma teacher only when they have broken open the great matter with him.

11

Again, there was a priest named Chuan, a descendant of priest Qingyuan, Zen Master Fuyan of Longmen. This Chuan, a librarian, also had a document of heritage. At the beginning of Jiading Era [1208–24], when librarian Chuan was sick, senior monk Ryūzen, a Japanese, took good care of him. Because Ryūzen worked hard, librarian Chuan, grateful for help during his illness, took out his document of heritage and let Ryūzen see it, saying, "This is a thing not commonly shown, but I will let you pay homage to it."

About eight years after that, in the autumn of the sixteenth year of Jiading Era [1223], when I was first staying at Mt. Tiantong, senior Ryūzen politely requested of librarian Chuan that he show this document of heritage to me. In this document of heritage, the names of the forty-five ancestors from the Seven Buddhas through Linji were lined up, and the names and monograms of masters after Linji were written inside a drawn circle. The name of the new heir was written at the end under the date. In this way a difference was made between the masters before and after Linji.

12

My late master, abbot of Mt. Tiantong, strictly prohibited students from unjustifiably claiming to have received dharma heritage. His assembly was an ancient buddha's assembly, restoring the monastic tradition. He himself did not wear a brocade robe. Although he had received the brocade robe of Zen master Daokai of Mt. Furong, he did not use it even during formal lecture. In fact, he never wore a brocade robe in his entire lifetime as an abbot. Those who were knowledgeable, as well as those who were not, admired him and respected him as a true master.

My late master, old buddha, often admonished all Buddhists in his lectures:

> Recently, there are a number of monks who borrow the name of the ancestor way, wear robes unsuitably, grow their hair, and get by in the world by having their distinguished titles registered. What a pity! Who can help them? I only regret that so few elders in this world have way-seeking mind and practice the way. Those who have seen or heard of the significance of the document of heritage or dharma heritage are even rarer—not one person out of a hundred or a thousand. Thus the ancestor way has declined.

When he said this, the other elders in China did not contradict him.

Thus, when you make sincere effort in the way, you will understand the document of heritage. To understand this is the study of the way.

13

On the document of heritage of the Linji lineage, the student's name is written, followed by the words "He has studied with me," "He has joined my assembly," "He has entered my room," or "He has had heritage from me." Then the names of the ancestors of the past are written in the traditional sequence.

Also in the Linji School there is an oral instruction that the heritage is not given by the first teacher or the last teacher, but by the right teacher; this is the principle of direct heritage.

14

One of the Linji lineage's documents of heritage, which I actually saw, is written as follows:

> Librarian Liaopai, a courageous man, is my disciple. I have attended priest Zonggao of Mt. Jing. Zonggao inherited from Keqin of Mt. Jia. Keqin inherited from Fayan of Yangqi. Fayan inherited from Shouduan of Haihui. Shouduan inherited from Fanghui of Yangqi. Fanghui inherited from Chu-

yuan, Ciming. Chuyuan inherited from Shanzhao of Fenyang. Shanzhao inherited from Xingnian of Mt. Shou. Xingnian inherited from Yanzhao of Fengxue. Yanzhao inherited from Huiyong of Nanyuan. Huiyong inherited from Cunjiang of Xinghua. Cunjiang is the heir of the great ancestor Linji.

This document was given by Deguang, Zen Master Fozhao of Mt. Ayuwang, to Wuji Liaopai. And when Wuji was the abbot of Mt. Tiantong, Chiyu, a junior priest, privately brought it to Liaoran Hall and showed it to me. It was the twenty-first day of the first month, the seventeenth year of Jiading Era [1224] of Great Song. What a joy it was! It was only possible by the inconceivable help of buddha ancestors. I saw it, after offering incense and paying homage to it.

The reason I requested to see this document of heritage was that Director Shiguang personally told me about it in Jiguang Hall around the seventh month of the previous year.

So I asked Shiguang, "Who keeps it?"

He said, "It is in the master abbot's quarters. If you request politely, you will be able to see it." After I heard this, day and night I wanted to see it. Then later I rendered my wholehearted request to the junior priest Chiyu.

The document was written on a mounted piece of white silk. The outside of the scroll was made of red brocade; the axis ends were of jade. It was about nine *sun** in height and over seven *shaku** long. Most people were not allowed to see it.

I thanked Chiyu. Also, I went to see Abbot Wuji immediately, offered incense and thanked him. Then he said, "Few people know about this, and now you do, elder. This is a fulfillment of your practice in the way." I was very pleased.

15

When I visited Mt. Tiantai and Mt. Yadang later in Baoqing Era [1225–27], I went to Wannian Monastery of Pingtian, on Mt. Tiantai. The abbot there was priest Yuanzi of Fu Region, who had succeeded former abbot Zhongjian after his retirement, and under whom the monastery had prospered.

Upon my first greeting him, Abbot Yuanzi talked about the teaching of the buddha ancestors. When he mentioned Yangshan's heritage from Great

Guishan, he said, "You haven't seen the document of heritage here in my quarters, have you?"

I replied, "No, unfortunately I haven't."

Abbot Yuanzi got up, took out the document of heritage, and, holding it up, said:

Following the dharma admonition of buddha ancestors, I have not shown this even to a close disciple or an old attendant monk. But when I went to the city to see the governor and stayed there as I do occasionally, I had a dream. In this dream a distinguished priest who seemed to be Zen master Fachang of Mt. Damei appeared, holding up a branch of plum blossoms. He said, "If a true man comes who has disembarked from a boat, do not withhold these flowers." And he gave me the plum blossoms. Still in the dream I exclaimed, "Why shouldn't I give him thirty blows before he leaves the boat?" Then before five days had passed, you came to meet me, elder. Of course you have disembarked from a boat, and this document of heritage is written on a brocade that has a design of plum blossoms. Since you must be the one Damei was referring to, in accordance with the dream I have taken this document out. Do you wish to inherit dharma from me? I would not withhold it if so.

I could not help being moved. Although I should have requested to receive a document of heritage from him, I only offered incense, bowed, and paid homage to him with deep respect. At that time there was present an incense attendant named Faning. He said that it was the first time he had ever seen the document of heritage.

I said to myself, "This event indeed could not have happened without the inconceivable help of buddha ancestors. As a foolish man from a remote country, by what fortune have I been able to see a document of heritage once again?" Tears wet my sleeves. At that time the Vimalakīrti Hall and Dashe Hall of Mt. Tiantai were quiet, without anyone around.

This document of heritage was written on white brocade with a pattern of fallen plum blossoms. Its height was over nine *sun*, and its length over one *hiro*.* Its axis ends were made of yellow jade. The outside of the scroll was brocade.

On my way back to Tiantong from Mt. Tiantai, I stayed at the entry hall of Husheng Monastery, on Mt. Damei. At that time I had an auspicious dream that the ancestor Damei came up to me and gave me a branch of plum blossoms in full bloom. This image of the ancestor was worthy of great respect. The branch was one *shaku* tall and one *shaku* wide. Aren't these plum blossoms as rare as an udumbara blossom? This dream was just as real as being awake. I have never before told this story to anyone in China or Japan.

16

The document of heritage written in our lineage from Dongshan is different from that written in the Linji and other lineages.

Our document of heritage was originally written in the mind of buddha ancestors. Great ancestor Qingyuan wrote it in front of the Sixth Ancestor Caoxi with the pure blood taken from his own finger and then correctly transmitted it. It has been said that his blood was mixed with Caoxi's blood when it was written. It has also been said that the ceremony of harmonizing blood was done by the First and Second Ancestors. Such statements as "This is my heir" or "He has studied with me" are not written on our document of heritage, but only the names of ancestors, including the Seven Buddhas, are written.

Thus, Caoxi's blood-spirit is graciously harmonized with Qingyuan's pure blood, and Qingyuan's pure blood is intimately harmonized with Caoxi's own blood. Only great ancestor Qingyuan directly received the seal of realization in this way, and no other ancestors can be compared with him. Those who know this agree that buddha-dharma has been transmitted only through Qingyuan.

Postscript

My late master, abbot of Tiantong, said, "All buddhas have dharma heritage without fail. That is to say, Shākyamuni Buddha inherited dharma from Kāshyapa Buddha. Kāshyapa Buddha inherited from Kanakamuni Buddha. Kanakamuni Buddha inherited dharma from Krakucchanda Buddha. Accept faithfully that buddhas have inherited from buddhas in this way until now. This is the way of studying about buddhas."

Then I said, "Shākyamuni Buddha came out into the world and attained the way after the parinirvāna of Kāshyapa Buddha. Furthermore, how could the buddha of the present eon inherit from the buddha of the previous eon? What is the meaning of this?"

My late master said, "What you mentioned is the view of scriptural schools or the way of the ten stages and three classes of bodhisattvas, which is different from the way of direct heritage of buddha ancestors. Our way of transmitting between buddhas and buddhas is not like that.

"We understand that Shākyamuni Buddha did inherit dharma from Kāshyapa Buddha. And we study that Kāshyapa Buddha entered parinirvāna after giving dharma heritage to Shākyamuni Buddha. If Shākyamuni Buddha had not inherited dharma from Kāshyapa Buddha, it would be the same as heretics who believe in spontaneous enlightenment. Who, then, could believe in Shākyamuni Buddha?

"Because of this heritage from buddha to buddha until now, each of the buddhas is a correct heir. They are not lined up, nor are they gathered together, but just inherit from each other. Thus we understand.

"It has nothing to do with measurements that are taught in various Āgama Schools,* such as eons or lifetimes. If you say that dharma heritage started from Shākyamuni Buddha, it would be only about two thousand years old, which is not so old. And the heritage would range only over forty generations, which is rather new. But buddha heritage should not be understood this way. We understand that Shākyamuni Buddha inherited dharma from Kāshyapa Buddha, and Kāshyapa Buddha inherited dharma from Shākyamuni Buddha. When you understand this way, it is the true dharma heritage of all buddhas and all ancestors."

Then, for the first time, I not only accepted that there is dharma heritage of buddha ancestors, but I was able to get out of the old pit I had been in up to that time.

On the twenty-seventh day, third month, second year of Ninji [1241], this was written at Kannondōri Kōshō Hōrin Monastery by monk Dōgen, who has transmitted dharma from China.

                    Translated by Lew Richmond and Kazuaki Tanahashi

All-Inclusive Study*

HENZAN[1]

1

The great way of buddha ancestors is to penetrate the ultimate realm, soaring with no strings attached or like clouds shooting below your feet.

This being so, "The world of blossoming flowers arises,"* and "I am always intimate with this."* Accordingly, sweet melon has a sweet stem, bitter gourd has its bitter root. Sweet melon and its stem are sweet through and through. Thus the way has been studied thoroughly.

2

Great Master Zongyi of Xuansha was called upon by his master Xuefeng, who said, "Since you've prepared a traveling bag, why don't you go toward all-inclusive study?"

Xuansha said, "Bodhidharma did not come to the eastern land. The Second Ancestor did not go to the western country."

Xuefeng was deeply impressed with this.[2]

"All-inclusive study" means here to study as cartwheels,* where "Sacred truth doesn't do anything.* What degrees can there be?"

3

When Zen Master Dahui of Nanyue first went to meet Huineng, the old buddha of Caoxi, the old buddha said, "What is it that thus comes?"*

Dahui all-inclusively studied that lump of mud for eight years and then presented this move to the ancient buddha. "I understand now. When I first came here you instructed me: 'What is it that thus comes?' "

Then the ancient buddha of Caoxi said, "What do you understand?"

Dahui said, "Speaking about it won't hit the mark."

This is the actualization of all-inclusive study, the realization of eight years.

The old buddha of Caoxi said, "Does it rest on practice and realization?"

Dahui said, "It is not that there is no practice and no realization, it is just that they cannot be defiled."

Then Caoxi said, "I am like this, you are like this, and all the buddha ancestors in India are also like this."³

After this Dahui studied all-inclusively for eight more years; counting from beginning to end it is an all-inclusive study of fifteen years.⁴

To "thus come" is all-inclusive study. To open up the hall and see all buddhas and all ancestors where "Speaking about it won't hit the mark" is all-inclusive study.

Since entering into and seeing the picture* there have been sixty-five hundred thousand myriad billions of turning bodies* of all-inclusive study. Leisurely entering the monastery and leisurely leaving the monastery is not all-inclusive study. Seeing with the entire eyeball* is all-inclusive study. Striking all the way through is all-inclusive study. To understand that the skin of the face is very thick* is all-inclusive study.

4

The meaning of "all-inclusive study" as asserted by Xuefeng does not mean that he encouraged Xuansha to leave the monastery or go north or come south. His expression provoked the all-inclusive study of Xuansha's words "Bodhidharma did not come to the eastern land. The Second Ancestor did not go to the western country."

Xuansha's words "Bodhidharma did not come to the eastern land" do not confusedly state that Bodhidharma did not come although he actually did come. But they mean that there is not an inch of land on earth. This "Bodhi-

dharma" is the tip of the life vein.* Even if the entire eastern land appears
to accompany him, his body is not turned, nor is it moved by the words.
Because Bodhidharma did not come to the eastern land, he faces the eastern
land.⁵ Even if the eastern land sees the buddha face, the ancestor face, it is
not that Bodhidharma came to the eastern land. To reach for a buddha
ancestor is to lose his nostrils.*

The lands do not lie to east or west. East-and-west has nothing to do with
lands. "The Second Ancestor did not go to the western country" means that
to study all-inclusively the western country, you need not go to the western
country. Should the Second Ancestor go to the western country, he would
miss his arm. What then is the meaning of the Second Ancestor's not going
to the western country? He leaped into the eyeball of the blue-eyed one;*
there was no need to go to the western country. Had he not leaped into the
blue eyes, he should have gone to the western country. Gouging out Bodhidharma's eyeball is all-inclusive study. To go to the western country or to
go to the eastern land is not all-inclusive study. To visit Tiantai or Nanyue
or to reach Wutai or heaven is not all-inclusive study. If Four Seas and Five
Lakes* are not penetrated, it is not all-inclusive study. To go back and forth
on the Four Seas and Five Lakes is not to allow the Four Seas and Five Lakes
to study all-inclusively. By treading back and forth you will make the road
smooth, the ground beneath your feet will become smooth, but all-inclusive
study will be lost.

Because Xuansha studied all-inclusively the understanding of "The entire universe of the ten directions is the true human body," he reached the
understanding of "Bodhidharma did not come to the eastern land. The
Second Ancestor did not go to the western country."

All-inclusive study means "If the top of a stone is large, the bottom is
large. If the top of the stone is small, the bottom is small."⁶ Without changing the top of a stone you allow the stone to be large or to be small. To study
a hundred thousand myriad things only as a hundred thousand myriad
things is not yet all-inclusive study. To turn a hundred thousand myriad
bodies even in half a statement is all-inclusive study. For example, "To just
hit the earth when you hit the earth" is all-inclusive study. Merely hitting
the earth once, hitting the sky once, or hitting the four quarters and eight
directions once is not all-inclusive study. But Juzhi's studying with Tianlong and attaining one finger* is all-inclusive study. Juzhi's raising just one
finger is all-inclusive study.

5

Xuansha taught the assembly, "Shākyamuni Buddha and I studied together."

A monk came up and asked, "I wonder, who did you two study with?"

The master said, "We studied with the third son of Xie* on a fishing boat."[7]

Old man Shākyamuni's study from beginning to end is itself studying together with old man Xuansha. Xuansha's study from beginning to end is studying closely together with old man Shākyamuni. Between old man Shākyamuni and old man Xuansha, there is no one study that is more complete or incomplete than another. This is the meaning of all-inclusive study. Old man Shākyamuni is an ancient buddha because he studied together with old man Xuansha. Old man Xuansha is a descendant because he studied together with old man Shākyamuni. You should study all-inclusively the meaning of this.

You should understand these words: "We studied with the third son of Xie on a fishing boat." This is to study all-inclusively in pursuit of the moment when old man Shākyamuni and old man Xuansha studied together at the same time. When Xuansha saw the third son of Xie on the fishing boat, they were sharing study. When the third son of Xie saw the bald-headed fellow on Mt. Xuansha, they were sharing study.

Studying together or not studying together—you should allow yourself and others to reflect on this. Old man Xuansha and old man Shākyamuni studied together, studied all-inclusively. Together you should study all-inclusively: "With whom did the third son of Xie and Xuansha study?"

If the meaning of all-inclusive study does not appear, then studying the self is not attained, studying the self is not complete; studying others is not attained, studying others is not complete; studying a true person is not attained, studying yourself is not attained; studying the fist* is not attained, studying the eyeball is not attained; self hooking self is not attained, catching the fish without a hook is not attained.

If you master all-inclusive study, all-inclusive study is dropped away. When the ocean is dry, no bottom is visible. When the man is dead, no mind remains. "The ocean is dry" means the entire ocean is completely dry. The ocean is dry and you cannot see the bottom. Not remaining and completely remaining—both are the person's mind. When the person is dead, the mind does not remain. When death is taken up, the mind does not remain. This being so, you should know that the entire person is mind, the entire mind is the person. In this way you should investigate thoroughly from top to bottom.

6

My late master, old buddha of Tiantong, was once asked to give a discourse when accomplished priests, who were elders from various places, assembled. He ascended the seat and said:

> The great road has no gate. It leaps out from the heads of all of you. The sky has no road. It enters into my nostrils. In this way we meet as Gautama's bandits, or Linji's troublemakers. Ha! The great house tumbles down and spring wind swirls. Astonished, apricot blossoms fly and scatter—red.[8]

This discourse was given when my late master, old buddha, was abbot of Qingliang Monastery in Jiankang Prefecture, when he was visited by the temple elders from various places. These accomplished priests and my late master had known each other as teacher and disciples or had been students together. He had friends like this in all directions. They got together and asked him for a discourse. Elders who did not have a teaching phrase were not his associates and were not included. Only the most venerable priests were requested to attend.

My late master's all-inclusive study cannot be fully accomplished by everyone. There has not been an ancient buddha like my late master for two or three hundred years in Great Song. As "The great road has no gate," it is four or five thousand avenues of pleasure quarters, two or three myriads of wind-and-string pavilions.[9]

But when the great road leaps out it leaps out from the head, not from anywhere else. In the same way it enters the nostrils. Both leaping out and entering are studies of the way. Those who have not leaped out of the head or inhaled the body through the nostrils are not students of the way or persons of all-inclusive study. You should just study the meaning of all-inclusive study with Xuansha.

7

Long ago the Fourth Ancestor studied with the Third Ancestor for nine years. This is all-inclusive study. Later Zen master Puyuan of Nanquan lived in Chiyang for almost thirty years. This is all-inclusive study without leaving the mountain. Yunyan, Daoyu [Yuanzhi], and others engaged in study when they were at Mt. Yao for forty years. This is all-inclusive study. Long ago the Second Ancestor studied at Mt. Song for eight years. He studied all-inclusively the skin, flesh, bones, and marrow.

8

All-inclusive study is just single-minded sitting, dropping away body and mind. At the moment of going there, you go there; at the moment of coming here, you come here. There is no gap. Just in this way, the entire body studies all-inclusively the great road's entire body.

Stepping over the head of Vairochana is samādhi without conflict. To attain this firmly is to step over the head of Vairochana.

The complete practice of all-inclusive study by leaping out is gourd leaping out from gourd. For a long time the gourd's head has been the practice place. Its vital force is vines. Gourd studies gourd all-inclusively. In this way a blade of grass is actualized. This is all-inclusive study.

On the twenty-seventh day, eleventh month, first year of Kangen [1243], this was taught in a grass-thatched hut at the foot of Yamashi Peak, Echizen Province.

Translated by Mel Weitsman and Kazuaki Tanahashi

*Going beyond Buddha**

BUKKŌJŌJI[1]

I

Reverend ancestor, Great Master Wuben of Mt. Dong (Dongshan), Yun Region, is the direct heir of Great Master Wuzhu of Mt. Yunyan, Tan Region. He is the thirty-eighth going-beyond ancestor from the Tathāgata. He is the thirty-eighth ancestor going beyond himself.

Master Dongshan once taught the assembly, "Concerning realization-through-the-body[2] of going beyond buddha, I would like to talk a little."

A monk said, "What is this talk?"

The master said, "When I talk you don't hear it."

The monk said, "Do you hear it, sir?"

The master said, "Wait till I don't talk, then you hear it."[3]

The words spoken here, "going beyond buddha," originally came from master Dongshan. Other buddha ancestors have studied his words and realized through-the-body going beyond buddha. You should know that going beyond buddha is neither causality nor fruition.[4] However, there is realization-through-the-body and complete attainment of "you don't hear it"[5] at the moment of talking.

If you do not get beyond buddha, you do not realize through-the-body going beyond buddha. Without talking* you do not realize through-the-

203

body going beyond buddha. Going beyond buddha and talking neither reveal each other nor hide each other, neither give to nor take from each other. This being so, talking brings forth going beyond buddha.

When going beyond buddha is actualized, you do not hear. "You do not hear" means buddha-going-beyond-buddha is not heard by the self. At the time of talking you do not hear. You should know that talking is not stained* by either hearing or not-hearing. It is not concerned with hearing or not-hearing.

You are concealed* within not-hearing. You are concealed within talking. It is like meeting a person and not meeting a person; being thus and not thus. When you talk you do not hear. The meaning of "not-hearing" is that you are not hindered by the tongue, you are not hindered by the ears, you are not drilled by the eyes, you are not shielded* by body and mind. This is not-hearing. Do not try to take this up and regard it as talking. Not-hearing is not talking. It is just that at the time of talking you do not hear. The reverend ancestor's words "When I talk you don't hear it" mean that talking, from beginning to end, is just like wisteria vines entangled with each other. Talking is entangled with talking, it is permeated by talking.

The monk said, "Do you hear it, sir?" This does not mean that he is asking if the master hears the talking; he is not asking about the master or his talking. Instead, the monk is asking whether he should study direct hearing as the master talks. That is to say, he is asking whether talking is talking and hearing is hearing. Even if you can say something about it, it is beyond your speech.

You should examine clearly the words of reverend Dongshan, "Wait till I don't talk, then you hear it." At the moment of talking, there is no direct hearing. Direct hearing comes forth at the moment of not-talking.

It is not that you unfortunately miss the moment of not-talking and must wait for not-talking. Direct hearing is not merely observing. It is true observation. It is not at the moment of direct hearing that talking goes away and is confined. It is not at the time of talking that direct hearing hides its body in the eyes of talking and resounds like thunder. It is just that you do not hear at the time of talking, you directly hear at the time of not-talking.

This is the meaning of "I would like to talk a little" and "realization-through-the-body of going beyond buddha." That is to realize through-the-body direct hearing at the time of talking. This being so, master Dongshan said, "Wait till I don't talk, then you hear it." However, going beyond buddha is not before the Seven Buddhas. It is the Seven Buddhas going beyond.

2

Reverend ancestor, Great Master Wuben, taught the assembly, "You should know someone going beyond buddha."

A monk asked, "Who is someone going beyond buddha?"

The master said, "Not-buddha."*

Later Yunmen interpreted this: "The name is unattainable, the form is unattainable, therefore he is 'not'."

Baofu said, "Buddha-not."

Fayan also said, "Provisionally he is called buddha."⁶

The buddha ancestor going beyond a buddha ancestor is reverend Dongshan. The reason is that though there are many other buddhas and ancestors they have never dreamed of the words "going beyond buddha." If this is spoken to Deshan or Linji, they will disregard it. Neither Yantou nor Xuefeng would get hold of the fist* even if they were to crush and grind their bodies. The reverend ancestor's words "realization-through-the-body of going beyond buddha," "I would like to talk a little," and "You should know someone going beyond buddha" cannot be fully realized merely by practice and enlightenment through one, two, three, four, five eons, or one hundred great eons. Only those who study the inconceivable road can realize it.

Know that there is someone going beyond buddha. This is the full activity of rousing the intention. So you should understand going beyond buddha by taking up an ancient buddha and raising a fist. To see through this is to know someone who goes beyond buddha and someone who goes beyond not-buddha. The words of Dongshan do not mean that you should be someone who goes beyond buddha, or that you should meet someone who goes beyond buddha. He just means that you should know that there is someone who goes beyond buddha. The key to this barrier is not-knowing* someone who goes beyond buddha, and not-knowing someone who goes beyond not-buddha.

Someone who goes beyond buddha in this way is not-buddha. When you are asked "What is not-buddha?", you should consider: You do not call him not-buddha because he precedes buddha. You do not call him not-buddha because he follows buddha. You do not call him not-buddha because he surpasses buddha.

He is not-buddha merely because he is going-beyond-buddha. "Not-buddha" is so called because buddha's face is dropped away, buddha's body and mind are dropped away.

3

Zen master Kumu of Jingyin, Dongjing (whose initiatory name is Facheng, an heir of Furong), taught the assembly, "As I know about going beyond buddha, I have something to say. Answer now, good students! What is going beyond buddha? This man has a child who does not have six sense-organs* and lacks seven consciousnesses.* He is a great *icchantika*,* a kind of not-buddha. When he meets a buddha he kills the buddha, and when he meets an ancestor he kills the ancestor. The heavens cannot contain this person. Hell does not have a gate to let him in. All of you! Do you know this man?"

After waiting for a while he said, "If you don't see *saindhava*,* it's like talking a lot in deep sleep."[7]

"Not having six sense-organs" can be described as "The eyeballs have become tallow beads, the nostrils have become bamboo pipes, and the skull has turned into a shit dipper. What is the meaning of all this?"[8]

In this way, the six sense-organs are not there. Because there are no six sense-organs, he has gone through the forge and bellows and has become a metal buddha. He has gone through a great ocean and has become a clay buddha. He has gone through the fire and has become a wooden buddha.[9]

"Lacking seven consciousnesses" means this person is a broken wooden dipper.* Although he kills a buddha, he meets the buddha. Because he meets a buddha, he kills the buddha. If he tries to enter the heavens, the heavens are annihilated. If he goes toward hell, hell will burst immediately. If he meets face to face, his face breaks into a smile and there is no *saindhava*. Although he is in deep sleep, he talks a lot.

Understand that this means all the mountains and the entire land know the self. Jewels and stones are all crushed into pieces. You should quietly study and pursue this teaching of Zen Master Kumu. Do not neglect it.

4

Zen Master Hongjue of Mt. Yunju went to study with great master Dongshan. Dongshan said, "What is your name?"

Yunju said, "Daoying."

Dongshan said, "Say something beyond that."

Yunju said, "When I say something beyond, I am not called Daoying."

Dongshan said, "When I was with Yunyan we spoke just like this."[10]

You should examine in detail the words between this master and disciple. "When I say something beyond, I am not called Daoying" is Daoying's going beyond. You should understand that in addition to usual Daoying there is someone beyond, who is not called Daoying. From the moment "When I say something beyond, I am not called Daoying" is actualized, he is truly Daoying.

However, you should not say that he is Daoying when he is going beyond. When he was asked by Dongshan, "Say something beyond that," even if he had replied, "When I say something beyond, I am called Daoying," it would still be the words of going beyond. Why is it so? Daoying immediately leaps into the top of the head* and hides his own body.* Since he hides his own body, his form is revealed.

5

Zen master Benji of Caoshan studied with reverend ancestor Dongshan. Dongshan said, "What is your name?"

Caoshan said, "Benji."

Dongshan said, "Say something beyond that."

Caoshan said, "I will not say."

Dongshan asked again, "Why will you not say?"

Caoshan said, "No-name Benji." Dongshan approved it.[11]

It is not that there is nothing to say in going beyond, but here there is no saying. Why did he not say? Because of no-name Benji. Therefore, saying in going beyond is no-saying. No-saying in going beyond is no-name. Benji of no-name is saying going beyond. Because of this, he is Benji no-name.

Thus there is no-Benji. No-name drops away. Benji drops away.

6

Zen master Baoji of Panshan said, "The single path of going beyond—a thousand sages, no transmission."[12]

"The single path of going beyond" is the utterance of Baoji alone. He did not say "buddha going beyond" or "someone going beyond," but he said "the single path of going beyond."

It means that even if thousands of sages appear all together, the single path of going beyond is not transmitted. "No transmission" means a thousand sages protect that which is not transmitted. You may be able to understand in this way. But there is something further to say about this. It is not that a thousand sages or a thousand wise people do not exist, but that a single path of going beyond is not merely the realm of the sages or of the wise.

7

Zen master Guangzuo of Mt. Zhimen was once asked by a monk, "What is going beyond buddha?"

He said, "To carry sun and moon on the end of a staff."[13]

This means that you are completely covered by the sun and moon on top of a staff. This is buddha going beyond. When you penetrate the staff that carries sun and moon, the entire universe is dark. This is buddha going beyond. It is not that the sun and moon are the staff. "On the end of a staff" means the entire staff.

8

Zen master Daowu of Tianhuang Monastery visited the assembly of Great Master Wuji of Shitou. Daowu asked, "What is the fundamental meaning of buddha-dharma?"

Shitou said, "Not to attain, not to know."

Daowu said, "Is there some turning point* in going beyond, or not?"

Shitou said, "The vast sky does not hinder white clouds from flying."[14]

Now, Shitou is the second generation from Caoxi. Priest Daowu of Tianhuang Monastery is the younger dharma brother of Yaoshan. Daowu once asked Shitou about the fundamental meaning of buddha-dharma. This is not a question asked by beginners or those just recently started. Daowu asked this question when he was ready to understand the fundamental meaning if he heard it.

Shitou said, "Not to attain, not to know." Understand that in buddha-dharma the fundamental meaning is in the first thought,* as well as in the ultimate level.

This fundamental meaning is not-attaining.* It is not that there is no aspiration for enlightenment, no practice, or no enlightenment. But simply, not-attaining.

The fundamental meaning is not-knowing. Practice-enlightenment is not nonexistent or existent, but is not-knowing, not-attaining.

Again, the fundamental meaning is not-attaining, not-knowing. It is not that there is no sacred truth, no practice-enlightenment, but simply not-attaining not-knowing.

Daowu said, "Is there some turning point in going beyond, or not?" It means that when the turning point is actualized, going beyond is actualized. "Turning point" is a provisional expression. The provisional expression is all buddhas, all ancestors. In saying this, there is going beyond. Although there is going beyond, do not neglect not-going-beyond in saying this.

"The vast sky does not hinder the white clouds from flying." These are Shitou's words. The vast sky does not hinder the vast sky. Just as the vast sky does not hinder the vast sky from flying, white clouds do not hinder white clouds. White clouds fly with no hindrance. White clouds' flying does not hinder the vast sky's flying. Not hindering others is not hindering self.

It is not that self and others need or have no hindrance. None of these requires no-hindrance or remains in no-hindrance. This is the no-hindrance brought out in the phrase "The vast sky does not hinder the white clouds from flying."

Right now, raise the eyebrow of the eye of study and see through the coming forth of buddhas, ancestors, self, and others. This is a case of asking one question and answering ten. In asking one question and answering ten, the person who asks one question is the true person; the person who answers ten is the true person.

9

Huangbo said, "Those who have left home should understand things which have come from the past. Great master Farong of Niutou, a disciple of the Fourth Ancestor, explains both vertical and horizontal but does not know the key to the barrier of going beyond. With your own eyes and brain you should discern the correct school from the incorrect."[15]

Huangbo's words "things which have come from the past" mean that which has been correctly transmitted from buddha ancestors. This is called the treasury of the true dharma eye, the inconceivable mind of nirvāna. Although it is in yourself, you should understand it. Although it is in yourself, it is beyond your understanding. Those who have not received correct buddha-to-buddha transmission have never dreamed of it.

Huangbo, as the dharma heir of Baizhang, exceeds Baizhang and, as a dharma descendant of Mazu, exceeds Mazu. In three or four generations of the ancestor school, there was no one who could stand shoulder to shoulder with Huangbo. Huangbo alone made it clear that Niutou did not have two horns.[16] Other buddha ancestors had not noticed.

Zen master Farong of Mt. Niutou was a respected teacher, a disciple of the Fourth Ancestor. His discourse, horizontal and vertical, when compared with that of Indian or Chinese sūtra masters and treatise masters, was not less. But regrettably he did not speak of the key to the barrier of going beyond.

If you do not have the key to the barrier of things which have come from the past, how can you discern correct from incorrect in buddha-dharma? You are merely someone who studies words and phrases. Therefore, the knowing, practicing, and realizing of the key to the barrier of going beyond is not something ordinary people can accomplish. Where there is true endeavor, the key is realized.

"Going beyond buddha" means that you reach buddha, and going further, you continue to see buddha. It is not the same as sentient beings' seeing buddha.* Therefore if your seeing buddha is merely the same as sentient beings' seeing buddha, it is not seeing buddha. If your seeing buddha is merely the same as sentient beings' seeing buddha, it is seeing buddha mistakenly; how can you experience going beyond buddha?

You should know that Huangbo's words "going beyond" cannot be understood by the careless people of these times. Their dharma discourses cannot reach to that of Farong. Even if their dharma discourses equaled that of Farong, they are merely Farong's dharma brothers. How can they have the key to the barrier of going beyond? Other bodhisattvas of ten stages or three classes can never have the key to the barrier of going beyond. How can they open and close the barrier of going beyond? This is the eye of study. One who has the key to the barrier of going beyond goes beyond buddha, realizing through-the-body, going beyond buddha.

On the twenty-third day, third month, third year of Ninji [1242], this was taught to the assembly at Kannondōri Kōshō Hōrin Monastery.

Translated by Mel Weitsman and Kazuaki Tanahashi

PART FIVE

Poems

Waka Poems[1]

Awake or asleep
in a grass hut,
what I pray for is
to bring others across
before myself.

Although this ignorant self
may never become a buddha
I vow to bring
others across
because I am a monk.

How august!
Studying the old words
of the Seven Buddhas
you pass beyond
the six realms.

MOUNTAIN SECLUSION

I won't even stop
at the valley's brook
for fear that
my shadow
may flow into the world.

BOWING FORMALLY

A snowy heron
on the snowfield
where winter grass is unseen
hides itself
in its own figure.

VIEWING PEACH BLOSSOMS AND REALIZING THE WAY

In spring wind
peach blossoms
begin to come apart.
Doubts do not grow
branches and leaves.

ON NONDEPENDENCE OF MIND

Water birds
going and coming
their traces disappear
but they never
forget their path.

THE BODY BORN BEFORE THE PARENTS

The village I finally reach
deeper than the deep mountains
indeed
the capital
where I used to live!

ON THE TREASURY OF THE TRUE DHARMA EYE

Waves recede.
Not even the wind ties up
a small abandoned boat.
The moon is a clear
mark of midnight.

Translated by Brian Unger
and Kazuaki Tanahashi

Chinese-style Poems[2]

SECLUSION

Evening zazen hours advance. Sleep hasn't come yet.
More and more I realize mountain forests are good for efforts in the way.
Sounds of the valley brook enter the ears, moonlight pierces the eyes.
Outside this, not one further instant of thought.

SECLUSION

The ancestor way came from the west; I transmitted it east.
Polishing the moon, plowing clouds, I long for ancient wind.
How can worldly red dusts blow here?
Deep mountain snowy evening—thatched hut—inside.

ON A PORTRAIT OF MYSELF

Cold lake, for thousands of yards, soaks up sky color.
Evening quiet: a fish of brocade scales reaches bottom, then goes
first this way, then that way; arrow notch splits.
Endless water surface moonlight brilliant.

SNOW

All my life false and real, right and wrong tangled.
Playing with the moon, ridiculing wind, listening to birds. . . .
Many years wasted seeing the mountain covered with snow.
This winter I suddenly realize snow makes a mountain.

SPRING SNOW NIGHT

Snowdrifts like those at Shaolin, in the old days.
Whole sky, whole earth, whole spring—new.
Inheriting the robe, attaining the marrow—to join the ancestors
who would spare himself standing in snow through the night?

GIVEN TO A ZEN PERSON WHO REQUESTED A POEM

Mind itself is buddha.
Practice is difficult. Explanation is not difficult.
Not-mind. Not-buddha.
Explanation is difficult. Practice is not difficult.

FOR ATTENDANT WANG

Vast, boundless world—waxing and waning.
What person reaches this realm and understands without delusion?
Iron ox shuts off the Milky Way.
At the summit, Vairochana follows at your heels.

illumination
Mahavairochana = central deity of
esoteric Buddhism

GIVEN TO A ZEN PERSON

Where the great function turns, entire sky moves.
Penetrate; no trace on thread road.
Alone I sing in the balcony, only moon color
dyes clouds. Winter shower moistens burning haze.

SUN REFLECTED—HOUR OF THE SHEEP

Within the sun-face eye, round moon-face.
Attaining the sūtra covers the eye; eye becomes sūtra.
Study, mastery—ultimately nothing outside.
Cloud in the blue sky, water in a jar.

> Translated by David Schneider and Kazuaki Tanahashi

DIRECT MIND SEEING THE MOON, SIXTEENTH NIGHT

Contemplate on the sixteenth-night kōan.
When body moon tries for fullness, mind moon starts to fade.
If you have a clear idea of moon, a moon will be born.
But how can mid-autumn moon be grasped?

IN RESPONSE TO INSPECTOR WANG'S POEM

Speech and silence—absolutely the same: extremely subtle and profound.
A good remedy was prescribed a long time ago.
Piercing the sky, embracing the earth—no end to it.
An immense escarpment glowing with mysterious light.

GIVEN TO COURIER NAN

An explosive shout cracks the great empty sky.
Immediately clear self-understanding.
Swallow up buddhas and ancestors of the past.
Without following others, realize complete penetration.

THE POINT OF ZAZEN, AFTER ZEN MASTER HONGZHI[3]

The hub of buddhas' activity,
the turning of ancestors' hub—
it moves along with your nonthinking
and is completed in the realm of nonmerging.
As it moves along with your nonthinking

its appearance is immediate.
As it is completed in the realm of nonmerging
completeness itself is realization.
If its appearance is immediate
you have no defilement.
When completeness is realization
you stay in neither the general nor the particular.
If you have immediacy without defilement
immediacy is "dropping away" with no obstacles.
Realization, neither general nor particular,
is effort without desire.
Clear water all the way to the bottom;
a fish swims like a fish.
Vast sky transparent throughout;
a bird flies like a bird.

DURING SECLUSION

All that's visible springs from causes intimate to you.
While walking, sitting, lying down, the body itself is complete truth.
If someone asks the inner meaning of this:
"Inside the treasury of the dharma eye a single grain of dust."

UPON LOOKING AT MR. RAN'S LAST WORDS

Clearly nothing is sacred—hard as iron.
Tested in a raging furnace it melts like snow.
Let me ask you, where does it go?
When the breakers are high, what kind of moon do you see?

DEATH POEM[4]

Fifty-four years lighting up the sky.
A quivering leap smashes a billion worlds.
            Hah!
Entire body looks for nothing.
Living, I plunge into Yellow Springs.

Translated by Philip Whalen and Kazuaki Tanahashi

Appendixes

Reading the
Record of Eihei Dōgen

Ryōkan (1758–1831)

On a somber spring evening around midnight,
rain mixed with snow sprinkled on the bamboos in the garden.
I wanted to ease my loneliness but it was quite impossible.
My hand reached behind me for the *Record of Eihei Dōgen*.
Beneath the open window at my desk,
I offered incense, lit a lamp, and quietly read.
Body and mind dropping away is simply the upright truth.
In one thousand postures, ten thousand appearances, a dragon toys with the jewel.
His understanding beyond conditioned patterns cleans up the current corruptions;
the ancient great master's style reflects the image of India.

I remember the old days when I lived at Entsū Monastery
and my late teacher lectured on the *True Dharma Eye*.
At that time there was an occasion to turn myself around,
so I requested permission to read it, and studied it intimately.
I keenly felt that until then I had depended merely on my own ability.
After that I left my teacher and wandered all over.
Between Dōgen and myself what relationship is there?
Everywhere I went I devotedly practiced the true dharma eye.
Arriving at the depths and arriving at the vehicle—how many times?
Inside this teaching, there's never any shortcoming.
Thus I thoroughly studied the master of all things.

Now when I take the *Record of Eihei Dōgen* and examine it,
the tone does not harmonize well with usual beliefs.
Nobody has asked whether it is a jewel or a pebble.
For five hundred years it's been covered with dust
just because no one has had an eye for recognizing dharma.
For whom was all his eloquence expounded?
Longing for ancient times and grieving for the present, my heart is exhausted.

One evening sitting by the lamp my tears wouldn't stop,
and soaked into the records of the ancient buddha Eihei.
In the morning the old man next door came to my thatched hut.
He asked me why the book was damp.
I wanted to speak but didn't as I was deeply embarrassed;
my mind deeply distressed, it was impossible to give an explanation.
I dropped my head for a while, then found some words.
"Last night's rain leaked in and drenched my bookcase."

                              Translated by Daniel Leighton and Kazuaki Tanahashi

Chinese Transliteration: Comparative Table

PINYIN	WADE-GILES		PINYIN	WADE-GILES
a	a		can	ts'an
ai	ai		cang	ts'ang
an	an		cao	ts'ao
ang	ang		ce	ts'ê
ao	ao		cen	ts'ên
			ceng	ts'êng
ba	pa		cha	ch'a
bai	pai		chai	ch'ai
ban	pan		chan	ch'an
bang	pang		chang	ch'ang
bao	pao		chao	ch'ao
bei	pei		che	ch'ê
ben	pên		chen	ch'ên
beng	pêng		cheng	ch'êng
bi	pi		chi	ch'ih
bian	pien		chong	ch'ung
biao	piao		chou	ch'ou
bie	pieh		chu	ch'u
bin	pin		chua	ch'ua
bing	ping		chuai	ch'uai
bo	po		chuan	ch'uan
bou	pou		chuang	ch'uang
bu	pu		chui	ch'ui
			chun	ch'un
ca	ts'a		chuo	ch'o
cai	ts'ai			

PINYIN	WADE-GILES	PINYIN	WADE-GILES
ci	tz'ŭ	gai	kai
cong	ts'ung	gan	kan
cou	ts'ou	gang	kang
cu	ts'u	gao	kao
cuan	ts'uan	ge	kê, ko
cui	ts'ui	gei	kei
cun	ts'un	gen	kên
cuo	ts'o	geng	kêng
		gong	kung
da	ta	gou	kou
dai	tai	gu	ku
dan	tan	gua	kua
dang	tang	guai	kuai
dao	tao	guan	kuan
de	tê	guang	kuang
dei	tei	gui	kuei
deng	têng	gun	kun
di	ti	guo	kuo
dian	tien		
diao	tiao	ha	ha
die	tieh	hai	hai
ding	ting	han	han
diu	tiu	hang	hang
dong	tung	hao	hao
dou	tou	he	ho
du	tu	hei	hei
duan	tuan	hen	hên
dui	tui	heng	hêng
dun	tun	hong	hung
duo	to	hou	hou
		hu	hu
e	ê, o	hua	hua
en	ên	huai	huai
eng	êng	huan	huan
er	êrh	huang	huang
		hui	hui
fa	fa	hun	hun
fan	fan	huo	huo
fang	fang		
fei	fei	ji	chi
fen	fên	jia	chia
feng	fêng	jian	chien
fo	fo	jiang	chiang
fou	fou	jiao	chiao
fu	fu	jie	chieh
		jin	chin
ga	ka		

PINYIN	WADE-GILES		PINYIN	WADE-GILES
jing	ching		lu	lu
jiong	chiung		luan	luan
jiu	chiu		lun	lun
ju	chü		luo	lo
juan	chüan		lü	lü
jue	chüeh		lüan	lüan
jun	chün		lüe	lüeh
			lun	lun, lün
ka	k'a			
kai	k'ai		ma	ma
kan	k'an		mai	mai
kang	k'ang		man	man
kao	k'ao		mang	mang
ke	k'ê, k'o		mao	mao
ken	k'ên		me	mê
keng	k'êng		mei	mei
kong	k'ung		men	mên
kou	k'ou		meng	mêng
ku	k'u		mi	mi
kua	k'ua		mian	mien
kuai	k'uai		miao	miao
kuan	k'uan		mie	mieh
kuang	k'uang		min	min
kui	k'uei		ming	ming
kun	k'un		miu	miu
kuo	k'uo		mo	mo
			mou	mou
la	la		mu	mu
lai	lai			
lan	lan		na	na
lang	lang		nai	nai
lao	lao		nan	nan
le	lê		nang	nang
lei	lei		nao	nao
leng	lêng		ne	nê
li	li		nei	nei
lia	lia		nen	nên
lian	lien		neng	nêng
liang	liang		ni	ni
liao	liao		nian	nien
lie	lieh		niang	niang
lin	lin		niao	niao
ling	ling		nie	nieh
liu	liu		nin	nin
long	lung		ning	ning
lou	lou		niu	niu

PINYIN	WADE-GILES		PINYIN	WADE-GILES
nong	nung		re	jê
nou	nou		ren	jên
nu	nu		reng	jêng
nuan	nuan		ri	jih
nun	nun		rong	jung
nuo	no		rou	jou
nü	nü		ru	ju
nüe	nüeh		ruan	juan
			rui	jui
ou	ou		run	jun
			ruo	jo
pa	p'a			
pai	p'ai		sa	sa
pan	p'an		sai	sai
pang	p'ang		san	san
pao	p'ao		sang	sang
pei	p'ei		sao	sao
pen	p'ên		se	sê
peng	p'êng		sen	sên
pi	p'i		seng	sêng
pian	p'ien		sha	sha
piao	p'iao		shai	shai
pie	p'ieh		shan	shan
pin	p'in		shang	shang
ping	p'ing		shao	shao
po	p'o		she	shê
pou	p'ou		shei	shei
pu	p'u		shen	shên
			sheng	shêng
qi	ch'i		shi	shih
qia	ch'ia		shou	shou
qian	ch'ien		shu	shu
qiang	ch'iang		shua	shua
qiao	ch'iao		shuai	shuai
qie	ch'ieh		shuan	shuan
qin	ch'in		shuang	shuang
qing	ch'ing		shui	shui
qiong	ch'iung		shun	shun
qiu	ch'iu		shuo	shuo
qu	ch'ü		si	ssŭ, szŭ
quan	ch'üan		song	sung
que	ch'üeh		sou	sou
qun	ch'ün		su	su
			suan	suan
ran	jan		sui	sui
rang	jang		sun	sun
rao	jao			

PINYIN	WADE-GILES	PINYIN	WADE-GILES
suo	so	ya	ya
		yai	yai
ta	t'a	yan	yen
tai	t'ai	yang	yang
tan	t'an	yao	yao
tang	t'ang	ye	yeh
tao	t'ao	yi	i, yi
te	t'ê	yin	yin
teng	t'êng	ying	ying
ti	t'i	yong	yung
tian	t'ien	you	yu
tiao	t'iao	yu	yü
tie	t'ieh	yuan	yüan
ting	t'ing	yue	yüeh
tong	t'ung	yun	yün
tou	t'ou		
tu	t'u	za	tsa
tuan	t'uan	zai	tsai
tui	t'ui	zan	tsan
tun	t'un	zang	tsang
tuo	t'o	zao	tsao
		ze	tsê
wa	wa	zei	tsei
wai	wai	zen	tsên
wan	wan	zeng	tsêng
wang	wang	zha	cha
wei	wei	zhai	chai
wen	wên	zhan	chan
weng	wêng	zhang	chang
wo	wo	zhao	chao
wu	wu	zhe	chê
		zhei	chei
xi	hsi	zhen	chên
xia	hsia	zheng	chêng
xian	hsien	zhi	chih
xiang	hsiang	zhong	chung
xiao	hsiao	zhou	chou
xie	hsieh	zhu	chu
xin	hsin	zhua	chua
xing	hsing	zhuai	chuai
xiong	hsiung	zhuan	chuan
xiu	hsiu	zhuang	chuang
xu	hsü	zhui	chui
xuan	hsüan	zhun	chun
xue	hsüeh	zhuo	cho
xun	hsün	zi	tzŭ

PINYIN	WADE-GILES		PINYIN	WADE-GILES
zong	tsung		zui	tsui
zou	tsou		zun	tsun
zu	tsu		zuo	tso
zuan	tsuan			

MAPS OF ZEN SITES IN CHINA

Hebei

Mt. Yan

Mt. Pan △

Mt. Wutai △

Shanxi

• Zhen

• Zao

• Taiyuan

• Fenyang

Shandong

Ye

Lake Furong ▷

Shanxi

Mt. Mayu
△ • Dongjing
Luoyang • △ Mt. Song

Huang River

Changan △ Mt. Shou
Mt. Xionger • She

Jiangsu

△ Mt. Danxia **Henan** **Anhui**

• Nanyang Mt. Ding △

• Deng • Jinling (Jiankang)

Mt. Niutou

Mt. Dong △ Huating •

• Sui Mt. Nanquan •

Hubei Mt. Dayang △ Mt. Baizhao △ Mt. Touzi

△ Huangmei • △ Mt. Sikong

Chang (Yangzi) River Mt. Shuangfeng △ △

Mt. Wuzu **Zhejiang**

(Mt. Pingmao) △

• Jing Mt. Yunju △ (see Map 2)

△ Mt. Jia • Rao

△ Mt. Yao△ △ Mt. Shimen

Mt. Liang △ Lake △ Mt. Baizhang

Mt. De △ Dongting △ Mt. Huangbo • Zhongling

△ Mt. Longya Mt. Dong △ Mt. Su

Mt. Gui (Mt. Dagui) △ Changsha • △

Mt. Shishuang △ △ Mt. Yangqi Mt. Cao △

Nanyue (Mt. Heng) △ **Jiangxi**

Mt. Qingyuan △ Mt. Lingyun △

Hunan △ Mt. Xuefeng △

Yunyan

Fujian

△ Mt. Yunmen

Caoxi • Zhang •

Guangdong

Xin •

Map 2

ZHEJIANG

Mt. He △

Mt. Jing
△

Mt. Bei   Hang
△   •

Mt. Nan △

Mt. Taibo
(Mt. Tiantong)

Ming
Mt. Xuedou △   •   △   △ Mt. Ayuwang

Mt. Damei △

Mu •

Zhe River

Mt. Tiantai △

Zhejiang Province

Mt. Ruiyan △

Mt. Yandang
△

Yongjia •

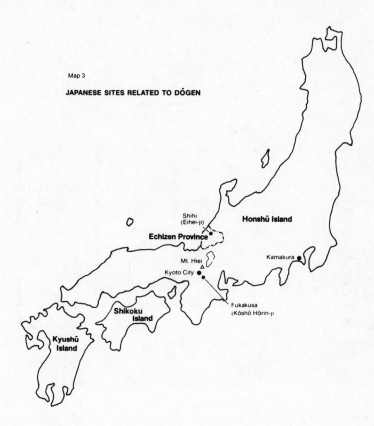

Map 3

JAPANESE SITES RELATED TO DŌGEN

Lineage Charts
of Chinese Zen Masters

EARLIER MASTERS

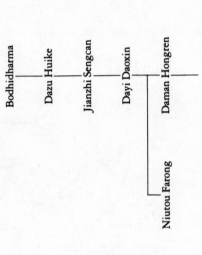

Bodhidharma

Dazu Huike

Jianzhi Sengcan

Dayi Daoxin

Daman Hongren

Niutou Farong

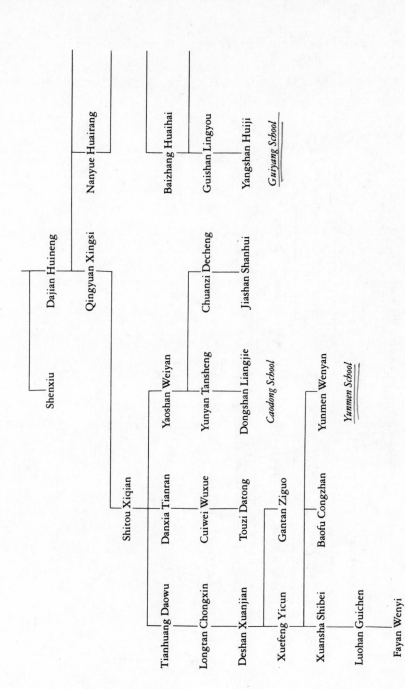

Dajian Huineng

Shenxiu

Qingyuan Xingsi   Nanyue Huairang

Shitou Xiqian

Baizhang Huaihai

Guishan Lingyou

Yangshan Huiji

Guiyang School

Yaoshan Weiyan   Chuanzi Decheng

Danxia Tianran

Yunyan Tansheng   Jiashan Shanhui

Cuiwei Wuxue

Dongshan Liangjie

Touzi Datong

Caodong School

Gantan Ziguo

Yunmen Wenyan

Tianhuang Daowu

Baofu Congzhan

Yunmen School

Longtan Chongxin

Deshan Xuanjian

Xuefeng Yicun

Xuansha Shibei

Luohan Guichen

Fayan Wenyi

Fayan School

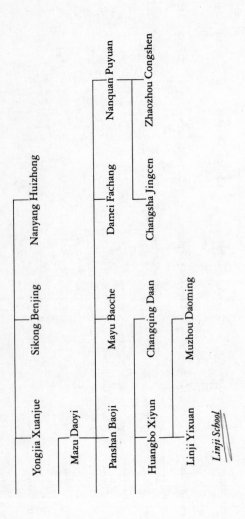

Yongjia Xuanjue

Sikong Benjing

Nanyang Huizhong

Mazu Daoyi

Panshan Baoji

Mayu Baoche

Damei Fachang

Nanquan Puyuan

Huangbo Xiyun

Changqing Daan

Changsha Jingcen

Zhaozhou Congshen

Linji Yixuan

Muzhou Daoming

Linji School

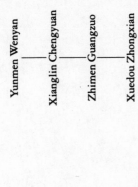

YUNMEN SCHOOL

Yunmen Wenyan
Xianglin Chengyuan
Zhimen Guangzuo
Xuedou Zhongxian

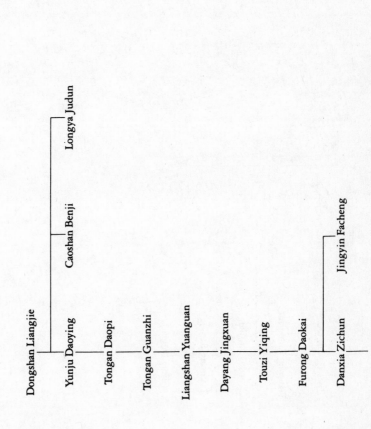

CAODONG SCHOOL

Dongshan Liangjie
Caoshan Benji
Longya Judun
Yunju Daoying
Tongan Daopi
Tongan Guanzhi
Liangshan Yuanguan
Dayang Jingxuan
Touzi Yiqing
Furong Daokai
Danxia Zichun
Jingyin Facheng

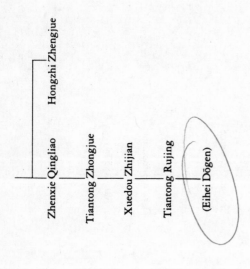

Hongzhi Zhengjue

Zhenxie Qingliao

Tiantong Zhongjue

Xuedou Zhijian

Tiantong Rujing

(Eihei Dōgen)

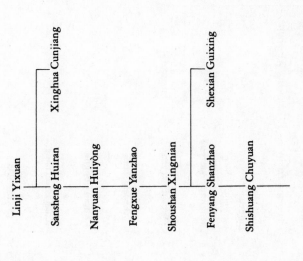

LINJI SCHOOL

Linji Yixuan — Sansheng Huiran
— Xinghua Cunjiang — Nanyuan Huiyong — Fengxue Yanzhao — Shoushan Xingnian — Fenyang Shanzhao — Shexian Guixing
— Shishuang Chuyuan

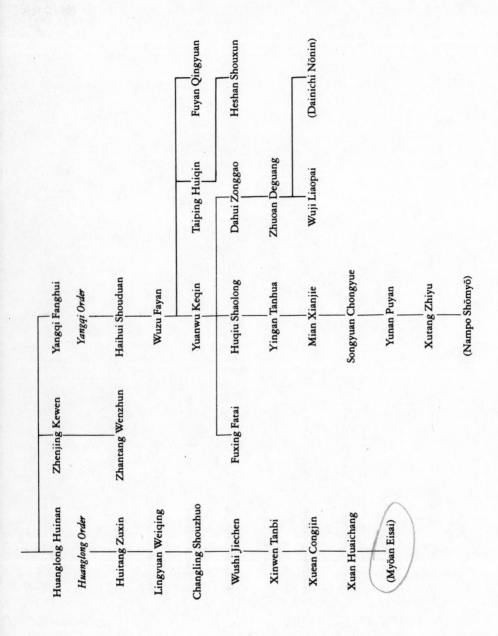

Huanglong Huinan ─┬─ Zhenjing Kewen ─── Yangqi Fanghui

Huanglong Order   *Yangqi Order*

Huitang Zuxin   Zhantang Wenzhun   Haihui Shouduan

Lingyuan Weiqing   Wuzu Fayan

Changling Shouzhuo   Yuanwu Keqin ─┬─ Taiping Huiqin ─┬─ Fuyan Qingyuan
                                                       │   └─ Heshan Shouxun
                                                       └─ Dahui Zonggao

Wushi Jiechen   Fuxing Fatai   Huqiu Shaolong ─── Zhuoan Deguang

Xinwen Tanbi   Yingan Tanhua   Wuji Liaopai ─── (Dainichi Nōnin)

Xuean Congjin   Mian Xianjie

Xuan Huaichang   Songyuan Chongyue

(Myōan Eisai)   Yunan Puyan

                                         Xutang Zhiyu

                                         (Nampo Shōmyō)

Notes

Notes to Introduction
1. "Kenzei's Biography of Dōgen."*
2. TTDE, "Document of Heritage," section 14.
3. TTDE, "Face-to-Face Transmission," section 2.
4. "On the Endeavor of the Way," section 2.
5. TTDE, "Face-to-Face Transmission," section 10.
6. Frontispiece of this book.
7. "Anthology of Enlightenment Poems by the Ancestor of Sanshō."*
8. "Anthology of Enlightenment Poems by the Ancestor of Sanshō."*
9. TTDE, "Undivided Activity," section 5.
10. TTDE, "The Time-Being," section 14.
11. "Anthology of Enlightenment Poems by the Ancestor of Sanshō."*
12. TTDE, "The Time-Being," section 1.
13. TTDE, "The Time-Being," section 4.
14. TTDE, "Undivided Activity," section 4.
15. TTDE, "Actualizing the Fundamental Point," section 12.
16. TTDE, "Actualizing the Fundamental Point," section 11.
17. TTDE, "Mountains and Waters Sūtra," section 22.
18. "Guidelines for Studying the Way," section 9.
19. TTDE, "Undivided Activity," section 1.
20. "Anthology of Enlightenment Poems by the Ancestor of Sanshō."*
21. Yasunari Kawabata, *Japan the Beautiful and Myself.* Translated by Edward G. Seiden-sticker (Tokyo: Kōdansha, 1969).
22. TTDE, "The Point of Zazen."
23. TTDE, "Twining Vines," section 6.
24. TTDE, "Face-to-Face Transmission," section 1.

25. The commentaries mentioned above are included in Nyoten Jimbo and Bun'ei Andō, eds., *Shōbōgenzō Chūkai Zensho* (Collected Commentaries of TTDE).

26. See Appendix, "Reading the *Record of Eihei Dōgen*" by Ryōkan.

27. Tetsurō Watsuji, "Shamon Dōgen" (Monk Dōgen) in *Nihon Seishin-shi Kenkyū* (Studies of Japanese Spiritual History) (Tokyo: Iwanami Shoten, 1926).

28. Hajime Tanabe, *Shōbōgenzō no Tetsugaku Shikan* (Personal Views on the Philosophy of TTDE) (Tokyo: Iwanami Shoten, 1939).

29. Minoru Nishio and Yaoko Mizino, trans., *Shōbōgenzō Bendōwa Hoka* (Shōbōgenzō Bendōwa and Other Writings), vol. 14 of *Koten Nihon Bungaku Zenshū* (Collection of Japanese Classical Literature) (Tokyo: Chikuma Shobō, 1964). Minoru Nishio, Genryū Kagamishima, Tokugen Sakai, and Yaoko Mizuno, commentators, *Shōbōgenzō, Shōbōgenzō Zuimon-ki* (TTDE, TTDE: Record of Things Heard), vol. 81 of *Nihon Koten Bungaku Taikei* (Complete Collection of Japanese Classical Literature) (Tokyo: Iwanami Shoten, 1965). Kōshirō Tamaki, ed., *Dōgen-shū* (Works of Dōgen), vol. 2 of *Nihon no Shisō* (Japanese Thoughts) (Tokyo: Chikuma Shobō, 1969). Tōru Terada and Yaoko Mizuno, commentators, *Dōgen*, vols. 12 and 13 of *Nihon Shisō Taikei* (Complete Collection of Japanese Philosophical Works) (Tokyo: Iwanami Shoten, 1970 and 1972). Kōshirō Tamaki, trans., *Dōgen: Shōbōgenzō*, vol. 7 of *Nihon no Meicho* (Notable Books of Japan) (Tokyo: Chūōkōron-sha, 1971).

30. Sōichi Nakamura, Sōjun Nakamura, and Kazuaki Tanahashi, trans., *Zen'yaku Shōbōgenzō* (Complete Translation of TTDE) (Tokyo: Seishin Shobō, 1968–1972). Kenchin Takahashi, trans., *Gendaiyaku Shōbōgenzō* (Modern Version of TTDE) (Osaka: Risō-sha, 1971 and 1972). Fumio Masutani, trans., *Gendaigoyaku Shōbōgenzō* (Modern Version of TTDE) (Tokyo: Kadokawa Shoten, 1973–1975). Kazuo Nishijima, trans., *Gendaigoyaku Shōbōgenzō* (Modern Version of TTDE) (Tokyo: Bukkyō-sha, 1975).

31. See Bibliography.

32. A revised translation is included in this book under the title "Actualizing the Fundamental Point."

Notes to "Rules for Zazen"

1. 坐禪儀. Presented as a lecture at Yoshimine Temple in the eleventh month of 1343, four months after Dōgen's community had moved to Echizen Province from the suburbs of Kyoto. Eleventh fascicle of the primary (seventy-five-fascicle) version of the *Treasury of the True Dharma Eye*. Like all other fascicles of TTDE, *Zazen-gi* was written in Japanese—a combination of Chinese ideographs pronounced in the Japanese way, and Japanese phonetics.

   Other translations: Bielefeldt, "Fukan Zazen-gi," pp. 233–37. Nishiyama and Stevens, vol. 1, pp. 39–40, "The Rule for Zazen." Waddell and Abe, "Dōgen's Fukanzazengi," pp. 127–28.

2. To abide in the realm of nonduality where settling oneself is not other than settling all things.

3. The practice of zazen itself is the actualization of buddha nature. Hence desiring to become a buddha is a mistake, since practice would then be separate from already being a buddha.

Notes to "Guidelines for Studying the Way"

1. 學道用心集. Written in Chinese as an independent work and taught in the spring of 1224, one year after Dōgen moved into Kannondōri Temple (later Kōshō Hōrin Mon-

astery). As a part of the first publication by Eihei-ji, this text was published in 1357 under the title, "The First Ancestor Eihei's Guidelines for Studying the Way" (Eihei Shoso Gakudō Yōjin-shū).

   Other translations: Kennett, pp. 123–38, "Important Aspects of Zazen." Yokoi, *Zen Master Dōgen*, pp. 48–57, "Points to Watch in Buddhist Training."

2.   Nāgārjuna's *Commentary on the Mahāprajñāpāramitā Sūtra,* chap. 23.

3.   *Analects,** "Lord Weiling."

4.   With the eye of enlightenment, practice is an everyday, ongoing activity which does not appear to have outstanding or extraordinary attributes.

5.   One should become free from the idea that the state of enlightenment is separate or apart from practice.

6.   Understanding that enlightenment is a distant goal apart from or different from one's own experience.

7.   *Shūrangama Sūtra,** chap. 6.

8.   清 明 日. Fifteenth day from the spring equinox: one of the seasonal festivals in East Asia.

9.   When Huineng, the Sixth Ancestor, saw the Fifth Ancestor at Mt. Huangmei for the first time, he "lost his face," that is, shed his worldly identity.

10.   See Glossary, *nonthinking.*

Notes to "Bodhisattva's Four Methods of Guidance"

1.   菩 提 薩 埵 四 攝 法. Written in the fifth month of 1243, probably at Kōshō Hōrin Monastery, shortly before Dōgen moved to Echizen Province. He did not include this fascicle, which was likely written for his lay students, in the primary version of TTDE probably because the primary version was compiled for trained monks. Included in the sixty-fascicle version of TTDE by Giun.

   Other translation: Nishiyama and Stevens, vol. 3, pp. 124–28.

2.   *Mahāprajñāpāramitā Sūtra,** chap. 469.

3.   *Ekottarāgama Sūtra,** chap. 24.

4.   According to the *Classified Materia Medica,** Emperor Taizong 太 宗 of the Tang Dynasty cut off his mustache, burned it, and gave it to his retainer Liji 李 勣, a cure prescribed by Liji's physician. "To cure disease" can also be translated as "to harmonize mind."

5.   See Glossary, *offering sand.*

6.   According to the *History of Jin,** Kongyu 孔 愉 pitied a caged tortoise and bought and freed it. Later he was appointed lord, and when he had his official seal cast the shape of a tortoise came out. He then knew he had attained his position through the help of the tortoise.

7.   According to *Requested by Children,** Yangbao 楊 寶 of the Later Han Dynasty tended an injured sparrow. Later the sparrow appeared in his dream and said he was a messenger of Grandmother Xi 西 王 母, a sorcerer, and left four white rings. Then Yangbao's family flourished for four generations.

8.   Minister Zhou's 周 公 anecdote described in the *Historical Records.**

9.   This is based on a poem by Bo Yuetian 白 樂 天, called "Poem of Three Comrades at Northern Window:"

> Who are the three comrades?
> Lute stopped playing.
> Wine is raised up.

> When wine is finished a song is sung.
> The three comrades lead one another
> going round and round endlessly.

10. *Guanzi,* * chap. 20.

Notes to "Regulations for the Auxiliary Cloud Hall"

1. 重雲堂式. Completed in the fourth year of 1239 when the annex monks' hall (*jūundō*) was built at Kōshō Hōrin Monastery. Written in Japanese, while all other monastic regulations were to be written in Chinese. Dōgen did not regard this text as a portion of TTDE, but one of his dharma descendants, Kōzen, included it in the ninety-five-fascicle version of TTDE in 1690.

2. Guest or host: disciple or master; in this case regular student or director of the hall.

3. The formal way of walking in the practice hall is to hold the hands in *shashu* position. Originally *shashu* meant to cover the right fist with the left hand over the chest. In the Sōtō School it is now common to cover the left fist with the right hand.

Notes to "Instruction for the Tenzo"

1. 典座教訓. Written in Chinese as an independent work at Kōshō Hōrin Monastery in the spring of 1237, two years after the official completion of the monastery. Published in 1667 by Eihei-ji as a part of the *Monastic Regulations of Zen Master Dōgen, the First Ancestor of the Sōtō School, Japan.* *

    Other translations: Kennett, pp. 175–90, "Instruction to the Chief Cook." Yokoi, *Regulations,* pp. 8–26. Dōgen and Uchiyama, pp. 3–19, "Instructions for the Zen Cook."

2. ALZSME, chap. 21. *Hongzhi's Capping Verses,* * case 91.

3. When Yangshan was plowing a rice field with Guishan, Yangshan said, "One side is low and one side is high." Guishan said, "Water will even it out." Yangshan replied, "We don't need to depend on water. The high place is already even and high; the low place is already even and low." Guishan approved him. JRTL, chap. 11.

4. Because Dōgen is addressing a tenzo, he mentions a vegetable leaf instead of using a familiar expression in Zen: "a blade of grass." See Glossary, *blade of grass.*

5. See Glossary, *Guishan's water buffalo.*

6. *Anthology on Ancestral Eminence,* * chap. 2.

7. The reality of all things is manifested in verbal expressions that are represented by one, two, three, four, five; and six, seven, eight, nine, ten.

8. According to Indian legend, Shākyamuni Buddha deliberately shortened his one-hundred-year lifespan, entering parinirvāna at the age of eighty and offering the unused twenty years for the benefit of future students of dharma.

9. Nāgārjuna's *Commentary on the Mahāprajñāpāramitā Sūtra,* * chap. 8.

10. *Anthology on Ancestral Eminence.* *

11. See Glossary, *Baizhang's ember.*

12. See Glossary, *senior Fu's realization.*

13. See Glossary, *Guishan blowing the unlit firewood.*

Notes to "Actualizing the Fundamental Point"

1. Written and given to a lay student, Koshū Yō, in the eighth month of 1233, a few months after Dōgen started writing TDE beginning with the fascicle "Perfection of

Great Wisdom" (*Maka Hannya Haramitsu*). In 1252, one year before his death, Dōgen wrote the colophon of *Genjō Kōan*, probably after some revision. Dōgen used this text as the opening fascicle of the primary version of TTDE.

Bokuzan Nishiari, a famous Sōtō priest and sectarian scholar, referred to this essay in his lecture given in 1922:

This fascicle is the skin, flesh, bones, and marrow of the Founder. The fundamental teaching of the Founder's lifetime is expounded in this fascicle. The buddha-dharma throughout his lifetime is revealed in this work. The ninety-five fascicles of the *Treasury of the True Dharma Eye* are the offshoots of this fascicle. (*Shōbōgenzō Keiteki*).

Other translations: Jaffe, "Commentary" pp. 14–22. Kennett, pp. 171–75, "The Problem of Everyday Life." Maezumi and Cook, "The Realization of the Kōan," p. 326. Masunaga, *Primer*, pp. 125–32. Nishiyama and Stevens, *Dōgen*, vol. 1, pp. 1–4. Tanahashi and Aitken, "Realization of Truth." Waddell and Abe, "Shōbōgenzō Genjōkōan."

2. As all things are inseparable from the Buddha's teaching, . . .

3. See Glossary, *no-self*.

4. When one practices to attain enlightenment it goes further and further out of reach, because practice and enlightenment are not separate. When one tries to attain enlightenment by excluding delusion one enters even further into separation, which is another form of delusion.

5. Same as realizing beyond realization. In this line the nonseparateness of awakening and delusion is indicated.

6. In direct realization subject and object include each other. In "darkness" everything is included and there is no sense of boundaries.

7. This metaphor comes from Nāgārjuna's "Verses on the Foundation of the Middle Way."

8. See Glossary, *phenomenal expression*.

9. Moon here is enlightenment, and water is the person.

10. Cf. "On the Endeavor of the Way," section 6:

The zazen of even one person at one moment imperceptively accords with all things and fully resonates through all time. Thus in the past, future, and present of the limitless universe this zazen carries on the buddha's teaching endlessly.

11. See Glossary, *four views on water*.

12. Dusty world and world beyond conditions refer to the realm of bondage and the realm of freedom.

13. Fish and bird refer to those who practice. Water and sky refer to the realm of practice.

14. Practice is not separate from enlightenment.

15. The person is not separate from enlightenment.

16. By enlightenment one is confirmed in one's original self.

17 . Cf. "On the Endeavor of the Way," section 6:

All this, however, does not appear within perception, because it is unconstructedness in stillness—it is immediate realization. If practice and realization were two things, as it appears in an ordinary person's view, each could be recognized separately. But what can be met with recognition is not realization itself, because realization is not reached by a deluded mind.

18. Wind refers to buddha nature; fanning refers to practice in pursuit of the way of en-

lightenment. The question is: If the buddha nature, which is unchanging, is inherent in every human being, why does one need to practice to become a buddha?

19. You know that the buddha nature is universal, but you do not know how it is realized.

20. FLMS, chap. 4.

Notes to "Birth and Death"

1. Undated. Not included in the primary or later version of TTDE by Dōgen. Kept in the treasurehouse of Eihei-ji as a part of the twenty-eight-fascicle version known as the "Secret TTDE." Included in Kōzen's ninety-five-fascicle version in 1690.

   Other translations: Kennett, pp. 163–64, "Life and Death." Masunaga, pp. 97–99. Nishiyama and Stevens, vol. 1, pp. 21–22, "Life and Death." Waddell and Abe, "Birth and Death."

2. JRTL, chap. 7.

3. JRTL, chap. 7.

Notes to "The Time-Being"

1. 有時. A compound of *u* (meaning some, being, having, existence) and *ji* (time). A common expression *uji* means "sometime," "at one time," or "for the time being," but Dōgen interprets it literally as "the time-being," indicating that time and existence are inseparable.

   Written on the first day of early winter (the tenth month), 1240, at Kōshō Hōrin Monastery. Twentieth fascicle of the primary version of TTDE.

   Other translations: Kapleau, pp. 295–99, "Being-Time." Kennett, pp. 164–71, "The Theory of Time." Masunaga, pp. 81–90. Nishiyama and Stevens, vol. 1, pp. 68–72, "Being-time." Waddell, "Being Time," pp. 116–29.

2. No exact source has been found, but it seems to be based on the words of Yaoshan Weiyan:

   If you want to know human endeavors, then purify this noble form, hold a jar, and carry a monk's bowl. If you try to escape from falling into the lower realms, first of all you should not give up these practices. It is not easy. You should stand on top of the highest peak and go to the bottom of the deepest ocean. This is not an easy practice, but you will have some realization. (JRTL, chap. 28)

3. Dōgen's summary of ordinary people's view of past and present.

4. When one experiences time without separation of past and present, the entire past is experienced at present.

5. Pine tree and bamboo both traditionally represent long life or a long span of time.

6. From the viewpoint that time flies away, past and future would have to be removed from the present.

7. Complete experience cannot be characterized as existing or nonexisting because these designations require an outside viewpoint.

8. The time-being is not limited to the concepts of existence or nonexistence.

9. The "him" in this reply refers to Shākyamuni Buddha and his transmission of the teaching by holding up a flower and winking. See also Glossary, *treasury of the true dharma eye*.

10. ALZSME, chap. 19.

11. Mountains and oceans are the buddha's body. Cf. "Mountains and Waters Sūtra," sec-

tion 1: "Mountains and waters right now are the actualization of the ancient buddha way."

12. ALZSME, chap. 12.

13. This refers to the following story, JRTL, chap. 11: A monk said, "What is the meaning of buddha-dharma?" The master (Lingyun Zhiqin) said, "While the donkey has not yet left, the horse has arrived."

"Horse and donkey" is a Zen expression meaning "this and that" or "one thing and another." Dōgen uses it in this case to mean something which has not left (donkey) and something which has not arrived (horse).

14. Experiences which are usually viewed as partial, incomplete, or falling short are nevertheless the time-being. Although they are not recognized as such, they are "fully" or "completely" what they are.

Notes to "Undivided Activity"

1. Presented as a lecture at the house of Yoshishige Hatano in the city of Kyoto in the twelfth month of 1242, while Dōgen was still residing at Kōshō Hōrin Monastery. Twenty-second fascicle of the primary version of TTDE.

Other translations: Nishiyama and Stevens, vol. 1, pp. 81–82, "The total activity of life and death." Waddell and Abe, "Total Dynamic Working," pp. 74–77.

2. As a complete, independent experience, without any reference to other moments, birth cannot be conceptualized dualistically.

3. In the midst of undivided activity or total experience, one cannot analytically view the experience from outside, judging with dualistic standards.

4. Birth is not viewed as permanent or impermanent.

5. Here, Dōgen challenges a conventional view that a person *was* born, and that the person *is* apart from his birth.

6. *Recorded Sayings of Zen Master Fuguo Yuanwu,** chap. 17.

7. Here, Dōgen presents the understanding that a person's birth at one moment is boundless and all-inclusive, yet this does not exclude others' births (which are likewise all-inclusive) at the same moment, or the person's birth at other moments, and similarly that the all-inclusive experience in birth does not obstruct the all-inclusive experience in death.

8. The "world," in which the boundless and all-inclusive experience takes place, is beyond the categories of dualistic standards.

9. An immediate, vivid activity.

10. An activity beyond conscious decision or control.

11. Realization cannot be grasped as something fixed or unchanging, and is not limited to the moment in which it is presently recognized.

Notes to "Body-and-Mind Study of the Way"

1. 身心學道. Presented as a lecture at Kōshō Hōrin Monastery, in the ninth month of 1242. Fourth fascicle of the primary version of TTDE.

Other translation: Nishiyama and Stevens, vol. 1, pp. 9–16, "Learning through the body and mind."

2. See Glossary, *What is it that thus comes?*

3. Dōgen here admonishes students to practice with many "wide-open eyeballs," and to investigate ordinary consciousness over and over again.

4.   Cf. FLMS, chap. 5: " 'What is the phrase that is truth-like?' The master (Jiashan Shanhui) said, 'The lotus leaf is perfectly round, . . .' "

5.   JRTL, chap. 28.

6.   *Tiansheng Extensive Record of Lamps,** chap. 9.

7.   *Recorded Sayings of Zen Master Yuanwu,** chap. 17.

Notes to "Mountains and Waters Sūtra"

1.   山 水 經. Mountains and waters are viewed as a sūtra, or actual expression of the Buddha's enlightenment. Presented as a lecture at Kōshō Hōrin Monastery, in the tenth month of 1240. Twenty-ninth fascicle of the primary version of TTDE. The original manuscript by Dōgen has been kept at Zenkyū-in, Toyohashi City, Aichi Prefecture.

     Other translations: Bielefeldt, "Shōbōgenzō-sansuikyō," pp. 19–34. Nishiyama and Stevens, vol. 2, pp. 163–70, "The Mountain and River Sūtra."

2.   "Riding the clouds" and "following the wind" represent the state of freedom in meditation.

3.   *Jiatai Record of the Universal Lamps,** chap. 3.

4.   In the realm of nonduality, mountains and human beings are not separate.

5.   In the realm of wholeness, one's experience goes beyond the limited span of time.

6.   Here again experience in meditation of the wholeness of mountains and human beings is indicated.

7.   From a nondualistic viewpoint, mountains have inconceivable function beyond stillness and motion.

8.   Form: *gyōmyō* 形 名, literally, forms and names.

9.   Because of the enlightenment that is manifested in mountains, buddha ancestors appear.

10. This expression usually means to be free from the bondage of object and mind, bur in this case the duality of object and mind where one is not completely free is suggested.

11. This means explaining mind and true nature separately. In other cases Dōgen uses this phrase in the sense that explaining mind is itself an expression of buddha nature.

12. The ultimate understanding of a buddha mind (*kenshin* 見 心) and that of buddha nature (*kenshō* 見 性). But in this case Dōgen criticizes viewing a buddha mind or buddha nature as fixed or substantial.

13. In China there are legends in which men became stones and stones became women (*Record of Extraordinary Stories*).*

14. The teacher and disciple are one upon transmitting dharma.

15. *Extensive Record of Yunmen, Zen Master Kuangzhen,** chap. 1.

16. See Glossary, *four views on water.*

17. *Great Treasure-Heap Sūtra,** chap. 87.

18. *True Scripture for Penetrating the Subtle.**

19. *Suvarna Prabhāsottama Sūtra,** chap. 1.

20. In the inner chamber of buddha ancestors there is no self and others.

21. "Song of the Realization of the Way" by Yongjia Xuanjue.

22. *Zhuangzi* (Chuangtzu), chap. 4.

23. See Glossary, *Chuanzi Decheng.*

Notes to "Spring and Autumn"

1.   春 秋. Presented as lectures in Echizen Province in 1244 while Daibutsu Monastery was under construction. Thirty-seventh fascicle of the primary version of TTDE.

Other translations: Cook, pp. 151–57, "Spring and Fall." Nishiyama and Stevens, vol. 2, pp. 33–36, "Spring and fall."

2. *Extensive Record of Zen Master Hongzhi,** chap. 4.

3. Making no difference.

4. *Jiatai Record of the Universal Lamps,** chap. 26.

5. *Go* is the Japanese name for the originally Chinese game *qi*, played by two people with black and white pebble-like markers on a square wooden board divided into 361 squares.

6. To swallow you up: to blind and defeat "you"; or to take away the separation between "you" and "me."

7. *Extensive Record of Zen Master Hongzhi,** chap. 4.

8. In *go* to have nine extra stones to play with is the maximum handicap. Dōgen indicates the separation between the two players by this device.

9. Indicates nonduality of the two players.

10. This phrase is based on a line of *Chu Anthology**:
    > If this vast water is clear I will wash the tassel on my hat.
    > And if it is muddy I will wash my feet.

11. *Recorded Sayings of Zen Master Yuanwu,** chap. 19.

12. *Blue Cliff Record,** case 43, capping verse.

13. *Recorded Sayings of Priest Changling.**

14. Looking for the sword indicates the futility of seeking the place of no heat or cold somewhere outside of oneself.

15. *Threaded-Pearl Capping Verses of the Zen School,** chap. 24.

16. See Glossary, *expression complete this moment*.

17. *Threaded-Pearl Capping Verses of the Zen School,** chap. 24.

18. *Threaded-Pearl Capping Verses of the Zen School,** chap. 24.

19. Dōgen's respectful way of indicating Dongshan's teaching which expresses the single dharma. There is no such sūtra in the canon.

20. Qingyuan Xingsi's word, JRTL, chap. 5.

Notes to "Plum Blossoms"

1. 梅華. Written in the eleventh month of 1243 soon after Dōgen had moved to Echizen Province. This essay is largely commentaries of poems from the *Recorded Sayings of Priest Rujing,** of which Dōgen received a copy from China in the previous year. Fifty-third fascicle of the primary version of TTDE.

    Other translations: Nishiyama and Stevens, vol. 2, pp. 145–51, "Plum blossoms."

2. Eleventh month of the lunar calendar.

3. RSPR, chap. 2.

4. See Glossary, *five petals*.

5. RSPR, chap. 1.

6. See Glossary, *five petals*.

7. RSPR, chap. 1.

8. RSPR, chap. 1.

9. RSPR, chap. 1.

10. Literally, "a brocade of Shu 蜀 and jewel of Benhe 卞和." The brocade from Western China, Shu, represents high quality. Benhe was a man of the Zhou Dynasty who discovered a precious uncut jewel in a mountain. He presented it to a king whose jeweler did not believe it was genuine, and the king had Benhe's left leg cut off. He presented

it to another king who for the same reason had Benhe's right leg cut off. Later he presented it to King Weu who had it polished and found it to be the true jewel. After centuries a king offered to trade fifteen castles for it.

11. Dōgen reversed Bodhidharma's words to Huike, "You have attained my marrow," in order to cut through fixed views.

12. RSPR, chap. 2.

13. RSPR, chap. 2.

14. RSPR, chap. 2.

15. *Jianzhong Jingguo Later Record of Lamps*,* chap. 30.

16. FLMS, chap. 7.

Notes to "Everyday Activity"

1. Presented as a lecture in the twelfth month of 1243 at a hut near Yamashi Peak, Echizen Province. Fifty-ninth fascicle of the primary version of TTDE.

    Other translations: Cook, pp. 205–10, "Everyday Life." Nishiyama and Stevens, vol. 1, pp. 107–10, "The everyday life of the Buddhas and Patriarchs."

2. ALZSME, chap. 28.

3. A portion of "Song of the Grass Hut" by Shitou.

4. FLMS, chap. 3; *Blue Cliff Record*,* case 26.

5. Rujing was the abbot of Jingci Monastery, then became the abbot of Jingde Monastery, Mt. Tiantong.

6. RSPR, chap. 2.

7. RSPR, chap. 1.

8. RSPR, chap. 1.

9. RSPR, chap. 1.

10. JRTL, chap. 9.

11. ALZSME, chap. 6.

12. RSPR, chap. 2.

Notes to "The Moon"

1. 都 機. Instead of using the usual character for "moon," 月 (*tsuki*), Dōgen uses the characters: *tsu*, meaning entire or total; and *ki*, meaning possibility, capacity, function, or working. This has a similar meaning to "undivided activity" (*zenki*).

    Written in the first month of 1243 at Kōshō Hōrin Monastery, immediately after "Undivided Activity" was delivered as a lecture. Twenty-third fascicle of the primary version of TTDE.

    Other translation: Nishiyama and Stevens, vol. 1, pp. 83–85, "Complete fulfillment."

2. From the *Suvarna Prabhāsottama Sūtra*,* chap. 24. The original phrases are usually read, "Buddha's true dharma body *is like empty sky* [猶 若 虛 空 (*yūnyaku kokū*)]. Responding to things forms appear. *It is like the moon in water* [如 水 中 月 (*nyo suichū getsu*)]." But Dōgen interprets the Chinese text in the way it is translated here.

3. JRTL, chap. 7.

4. Since the moonlight is not separate from the illuminated objects, there are no objects outside of the moonlight.

5. Other names for moon and sun.

6. Describing sun and moon.

7. From *Blue Cliff Record*,* case 79. Using the image of the moon, buddha nature in its

fullness is discussed. "Three or four" or "seven or eight" mean buddha nature is beyond measure, not increasing or decreasing.

8. From *Sūtra of Complete Enlightenment*,* "Vajragarbha Bodhisattva." Clouds here represent the one who practices. The moon represents enlightenment. The boat and shore are other images for the same things.

9. This indicates activity within the realm of nonduality, beyond stillness and motion.

10. Direct and complete experience at the present moment.

11. The original character for moon also means month. Hence, this line can also be read as "even if time's passing month by month is swift, it is beyond the beginning, middle, or end of every month." Dōgen indicates here the timelessness of the present moment.

12. Each phase of the moon is the entire moon.

Notes to "Painting of a Rice-cake"

1. Presented as a lecture at Kōshō Hōrin Monastery in the eleventh month of 1243. Twenty-fourth fascicle of the primary version of TTDE.

    Other translation: Nishiyama and Stevens, vol. 1, pp. 86–90, "A painting of a rice cake."

2. In order to emphasize the buddhas' direct embodiment of enlightenment, Dōgen says all buddhas *are* realization, instead of *have* realization.

3. In the realm of nonduality there is no differentiation between all buddhas and all things.

4. Since the actualization of enlightenment of all buddhas is all-inclusive, there cannot be separate actualizations which amass together.

5. Xiangyan Zhixian's words. JRTL, chap. 11.

6. Painted rice-cakes, which are usually understood as letters and words useless for realization, are not different from mountains and waters, which are regarded as actual expressions of the buddha's enlightenment as explained in "Mountains and Waters Sūtra."

7. The enlightenment of various buddhas cannot be separated from verbal expressions of enlightenment.

8. *Extensive Record of Yunmen, Zen Master Kuangzhen,* chap. 3. Also, *Blue Cliff Record,* case 77.

9. RSPR, chap. 1.

Notes to "On the Endeavor of the Way"

1. 辨道話. Dōgen's earliest known writing in Japanese. Completed as an independent essay on the day of the harvest moon (fifteenth day of the eighth month), 1231, three years after Dōgen came back from China and two years before he founded his first practice center, Kōshō Hōrin Monastery. According to Menzan's "Eliminating Wrong Views on the Treasury of the True Dharma Eye" (Shōbōgenzō Byakujakuketsu, 1738), the text had been handed down in a courtier's house in Kyoto. Included in Kōzen's ninety-five-fascicle version of TTDE as its opening fascicle.

    Other translations: Kennett, pp. 138–54, "Lecture on Training." Masunaga, pp. 133–61. Nishiyama and Stevens, vol. 1, pp. 147–61, "A story of Buddhist practice." Waddell and Abe, "Dōgen's Bendōwa."

2. All buddhas continuously realize dharma and are not attached to intellectual recognition of their realization. Sentient beings are not apart from dharma, but this realization does not appear in their knowledge.

3. According to the *Lotus Sūtra*,* "Skillful Means": At the Dharma Blossom Assembly on

Vulture Peak, five thousand arrogant people left, saying that they did not need to hear more of such teaching that was different from the teaching in the past. Shākyamuni Buddha did not stop them and said, "You may leave if you wish."

4. *Regulations for Zen Monasteries,* * chap. 8.

5. Sikong Benjing's words, JRTL, chap. 5.

6. JRTL, chap. 17. Also, TTDE, "Mind Itself Is Buddha" (Sokushin Zebutsu).

7. *Extensive Record of Zen Master Hongzhi,* * chap. 1.

8. According to the *Storehouse of Various Treasures Sūtra,* * chap. 9: An old monk, hearing some young monks talk about the four fruits of the way, asked them to give him the fruits. The young monks hit him on the back with a ball, saying, "This is the first fruit." At that moment the old monk attained the first fruit of the way, the stage of stream-enterer. By being hit four times, he attained all the four fruits of the way.

9. According to Nāgārjuna's *Commentary on the Mahāprajñāpāramitā Sutra,* * chap. 13, nun Utpala wore a nun's robe for fun in one of her former births. Because of that she became a nun in a subsequent birth at the time of Kāshyapa Buddha.

10. According to the *Storehouse of Various Treasures Sūtra,* * chap. 9: A lay woman offered a meal to an old and ignorant monk. Afterward, she asked him for a dharma talk, sitting upright with her eyes closed. Unable to explain dharma, the old monk ran away. While waiting, the woman attained the first fruit of the way. Later, when the woman thanked him, the monk felt ashamed. Thus, he also attained the first fruit of the way.

Notes to "Only Buddha and Buddha"

1. 唯佛與佛. Undated. Not included in the primary or additional version of TTDE by Dōgen. Together with "Birth and Death," this fascicle was included in an Eihei-ji manuscript called the "Secret Treasury of the True Dharma Eye." Kōzen included it in the ninety-five-fascicle version.

    Other translation: Nishiyama and Stevens, vol. 3, pp. 129–35.

2. Cf. *Lotus Sūtra,* * "Skillful Means": "Only a buddha and a buddha can thoroughly master the true suchness of all things."

3. Seeing is not self and not a creation of the self.

4. Zhenzhou Baoshou's words. JRTL, chap. 12.

5. Xingjiao Xiaoshou's words. *Record of the Forests,* * chap. 1.

Notes to "Twining Vines"

1. Presented as a lecture at Kōshō Hōrin Monastery on the seventh day, seventh month, first year of Kangen (1243), nine days before Dōgen left for Echizen Province. Thirty-eighth fascicle of the primary version of TTDE.

    Other translation: Nishiyama and Stevens, vol. 2, pp. 37–42, "Spiritual entanglement."

2. RSPR, chap. 2.

3. Akshobhya is regarded as the buddha of the Eastern Land. In the *Mahāprajñāpāramitā Sūtra,* * chap. 9, Shākyamuni Buddha showed this land to his disciples once but never again. Thus, nun Zongchi's answer to Bodhidharma expresses her understanding of nonattachment in the study of the way.

4. JRTL, chap. 3.

5. Branches, leaves, flowers, and fruit represent the various manifestations of enlightened activity of teachers and disciples, which is independent as well as universal.

6. *Recorded Sayings of Zen Master Zhenji of Zhaozhou,* * chap. 1.
7. Marrow is the entire experience of buddha-dharma. When it appears, differentiation
    is not apparent. Skin is also the entire experience of buddha-dharma, and in this way
    marrow and skin are not separable.
8. This appears to be an ordinary question, but Dōgen regards it as the expression of the
    truth itself. "How about that?" speaks to the unlimited, unnameable truth.
9. Cf. JRTL, chap. 3, in the note after describing Bodhidharma's death:
    When Songyun was on a mission in the Western District [Central Asia], in the Zheng-
    guang Era [519–525] during the reign of Emperor Xiaoming of Wei, he saw Bodhid-
    harma in the Onion Range [the Belaturgh Mountains in Turkistan].
    The book also quotes a story that another envoy saw Bodhidharma walking along toward
    India alone with one shoe in his hand.

Notes to "Face-to-Face Transmission"

1. Presented as a lecture at Yoshimine Temple, Echizen Province, in the tenth month of
    1243. Fifty-first fascicle of the primary version of TTDE.
        Other translation: Nishiyama and Stevens, vol. 2, pp. 137–44, "Direct, face-to-face
    transmission."
2. *Jianzhong Jingguo Later Record of Lamps,* * chap. 2.

Note to "Buddha Ancestors"

1. Presented as a lecture at Kōshō Hōrin Monastery in the first month of 1241. Fifty-
    second fascicle of the primary version of TTDE.
        Other translation: Nishiyama and Stevens, vol. 1, pp. 100–102, "Buddhas and
    Patriarchs."

Notes to "Document of Heritage"

1. Written at Kōshō Hōrin Monastery in the third month of 1241. Thirty-ninth fascicle
    of the primary version of TTDE. Dōgen rewrote this fascicle at least twice. An original
    manuscript by Dōgen known as the "Satomi Family manuscript" exists in a complete
    form. Fragments of another manuscript are owned by six temples and one private
    family.
        Other translation: Nishiyama and Stevens, vol. 2, pp. 178–86, "The seal of trans-
    mission."
2. Shākyamuni Buddha's enlightenment is outside of time.

Notes to "All-Inclusive Study"

1. Presented as a lecture at a hut near Yamashi Peak, Echizen Province, in the eleventh
    month of 1243. Fifty-seventh fascicle of the primary version of TTDE.
        Other translation: Nishiyama and Stevens, vol. 2, pp. 94–98, "Direct study under
    a master."
2. JRTL, chap. 18.
3. JRTL, chap. 5.
4. In the East Asian way of counting, a partial year is counted as a full year. In this case
    the end of the first eight years and the beginning of the second eight years overlap and
    are counted as one year together; hence $7 + 1 + 7 = 15$.

5. Because Bodhidharma did not stay in the realm of duality such as east or west, coming and going, he was a great teacher in China.

6. To see the equality in diverse forms.

7. ALZSME, chap. 23.

8. RSPR, chap. 1.

9. As the buddha way has no gate it includes all things.

Notes to "Going beyond Buddha"

1. Presented as a lecture at Kōshō Hōrin Monastery in the third month of 1342. Twenty-sixth fascicle of the primary version of TTDE.

   Other translation: Nishiyama and Stevens, vol. 2, pp. 1–7, "Continuous development beyond Buddha."

2. Mastery of the buddha way through zazen.

3. JRTL, chap. 15.

4. It is not concerned with the notion of a process or goal.

5. In this dialogue when Dongshan says, "When I talk you don't hear it," it appears to mean that the monk does not understand. However, Dōgen interprets the words "not hearing" as the direct experience of realization-through-the-body.

6. JRTL, chap. 15.

7. *Jiatai Record of the Universal Lamps*,* chap. 5.

8. Cf. FLMS, chap. 14: Xuedou said, "If someone has no eyeballs, how can the eyeballs be turned into tallow beads?"

9. Cf. *Blue Cliff Record*,* case 96: Zhaozhou said, "A metal buddha cannot go through the forge. A clay buddha cannot go through the water. A wooden buddha cannot go through the fire."

10. JRTL, chap. 17.

11. JRTL, chap. 17.

12. JRTL, chap. 7.

13. *Yuanwu's Record of Striking the Node*,* chap. 2, case 47.

14. JRTL, chap. 14.

15. JRTL, chap. 9.

16. "Niutou" literally means Ox Head. Dōgen indicates that Niutou looks like an ox or Zen master but is not a real thing.

Notes to Poems

1. A selection of Japanese thirty-one-syllable poems from the "Anthology of Dōgen Zen-ji's Waka" (Dōgen Zenji Waka-shū), vol. 2, pp. 411–16 of *Dōgen Zenji Zenshū*—a modern edition by Dōshu Ōkubo which is based on the *Anthology of Enlightenment Poems by the Ancestor of Sanshō.*

2. These are poems written in Chinese but usually read with the addition of Japanese grammatical aids and with Japanese pronunciation. All except the two poems indicated by the following notes have been taken from the *Extensive Record of Priest Eihei Dōgen*,* chap. 10.

3. Taken from TTDE, "The Point of Zazen" (Zazenshin).

4. The earliest source of this poem is the "Recorded Acts of the Three Ancestors of Eihei Monastery" (Eihei-ji Sanso Gyōgō-ki) by an unknown author before Ōei Era (1394–1428).

Selected Bibliography

Abe, Masao. "Dōgen on Buddha Nature." *The Eastern Buddhist* 4, no. 1 (1971): 28–71.

Bielefeldt, Carl. "The Fukan Zazen-gi and the Meditation Teachings of the Japanese Zen Master Dōgen." Ph.D. diss. University of California, Berkeley, 1980.

———. "Shōbōgenzō-sansuikyō." Master's thesis, University of California, Berkeley, 1972.

Cleary, Thomas, trans. *Record of Things Heard: From the Treasury of the Eye of the True Teaching. Shōbōgenzō-zuimonki, talks of Zen Master Dōgen, as recorded by Zen Master Ejō.* Boulder, Colo.: Prajñā Press, 1980.

———, ed. and trans. *Timeless Spring: A Sōtō Zen Anthology.* New York and Tokyo: Weatherhill, 1980.

Cook, Francis Dojun. *How to Raise an Ox: Zen Practice as Thought in Zen Master Dōgen's Shōbōgenzō, Including Ten Newly Translated Essays.* Los Angeles: Center Publications, 1978.

Deshimaru, Taisen. *Maître Dōgen: "Shōbōgenzō," Le Trésor de la Vraie Loi.* Paris: Le Courrier du Livre, 1970.

Dōgen, Zen Master, and Uchiyama Kōshō. *Refining Your Life: From Zen Kitchen to Enlightenment.* Translated by Thomas Wright. New York and Tokyo: Weatherhill, 1983.

Domoulin, Heinrich, S.J. *A History of Zen Buddhism.* Translated by Paul Peachey. Boston: Beacon Press, 1969.

Ekstein, Manfred, trans. *Dōgen Zenji's Shōbōgenzō: Die Schatzkammer der Erkenntnis des Wahren Dharma, Ursprungs-Texte des Zen.* Vol. 1. Zurich: Theseus-Verlag, 1975.

Iwamoto, Hidemasa, trans. *Syōbōgenzō-Zuimonki: Wortgetreue Niederschrift der Lehrreichen Worte Dōgen-Zenziz über der Wahren Buddhismus.* Tokyo: Sankibō, 1943.

Jaffe, Paul David. "The Shōbōgenzō Genjōkōan by Eihei Dōgen, and Penetrating Inquiries into the Shōbōgenzō Genjōkōan: A Commentary by Yasutani Hakuun." Master's thesis, University of California, Santa Barbara, 1979.

Kapleau, Philip, ed. *The Three Pillars of Zen: Teaching, Practice, and Enlightenment.* Boston: Beacon Press, 1967.

Kasulis, T. D. *Zen Action/Zen Person.* Honolulu: University Press of Hawaii, 1981.

Katagiri-roshi, Dainin. "Commentary on the Bodhisattva's Four Methods of Guidance (Bodaisatta Shishōhō) from Shōbōgenzō, by Dōgen-Zenji."*Udumbara* 1, no. 3 (1981): 3–29; 2, no. 4 (1982): 8–34.

Kennett, Roshi Jiyu. *Zen Is Eternal Life*. Emeryville, Calif.: Dharma Publishing, 1976.

Kim, Hee-jin. *Dōgen Kigen: Mystical Realist*. Tucson: University of Arizona Press, 1975.

Kodera, Takashi James. *Dōgen's Formative Years in China: An Historical Study and Annotated Translations of the Hōkyō-ki*. Boulder, Colo.: Prajñā Press, 1980.

Kotani, Shoyu, trans. *Rev. Koun Ejō's Shōbōgenzō Zuimonki: An Introduction to Sōtō Zen Buddhism*. Kurayoshi, Japan: Published by the translator, 1965.

LaFleur, William R., ed. *Dōgen Studies*. Honolulu: University of Hawaii Press, 1985.

Maezumi, Taizan Roshi, and Francis Dojun Cook, revisers. "Shōbōgenzō Genjō Kōan." Los Angeles: Zen Center of Los Angeles, 1977.

Masunaga, Reihō, trans. *A Primer of Sōtō Zen: A Translation of Dōgen's Shōbōgenzō Zuimonki*. Honolulu: East-West Center Press, 1971.

––––––. *The Sōtō Approach to Zen*. Tokyo: Layman Buddhist Society Press, 1958.

Matsunaga, Daigen and Alicia Matsunaga. *Foundation of Japanese Buddhism*. 2 vols. Los Angeles and Tokyo: Buddhist Books International, 1974–1976.

Nishiyama, Kōsen, and John Stevens. *Dōgen Zenji's Shōbōgenzō (The Eye and Treasury of the True Law)*. 4 vols. Sendai, Japan: Daihokkaikaku, 1975–1983.

Tanahashi, Kazuaki, and Robert Aitken, trans. "Genjō Kōan, Realization of Truth: A portion of the Shōbōgenzō, by Dōgen Zenji." *Diamond Sanga* 5, no. 3 (1965): 1–4.

Waddell, Norman, trans. "Being Time: Dōgen's Shōbōgenzō Uji." *The Eastern Buddhist* 12, no. 1 (1979): 114–29.

Waddell, Norman, and Masao Abe, trans. "Dōgen's Bendōwa." *The Eastern Buddhist* 5, no. 1 (1971): 124–57.

––––––, trans. "One Bright Pearl: Dōgen's Shōbōgenzō Ikka Myōju." *The Eastern Buddhist* 5, no. 2 (1971): 108–17.

––––––, trans. "Dōgen's Shōbōgenzō Zenki: Total Dynamic Working, and Shōji: Birth and Death." *The Eastern Buddhist* 5, no. 1 (1972): 70–80.

––––––, trans. "Shōbōgenzō Genjōkōan." *The Eastern Buddhist* 5, no. 2 (1972): 120–40.

––––––, trans. "Dōgen's Fukanzazengi and Shōbōgenzō Zazengi." *The Eastern Buddhist* 6, no. 2 (1973): 115–28.

––––––, trans. "The King of Samādhis Samādhi: Dōgen's Shōbōgenzō Sammai Ō Zammai." *The Eastern Buddhist* 7, no. 1 (1974): 118–21.

––––––, trans. "Shōbōgenzō Buddha-nature." *The Eastern Buddhist* 8, no. 2 (1975): 94–112; 9, no. 1 (1976): 87–105; 9, no. 2 (1976): 71–87.

Yokoi, Yūhō, trans. *Eihei-genzenji-shingi: Regulation for a Monastic Life by Eihei Dōgen*. Tokyo: Sankibō, 1973.

––––––, trans. *The First Step to Dōgen's Zen: Shōbōgenzō-zuimonki*. Tokyo: Sankibō, 1972.

––––––, with Daizen Victoria. *Zen Master Dōgen: An Introduction with Selected Writings*. New York and Tokyo: Weatherhill, 1976.

JAPANESE

Etō, Sokuō, ed. *Shōbōgenzō*. 3 vols. Tokyo: Iwanami Shoten, 1939–1943.

Jimbō, Nyoten, and Bun'ei Andō, eds. *Shōbōgenzō Chūkai Zensho* (Collected Commentaries of Shōbōgenzō). Tokyo: Shōbōgenzō Chūkai Zensho Kankō-kai, 1914.

Ōkubo, Dōshū, ed. *Dōgen Zenji Zenshū* (Complete Work of Zen Master Dōgen). 2 vols. Tokyo: Chikuma Shobō, 1969–1970.

Glossary and Index

Chinese names are shown in Pinyin transliteration, followed by ideograms used in East Asia. Their Japanese transliterations appear in parentheses. Names that have entries of their own are not followed by ideograms or Japanese in other references.

Translated titles of Chinese texts are followed by their original titles in Pinyin transliteration and in Chinese characters.

Sanskrit terms are indicated by the abbreviation "Skt."

Italicized foreign terms are Japanese unless otherwise specified. In accordance with Dōgen's usage, Japanese phonetic letters (*kana*) are used in a few cases instead of ideograms (*kanji*).

waging many brutal conquests, he realized the misery of war, and became a great
supporter of Buddhism and sent missionaries to foreign lands. A legendary biography
of him is found in the *King Ashoka Sūtra*. 45, 61

as it is. 129

aspiration for enlightenment. 發 心 (*hosshin*).

assembly. 61, 125, 128, 144, 148, 151, 168, 175, 180, 191, 203
  great. 119

asura. See *three heads and eight arms.*

attachment. 18, 69

attaining one finger. Cf. *Blue Cliff Record*, case 19: Priest Juzhi raised one finger whenever
asked a question.

attaining the marrow. See *skin, flesh, bones, and marrow.* 41

attaining the way. 成 道 (*jōdō*). *Jō* means becoming or completing. *Dō* (Chinese *dao*) in this
case is a translation of Skt. *bodhi* (enlightenment). Basically indicating Shākyamuni
Buddha's enlightenment under the bodhi tree. 44, 45, 53, 61, 63, 77, 106, 115, 137,
144, 147, 148, 152, 156, 159, 163

austerities. 37

autumn. 20, 138, 166
  colors. 65
  scene of. 162

auxiliary cloud hall. 重 雲 堂 (*jūundō*). A hall for zazen, eating, and sleeping, attached to the
main monks' hall. Zen monks are regarded as clouds and water, for they move about
freely with no permanent abode.

Avalokiteshvara. Skt. 觀 音 (Kannon), observer of voices; 觀 世 音 ´Kanzeon), observer of the
world voices; 觀 自 在 (Kanjizai), viewer at will. A bodhisattva of compassion, this deity
is widely worshipped and is sometimes portrayed with one thousand arms and an eye
on each hand. 38

Avatamsaka School. Skt. Huayan or Huayen School 華 嚴 宗 Established by Fazang 法 藏
(Hōzō), it flourished during the Tang Dynasty along with the Tiantai School before the
Zen School became dominant in China. Provided a theoretical background for much
Zen thought. The teaching is based on the principle in the *Avatamsaka Sūtra* of all
things interacting with one another without obstruction. As the Kegon School in Japan
it became one of the six schools of Buddhism in the Nara Period (710–794). 149

aversion. 18, 69

Avīchi Hell. Skt 阿 鼻 (Abi). 無 間 (Mugen). The hell of unceasing suffering, the worst of all
hells. 104

awakening. 1 覺 (*kaku*), meaning enlightenment. 2. 度 (*do*), bringing sentient beings across
the ocean of birth and death to the shore of enlightenment. Often translated as saving
(sentient beings). 12, 15, 17, 19, 69, 145
  broad. 146
  correct. 146
  great. 138, 180
  original. 146
  self. 147
  sentient beings. 163

Baizhang (Bozhang) Huaihai. 百 丈 懷 海 (Hyakujō Ekai). 749–814. Dharma heir of Mazu
Daoyi. Founder of Dazhi Shousheng Monastery 大 智 壽 聖 寺 at Daxiong Peak (Mt.

Baizhang), Hong Region 洪 州 (Jiangxi 江 西). Initiator of monastic regulations for Chinese Zen Buddhism. Teacher of Guishan Lingyou and Huangbo Xiyun. 62, 92, 125, 181, 182, 183, 210

Baizhang Qinggui. See *Baizhang Regulations.*

Baizhang Regulations. Baizhang Qinggui 百 丈 清 規 (Hyakujō Shingi). A book compiled by Baizhang Huaihai, which included the earliest Zen monastic rules. It has been lost but the outline is known through a later work, *Regulations for Zen Monasteries.*

Baizhang's ember. Cf. JRTL, chap. 9:

> Guishan Lingyou became tenzo in Baizhang's community. One day he went to the abbot's room and stood by his side. Baizhang said, "Who is it?" Guishan said, "It's Lingyou." Baizhang asked him, "Poke the ash to see if there is any fire." Guishan poked through the ash and said, "There is no fire." Baizhang stood up and, digging deeply into the ash, found a small glowing ember. He showed it and said, "Isn't this fire?" Guishan experienced realization and presented his understanding.

Baizhao (Bozhao) Zhiyuan. 白 兆 志 圓 (Hakuchō Shien). Ca. ninth century A.D. Dharma heir of Gantan Ziguo 感 潭 資 國 (Kantan Shikoku). Founder of Zhuqian Monastery 竺 乾 院, Mt. Baizhao (Mt. Bi 碧 山), An Region 安 州 (Hubei 湖 北), China.

ball. 158

bamboo. 78, 138
　pipes. 206
　pole. 138
　sound of. 158
　tall. 137, 138
　tube. 99

banner-pole. 158

Banzan Hōshaku. See *Panshan Baoji.*

Baoche. See *Mayu Baoche.*

Baoen Monastery (Jiangsu). See *Baoen Xuanze; Fayan Wenyi.*

Baoen Monastery (Shanxi). See *senior Fu of Taiyuan.*

Baoen Xuanze. 報 恩 玄 則 (Hōon Gensoku). Ca. ninth-tenth centuries A.D. Dharma heir of Fayan Wenyi. Abbot of Baoen Monastery, Jinling 金 陵 (Jiangsu 江 蘇), China.

Baofu Congzhan. 保 福 從 展 (Hofuku Jūten). d. 928. Dharma heir of Xuefeng Yicun. Founded Baofu Monastery, Zhang Region 漳 州 (Fujian 福 建), China, where he always had more than 700 students. 205

Baofu Monastery. See *Baofu Congzhen.*

Baoji. See *Panshan Baoji.*

Baolin Monastery. See *Dajian Huineng.*

Baoning Renyong. 保 寧 仁 勇 (Honei Nin'yū). Ca. eleventh century A.D. Dharma heir of Yangqi Fanghui, Linji School. Abbot of Baoning Monastery, Jinling 金 陵 (Jiangsu 江 蘇), China. 54

Baoqing Era. 176, 181, 185, 193

barrier. 16, 80, 82, 143, 205, 209, 210

Baso Dōitsu. See *Mazu Daoyi.*

beads. 51

beard. 45

beasts. 64, 167

School. Dharma heir of Jianzhi Sengcan. Taught for thirty years at Mt. Shuangfeng 双峰山 or West Mountain 西山, Huangmei 黄梅, Qi Region 蕲州 (Hubei 湖北). He had 500 students, the first large assembly in Zen Buddhism. Zen Master Dayi is his posthumous name.

Fourth Ancestor. 201, 209, 210

Dayuan. See *Guishan Lingyou.*

Dazheng. See *Nanyang Huizhong.*

Dazhi. See *Baizhang Huaihai.*

Dazhidu-lun. See *Commentary on the Mahāprajñāpāramitā Sūtra.*

Dazhi Shousheng Monastery. See *Baizhang Huaihai.*

Dazu Huike. 大祖慧可 (Daiso Eka). 487–593. Second Chinese Ancestor of the Zen School. According to JRTS, chap. 3, when he visited Bodhidharma at Shaolin Monastery and asked for instruction, Bodhidarma would not reply. Finally, while standing in the snow, Huike cut off his arm and gave it to Bodhidharma as a sign of his sincerity. Thus, he received instruction. Later he taught in the northern capital, Ye 鄴都 (Henan 河南). His posthumous names are Great Master Zhengzong Pujue 正宗普覺大師 (Shōshū Fukaku Daishi) and Zen Master Dazu (Daiso Zenji). 144, 168, 169, 171, 175, 184

Second Ancestor. 168, 170, 172, 180, 195, 197, 198, 199, 202

dead ash. 死灰 (*shikai*). Practice with no-seeking mind. 93

death. See *birth and death*; *great death.* 19, 70, 84, 85, 94, 163, 201

"*Death Poem.*" 219

decay and death. See *twelvefold causation of rebirth.*

decayed tree. 枯木 (*koboku*). Sitting zazen with no-seeking mind. 93, 112

Decheng. See *Chuanzi Decheng.*

decline of the dharma. See *three periods.*

defiled. 染汙 (*zenna*). Separated by dualistic conception. 87, 198

defilement. 219

degree. 階級 (*kaikyū*). See *Sacred truth doesn't do anything.*

degree of enlightenment equal to buddha's. See *ten stages and three classes of bodhisattvas.*

degree of inconceivable enlightenment. See *ten stages and three classes of bodhisattvas.*

Deguang. See *Zhuoan Deguang.*

delusion. 迷 (*mei; mayoi*); 惑 (*madoi*). 1. Lack of enlightenment. 2. Seen as not outside of enlightenment. 17, 21, 33, 42, 69, 93, 148, 150, 158, 165, 179, 180

land of. 144

delusion and enlightenment. 迷悟 (*meigo*).

Demmyō Daishi. See *Jiashan Shanhui.*

demon(s). 64, 137

faces. 135

dempō. See *dharma transmission.*

Deng Region. See *Xiangyan Zhixian.*

Denshin Hōyō. See *Huangbo Xiyun.*

Dentō-roku. See *Jingde Record of Transmission of Lamps.*

dependent origination. See *twelvefold causation of rebirth.*

Deshan Xuanjian. 德山宣鑑 (Tokusan Senkan). 780–865. His family name is Zhou 周. Well versed with the *Diamond Sūtra*, he was called Zhou Diamond. He tried to defeat Zen by argument, but became a Zen student instead. Dharma heir of Longtan Chongxin

dharma wheel. 法 輪 (*hōrin*). The buddha's discourse is called the wheel of dharma. The "wheel," a symbol of a monarch in ancient India, represented justice and the crushing of hindrances. 56, 93, 105, 116, 130, 163, 179

dharma words. 190

dhyāna. Skt. 靜 慮 (*jōryo*). Meditation. One of the six pāramitās. See also *Zen.*

dialectical thinking. 24

dialogue. 109, 110

diamond. 101

diamond seat. 金 剛 座 (*kongōza*). The name for the seat beneath the bodhi tree where Shākya-muni Buddha was sitting when he attained enlightenment. 29

differentiation. See *five ranks.* 20, 109, 110, 111, 154

dignified bearing. 威 儀 (*igi; iigi*). Expression of buddha-dharma through a monk's posture and behavior. 93

dignity. 47

Dingshan Shenying. 定 山 神 英 (*Jōsan Shin'ei*). Ca. ninth century A.D. Dharma heir of Gui-shan Lingyou. Lived at Mt. Ding, Chu Region 滁 州 (Anhui 安 徽), China. 74

directions. 92, 104

director. 50, 51, 52, 54, 157
  assistant. 54
  temple. 128

direct penetration. 6

direct transmission. 單 傳 (*tanden*). Literally, single-lined or unique transmission. Practice of a one-to-one, face-to-face transmission of dharma.

disciple. 50, 51, 52, 54, 157

discontinuity. 31

discourse. 166

discrimination. 56, 162

discriminatory consciousness. See *seven consciousnesses.*

divine heads. 135

do. See *awakening.*

dō. See *attaining the way.*

document of heritage. 嗣 書 (*shisho*). A genealogical record given by a teacher to a disciple as the proof of dharma transmission. The names of the buddha ancestors and the new heir are written by the heir and the teacher adds words of approval with his signature and seals. 6

"Document of Heritage." 186–96

Dōfuku. See *Daofu.*

Dōgen. 永 平 道 元 Eihei Dōgen. His initiatory name is 希 玄 Kigen. See Introduction.

Dōgo Enchi. See *Daowu Yuanzhi.*

dogs. 狗 子 (*kushi*). People who do not understand the way. 41, 110, 111, 116
  fierce. 111

Dōiku. See *Daoyu.*

doing zazen sitting upright. 端 坐 參 禪 (*tanza sanzen*).

dōji. See *identity-action.*

domain. See *inner chamber.* 125

Dongjing. See *Changling Shouzhuo.*

Dongshan Liangjie. 洞 山 良 价 (*Tōzan Ryōkai*). 807–869. Became a monk in childhood, stud-

the universe as a manifestation of Vairochana Buddha. The practice is based on rituals involving mudrās, mantras, and visualizations of various deities. See also *Shingon School*; *Tendai School*.

esoteric Buddhist rituals. 4, 23

esoteric school. 32

esoteric teaching. 4

essence. 144, 145

Essential Teaching of Transmission of Mind. See *Huangbo Xiyun*.

evening practice instruction (period). 暮 請 (*boshō*). Receiving personal instruction in the abbot's room. 52, 57

everyday activity. 家 常 (*kajō*). *Ka*—house, home, family, meaning the buddha's house or Buddhism. *Jō*—common, usual, normal, regular. 113, 131

"Everyday Activity." 124–8

examining. See *sankyū*.

exchanging your face. 換 面 (*kammen*). Exchanging one's face with one's true face. 178

exoteric Buddhism. 顕 教 (*kengyō*). Esoteric School's way of referring to the teachings of all other Buddhist schools.

exoteric school. 32

exoteric teaching. 4

expectation. 161

expedient phrases. 100

expedient practice. 3

expedient teaching/complete teaching. (*gonjitsu*). According to Tiantai understanding, all sūtras other than the *Lotus Sūtra* are regarded as provisional teachings. The *Lotus* is taught to be the "complete" or supreme teaching. 135

explanation. 217

expression. 80, 100, 137, 163

   complete. 127

   gentle. 47

   provisional. 209

expression complete this moment. ひ と と き の く ら ゐ (*hitotoki no kurai*). Literally, "position of one time." Dharma position or state of being itself (*hōi*) at each moment which carries entire time. 71

Extensive Record of Lamps. See *Tiansheng Extensive Record of Lamps*.

Extensive Record of Priest Eihei Dōgen. 永 平 道 元 和 尚 廣 錄 (Eihei Dōgen Oshō Kōroku), also called Eihei Kōroku. A collection of Dōgen's lectures, words, and poems compiled soon after his death by his students Sen'e, Ejō, and Gien. Published in 1672.

Extensive Record of Yunmen, Zen Master Kuangzhen. Yunmen Kuangzhen Chanshi Guanglu 雲 門 匡 眞 禪 師 廣 錄 (Ummon Kyōshin Zenji Kōroku). Sayings of Yunmen Wenyan, collected by his students after his death. Three chapters, published in 1076.

Extensive Record of Zen Master Hongzhi. Hongzhi Chanshi Guanglu 宏 智 禪 師 廣 錄 (Wanshi Zenji Kōroku), compiled by his students after his death. Completed in 1132.

extraordinary thing. 125

eye. 眼 (*gen*). 1. True seeing or understanding. 2. Essential meaning. 24, 54, 81, 105, 108, 117, 120, 138, 148, 166, 171, 176, 183, 184, 204, 216

   ancestor. 126

   celestial. 164

江 蘇), China. Author of many poems and commentaries including the *Ten Admonitions for the Zen School* 宗 門 十 句 論 (Shūmon Jikku-ron). His posthumous name is Zen Master Great-Fayan 大 法 眼 禪 師 (Daihōgen Zenji). Regarded as founder of the Fayan School.

Faying. Editor of *Threaded-Pearl Capping Verses of the Zen School.*

Fazang. See *Avatamsaka School.*

feeling. 受 (*ju*). One of the five skandhas. See also *twelvefold causation of rebirth.*

Fengxue Yanzhao. Shoushan Xingnian's teacher.

Fengyang. See *Deshan Xuanjian.*

Fifth Ancestor. See *Daman Hongren.*

fifth day of the fifth month. The day of the Dragon-boat Festival in China.

fighting spirits. See *six realms.*

final body. 最 後 身 (*saigoshin*). The state of being free from rebirth. That of an arhat; or in Mahāyāna, of a bodhisattva whose enlightenment is equal to buddha.

fined. Monks are asked to pay for a small portion of oil for the lamps, when they make careless mistakes. 52

fire on your head to be put out. See *saving your head from fire.* 50

first thought. 初 一 念 (*shoichinen*). Same as thought of enlightenment.

fish. Often represents freedom. 19, 20, 51, 71, 72, 104–6, 166, 200, 216, 219

fish's heart. 166

fishing pole. 110

fist. 拳 頭 (*kentō*). Raising a fist expresses direct understanding. 200, 205

Five Buddhas. 五 佛 (*gobutsu*). Mahāvairochana, Akshobhya, Ratnasambhava, Amitāyus (Amitābha), and Amoghasiddhi. Regarded as manifestations of the fivefold wisdom of Mahāvairochana. 149

five eyes. 五 眼 (*gogen*). Fleshly eyes, heavenly eyes, wisdom eyes, dharma eyes, and buddha eyes. Heavenly eyes are those of devas. Wisdom eyes are those of shrāvakas and pratyekabuddhas. Dharma eyes are those of bodhisattvas. 117

fivefold controlling power. 五 根 (*gokon*). 1. Trust. 2. Effort. 3. Mindfulness. 4. Concentration. 5. Wisdom. See also *thirty-seven bodhipākshikas.*

fivefold moral power. 五 力 (*goriki*). 1. Trust. 2. Effort. 3. Mindfulness. 4. Concentration. 5. Wisdom. See also *thirty-seven bodhipākshikas.*

fivefold wisdom. See *Five Buddhas.*

Five Gates. Same as Five Schools. 145

five great elements. 五 大 (*godai*). Four great elements (earth, water, fire, and air) plus space. 104

Five Lakes. 199

Five Lamps Merged in the Source. Wudeng Huiyuan 五 燈 會 元(Gotō Egen). Abbreviated edition of the five major records of Zen tradition in China. Probably edited by Dachuan Puji 大 川 普 濟 (Daisen Fusai, 1179–1253) of the Linji School. The five books are: *Jingde Record of Transmission of Lamps, Tiansheng Extensive Record of Lamps, Jianzhong Jingguo Later Record of Lamps, Arrayed Lamps of the Zen School Merged in Essence,* and *Jiatai Record of the Universal Lamps.*

Five Mountains. 五 山 (Gozan; Gosan). The highest-ranked Zen monasteries in China whose abbots were appointed by the emperor. Instituted during the reign of Emperor Ningzong of Southern Song, 1195–1225. 1. Wanshou Monastery 萬 壽 寺 Mt. Jing 徑 山, Hang Region 杭 州(Zhejiang 浙 江). 2. Lingyin Monastery 靈 隱 寺, Mt. Bei 北 山, Hang

It is like water whose nature remains the same. But as celestial beings, human beings, hungry ghosts, and fish do not carry the same effect (from past causations), they each see water differently. Celestial beings see it as jewels, people in the world see it as water, hungry ghosts see it as pus and blood, and fish see it as a palace.

Futō-roku. See *Jiatai Record of the Universal Lamps.*

future. 70, 75, 103, 121

Fuxing Fatai. 佛 性 法 泰 (Busshō Hōtai). Ca. twelfth century A.D. Dharma heir of Yuanwu Keqin, Linji School. Abbot of Mt. Dagui 大 潙 山, Tan Region 潭 州 (Hunan 湖 南), China. Zen Master Fuxing (Busshō Zenji) is his posthumous name. 112

Fuyan Qingyuan. 佛 眼 清 遠 (Butsugen Seion). 1067–1120. After studying precepts and the *Lotus Sūtra*, became dharma heir of Wuzu Fayan, Linji School, China. Also called Longmen 龍 門(Ryūmon). Zen Master Fuyan is his title given by the emperor. 191

Fuyō Dōkai. See *Furong Daokai.*

Fuzan. 23

fuzenna. See *nondefiled.*

fuzenna no shushō. See *undefiled practice and enlightenment.*

ga. See *self.*

gabyō. See *painted rice-cake; painting of a rice cake.*

Gachimen Butsu. See *Sun-face Buddha/Moon-face Buddha.*

gain, idea of. 34

Gantan Ziguo. Baizhao Zhiyuan's teacher.

Gantō Zenkatsu. See *Yantou Quanhuo.*

ganzei. See *eyeball.*

gate(s). 40, 90, 111, 147, 155, 201, 206
  authentic. 143
  front. 147

Gateless Gate. 無 門 關 Wumen Guan (Mumon-kan). One of the best known collections of kōans, along with *Blue Cliff Record* and *Book of Serenity*. Forty-eight cases, compiled by Wumen Huikai 無 門 慧 開 (Mumon Ekai) of the Linji School, China. Published in 1229. First brought to Japan by Kakushin 覺 心 in 1254. 89

ga ten hō. See *Dharma turns you, and also you turn dharma.*

Gautama. 115, 117, 118, 121

Gautama's bandits. 201

Gautama's eyeball vanished. Enlightenment that is free from enlightenment. See also *eyeball; dropping away.*

ge. See *hindrance.*

gedatsu. See *emancipation.*

gedō. See *heretics.*

gen. 眼 See *eye.*

gen. 現 See *actualization.*

general. An element of the five ranks. 20, 219

genjō. See *actualization.* 19

genjō kōan. See *actualizing the fundamental point.*

"*Genjo Kōan.*" 25

Gensha Shibi. See *Xuansha Shibei.*

gentle melancholy. 20

gimlet. A term used to indicate a sharp, penetrating Zen master. 89, 119

giving. 布 施 (*fuse*). One of the six pāramitās. Also one of the bodhisattva's four methods of guidance. See "Bodhisattva's Four Methods of Guidance" in the text. 44, 45

go. See *enlightenment.* 110

goat. 110

When Guishan Lingyou was studying with Baizhang, he was working together with Baizhang in the mountain. Baizhang said, "Fetch some fire." Guishan said, "Here you are." Baizhang said, "What is it?" Guishan picked up a dead branch, blew on it three times, and gave it to Baizhang. Baizhang acknowledged it.

Guishan Lingyou. 潙 山 靈 裕 (Isan Reiyū). 771–853. Dharma heir of Baizhang Huaihai. Along with his dharma brother Huangbo, he became a renowned Zen master of the Tang Dynasty. Taught at Mt. Gui (Mt. Dagui or Great-Guishan 大 潙 山), Tan Region 潭 州 (Hunan 湖 南), China, and raised excellent students including Yangshan Huiji. His words are collected in *Guishan's Guiding Stick* 潙 山 警 策 (Isan Kyōsaku). His post-humous name is Zen Master Dayuan 大 圓 禪 師 (Daien Zenji). Regarded as co-founder of the Guiyang School. 53, 57, 65, 127, 173, 194, 244(n.3)

Great. 64

Guishan's water buffalo. Cf. JRTL, chap. 9:

One day master Guishan taught the assembly, "After I have passed away I will become a water buffalo at the foot of the mountain. On the left side of the buffalo's chest the characters, "I am a monk of Guishan," will be written. When you call me the monk of Guishan, I will be a water buffalo. When you call me water buffalo, I will be a monk of Guishan. Then how are you going to call me?" 57

Guixing. See *Shexian Guixing.*

Guiyang School. 潙 仰 宗 (Igyō-shū). One of the Five Schools of Chinese Zen Buddhism, developed earlier than the other schools in the ninth century A.D. and perished in the tenth century. Named after Guishan Lingyou and Yangshan Huiji. 145

gūjin. 究 盡. Full, thorough practice. Complete mastery of the way.

Gutei. See *Juzhi.*

gyō. See *practice; impulses.*

gyōsoku. See *raising his foot.*

Gyōzan Ejaku. See *Yangshan Huiji.*

hachiman shisen. See *eighty-four thousand.*

hachi nansho. See *eight difficult situations.*

Haihui Shouduan. 海 會 守 端 (Kaie Shutan). 1025–1072. Dharma heir of Yangqi Fanghui, Linji School. Abbot of Haihui Monastery, Mt. Boyun 白 雲 山, Shu Region 舒 州 (Anhui 安 徽), China.

Haikyū. See *Minister Fang.*

hair, a single. 41

hair tuft. See *white hair tuft.*

Hajun. See *Pāpīyas.*

hakkai. See *eight precepts.*

Hakuchō Shien. See *Baizhao Zhiyuan.*

Hakuin Ekaku. See *Rinzai School.*

hakujushi. See *cypress tree.*

half a mango. In the last part of his life King Ashoka, after giving away everything to the Buddhist monks, had only half a mango left to him, which satisfied the entire community. (*King Ashoka Sūtra*, chap. 5) 45, 61

hammer. 147

hamokushaku. See *broken wooden dipper.*

hannya. See *prajñā.*

haramitsu. See *six pāramitās.*

jippō. See *ten directions.*

Jisai Daishi. See *Touzi Datong.*

jisshō sanken. See *ten stages and three classes of bodhisattvas.*

jissō. See *true suchness.*

jō. See *attaining the way; actualization.*

jō. See *everyday activity.*

jōdō. See *attaining the way.*

Jōin Hōjō. See *Jingyin Facheng.*

jōroku hasshaku. See *eight- or sixteen-foot body.*

jōroku konjin. See *sixteen-foot golden body.*

jōryo. See *dhyāna.*

Jōsan Shin'ei. See *Dingshan Shenying.*

Jōshū Jūshin. See *Zhaozhou Congshen.*

Jōshū Shinzai Zhenji Goroku. See *Recorded Sayings of Zen Master Zhenji of Zhaozhou.*

ju. 受. See *feeling.*

ju. 呪. See *mantra.*

jūaku. See *ten unwholesome actions.*

Judun. See *Longya Judun.*

Juefan Huihong. Editor of *Record of the Forests.*

jūgō. See *ten names.*

jūhōi/jūi. See *abiding in the phenomenal expression.*

jūji. See *ten stages and three classes of bodhisattvas.*

juko. See *capping verses.*

jūni bunkyō. See *twelve divisions.*

jūni innen. See *twelvefold causation of rebirth.*

jūni ji. See *twelve hours.*

juniors. 50, 75

jūni rinden. See *twelvefold causation of rebirth.*

Junsō. See *Emperor Shunzong.*

just this. 82

just this moment. 正當恁麼時 (*shōtō immo ji*). Literally, the very moment of suchness.

Jutsui-ki. See *Record of Extraordinary Stories.*

jūūndō. See *auxiliary cloud hall.*

Juzhi. 俱胝 (Kutei; Gutei). Ca. ninth century A.D. Dharma heir of Tianlong. Juzhi always responded to dharma questions by simply raising his finger.

Juzhi's one finger. See *attaining one finger.*

ka. See *everyday activity.*

Kaidō Soshin. Qingyuan Weixin's teacher.

Kaie Shutan. See *Haihui Shouduan.*

kaikyū. See *degree.*

kainō. See *turning the body and flapping the brain.*

Kaiō Gomyō. Editor of *Arrayed Lamps of the Zen School Merged in Essence.*

kaitō. See *turning your head.*

kajō. See *everyday activity.*

kakkei. 活計. Full, vital activity.

kaku. See *awakening; enlightenment.*

kakugai. See *world beyond conditions.*

Mahāprajñāpāramitā Sūtra. An extensive Mahāyāna sūtra, teaching that all phenomena are emptiness. A seventh-century Chinese translation by Xuanzhuang 玄 奘 (Genjō) contains 600 chapters.

Mahāvairochana. See *Vairochana.*

Mahāyāna. 大 乘 (*daijō*). The "great" vehicle or teaching of Buddhism, indicating either the Bodhisattva Vehicle, or the One Vehicle.

Mahāyāna Buddhist teaching(s). 14, 149, 156

Mahāyāna precepts. 4

Mahāyāna Shamatha and Vipashyanā. See *Nanyue Huisi.*

Maheshvara. See *eye at the top of the head.*

maitrī. See *compassion.*

Makakashō. See *Mahākāshyapa.*

make three bows and return standing. See *skin, flesh, bones, and marrow.*

malevolent spirit. 修 羅 (*shura*). Skt. *asura.* A fighting spirit. See also *six realms.*

manas. See *six sense-organs.*

māndāra. Skt. 曼 陀 羅 華 (*mandarage*). Blossoms of the heavenly world whose color and fragrance make people joyous. The plant has many leaves that give people shade and comfort. 117

mandarage. See *māndāra.*

mango. See *half a mango.*

manifestation. Japanese *genjō.* See *actualization.* 134, 163

manjushage. See *manjūshaka.*

manjūshaka. Skt. 曼 殊 沙 華 (*manjushage*). Soft, white blossoms, which are rained down by heavenly beings and free the viewers from wrong actions. 117

Manjushrī. 文 殊 (Monju). The bodhisattva of wisdom whose image is usually enshrined in the center of the monks' hall.

mano-vijñāna. See *seven consciousnesses.*

mantra. 眞 言 (*shingon*). Literally, true word; 呪 (*ju*), magical spell. Indicates a dhāranī, especially a short dhāranī. 155

Mantra School. See *Shingon School.* 149

many. See *the many and the one.*

Manzan Dōhaku. 23

Maoqiang/Xishi. 毛 嬙 (Mōshō), 西 施 (Seishi). Two beautiful women of ancient China described in *Zhuangzi* 莊 子. 31

Māra-Pāpīyas. See *Pāpīyas.*

mark. 101, 215
　hitting the. 43, 159, 198

marrow. 92, 118, 120, 169, 170, 172, 176, 180, 217, 252(n.7)

marrow is attained. 得 髓 (*tokuzui*). See *skin, flesh, bones, and marrow.*

ma sangin. See *three jin of hemp.*

masen. See *polishing a brick.*

master(s). 43, 105, 145, 150, 155, 158, 172, 178, 180, 189–92, 204, 207
　ancient. 55, 59
　authentic. 156
　correct. 183
　old. 112, 164
　real. 62

Mount Yunyan. See *Yunyan Tansheng*. 203

Mount Zhimen. 208

movement. 132

mu. 無. (Chinese *wu*). No, nothing, or nothingness. Cf. *Hongzhi's Capping Verses*, case 18:
　　. . . A monk asked Zhaozhou, "Does a dog have buddha nature or not?" Zhaozhou
　　said, "*Mu*."
　　Later this kōan was included in the *Gateless Gate*, as its first case. This *mu* is often
　　regarded as a complete denial of dualistic interpretations. 41

mud, lump of. 198

　within. 110

mud and water. See *splattered with mud and wet with water*.

muga. See *no-self*.

Mugai Gion. Editor of *Recorded Sayings of Zen Master Eihei Gen*.

Mugen. See *Unceasing Hell*.

mui. See *unconditioned*.

mujō jibaku. See *binding the self with no-rope*.

mujō jinsoku. See *impermanent world passing away swiftly*.

mujō zammai. See *samādhi without conflict*.

Mujū Daishi. See *Yunyan Tansheng*.

Mumon Ekai. Compiler of the *Gateless Gate*.

Mumon-kan. See *Gateless Gate*.

Mu Region. See *Muzhou Daoming*.

Muromachi Period. 23

Musai Daishi. See *Shitou Xiqian*.

Musai Ryōha. See *Wuji Liaopai*.

muscle. 138

mushi dokugo. See *realization without a teacher*.

mushotoku. See *not-attaining*.

Musōten. See *Heaven of No Thought*.

mutual heritage. 相嗣 (*sōshi*). Realization outside of time, beyond before and after. In the
　　merged realization of teacher and disciple, disciple inherits dharma from the teacher
　　and the teacher inherits dharma from the disciple. Cf. "Document of Heritage," section
　　4: "Shākyamuni Buddha inherited dharma from Kāshyapa Buddha. . . . Kāshyapa
　　Buddha inherited dharma from Shākyamuni Buddha." 187

Muzhou Daoming. 睦州道明 (Bokushū Dōmyō). Ca. ninth century. Dharma heir of Huangbo
　　Xiyun. Lived in Mu Region 睦州 (Zhejiang 浙江), China, and taught more than one
　　hundred students. Then left his students and made straw sandals to support his mother.
　　Also called venerable master Chen 陳尊宿 (Chin Sonshuku). 173

muzōsa. See *unconditioned*.

Myōan Eisai. 明庵栄西. 1141–1215. Became a monk of the Tendai School, Japan, at fifteen.
　　Went to China in 1168 and brought back Tiantai texts. Made a second visit to China
　　between 1185 and 1191 to study Zen Buddhism. Dharma heir of Xuan Huaichang
　　虛庵懷敞 (Kian Eshō), Linji School. Author of *On Raising Zen and Protecting the Nation*
　　興禪護國論 (Kōzen Gokoku-ron). Founded Kennin Monastery 建仁寺 in Kyoto.
　　Regarded as the founder of the Rinzai School, the Japanese form of the Linji School.
　　4, 5, 6, 144

myōjō. See *morning star*.

nirmāna-kāya. See *buddha body.*

nirvāna. Skt. 涅槃 (*nehan*). The state of enlightenment attained by Shākyamuni Buddha, or by any buddha. Literally, extinction of fire, meaning extinction of desires, or liberated from the cycle of birth, death, and rebirth. 14, 74, 79, 80, 90, 132, 154, 175, 209
  inconceivable mind of. 22, 151

Nishiari, Bokuzan. 244–5(n. 1)

Nishiyama, Kōsen. 25

Ni Sōji. See *nun Zongchi.*

Niutou Farong. 牛頭法融 (Gozu Hōyū). 594–657. Said to be a dharma heir of Fourth Ancestor Daoxin. His lineage is called Niutou School or Ox-head School 牛頭宗 (Gozu-shū), in contrast to Fifth Ancestor Hongren's Dongshan School 東山宗 (Tōzan-shū). His teaching emphasized thoroughness and logic. 209, 210

Niutou School. See *Niutou Farong.*

no. See *mu.*

no abiding. 41

no attaching. 41

no birth. 70, 117, 163

no-birth, no-death. 不生不死 (*fushō fushi*). Birth and death as the experience of nirvāna. See *nirvāna.* 71, 75

noble path. See *eightfold noble path.* 137, 179

no-death. See *no-birth, no-death.* 71

nodes in bamboo/knots in wood. 節目 (*setsumoku*). Hindrance of dualistic thinking; complicated theories. 36, 143

nōe. See *patched robe.*

no hindrance. 209

no hunger. 139

no-name. 207

nonattachment. 18

nonbeing. 79

nondefiled. 不染汗 (*fuzenna*). Not colored with dualistic separation, especially between practice and realization. See *What is it that thus comes?*

nondifference. 46

nonduality. 不二 (*funi*). Literally, not two. See *wholeness.* 16, 18

nongreed. 44

nonintending/nonintentionally. See *unconditioned.* 52

noninterfering. 112

nonmerging. 不回互 (*fuego*). No more merging in complete merging of realization. 218

nonscriptural nature. 22

nonseparate/nonseparateness. See *wholeness.*

nonthinking. 非思量 (*hishiryō*). Cf. TTDE, "The Point of Zazen" (Zazen-shin):
  When Great Master Hongdao of Yaoshan was sitting, a monk asked, "What is thinking in steadfast composure like?" The master said, "Think not-thinking." The monk said, "How do you think not-thinking?" The master said, "Nonthinking." 30, 88, 218
  In contrast to "thinking" 思量 (*shiryō*) and "not-thinking" 不思量 (fushiryō), "nonthinking" describes the unrestricted mind in zazen where one tries neither to develop nor to suppress thoughts which are continually arising.

Recorded Sayings of Priest Rujing. Rujing Heshang Yulu. 如淨和尚語錄 (Nyojō Oshō Goroku). Edited by Tiantong Rujing's students in 1229, soon after his death.

Recorded Sayings of Zen Master Eihei Gen. 永平元禪師語錄 (Eihei Gen Zenji Goroku). An abbreviated version of the *Extensive Record of Priest Eihei Dōgen,* edited by Dōgen's dharma brother Wuwai Yiyuan 無外義遠 (Mugai Gion) of Ruiyan Monastery, China, in 1264. Published in Japan in 1358.

Recorded Sayings of Zen Master Fuguo Yuanwu. Fuguo Yuanwu Chanshi Yulu 佛果圜悟禪師語錄 (Bukka Engo Zenji Goroku). Words of Yuanwu Kiqin, collected by his students after his death. Twenty chapters, published in the Ming Dynasty.

Recorded Sayings of Zen Master Zhenji of Zhaozhou. Zhaozhou Zhenji Chanshi Yulu 趙州眞際禪師語錄 (Jōshū Shinsai Zenji Goroku). Words of Zhaozhou Congshen edited by his students after his death. Three chapters. Completed in 953.

Record of Baoqing Era. 寶慶記 (Hōkyō-ki). Dōgen's record of Rujing's personal instructions to him, recorded during his stay at Mt. Tiantong between the first and third years of Baoqing Era (1225–1227). Written in Chinese. Edited by Ejō after Dōgen's death. Published in 1750. 4, 5

Record of Eihei Dōgen. 永平錄 (Eihei-roku). Probably refers to *Recorded Sayings of Zen Master Eihei Gen.* 24, 223, 224

Record of Extraordinary Stories. Shuyi-ji 述異記 (Jutsui-ki). A collection of mysterious stories attributed to Renfang 任昉 (Jimbō) [460–508].

Record of the Forests. Linjian-lu 林間錄 (Rinkan-roku). A collection of Zen Buddhist stories edited by Juefan Huihong 覺範慧洪 (Kakuhan Ekō) of the Linji School. Published in 1107.

Record of the Universal Lamps. See *Jiatai Record of the Universal Lamps.*

Record of Things Heard. See *Treasury of the True Dharma Eye: Record of Things Heard.*

reflection. 70, 71, 149

refraining from all unwholesome actions. See *to refrain from all unwholesome actions and to respectfully practice wholesome actions.*

Regulations for Zen Monasteries. Chanyuan Qinggui 禪苑清規 (Zennen Shingi). A Chinese collection of guidelines for a monastic life, written in the early twelfth century by Changlu Zongze 長蘆宗頤 (Chōro Sōsaku) of the Yunmen School. Published in 1103. 53, 54, 55, 61, 62, 64

"Regulations for the Auxiliary Cloud Hall." 7, 49–52

Reigen Isei. Teacher of Changling Shouzhuo.

reikai. See *cold ash.*

Reiun Shigon. See *Lingyun Zhiqin.*

remedy. 138, 218

Renfang. See *Record of Extraordinary Stories.*

Renju Tsūshū. See *Threaded-Pearl Capping Verses of the Zen School.*

renmo. See *suchness.*

Rentō Eyō. See *Arrayed Lamps of the Zen School Merged in Essence.*

Requested by Children. Mengqiu 蒙求 (Mōgyū). Anecdotes of ancient people compiled by Li Han 李瀚 (Ri Kan) of the later Jin Dynasty, China. Three chapters.

resonating with the way. 感應道交 (kannō dōko). Responding to the buddha's awakening of sentient beings.

Renyong. See *Baoning Renyong.*

repentence. 51, 145

sage of Huating. See *Jiashan Shanhui*.

sai. See *noon meal*.

Saichō. See *Tendai School*.

saigoshin. See *final body*.

saindhava. Skt. 仙 陀 婆 (*sendaba*). Meaning salt, vessel, water, and horse. According to the *Mahāparinirvāna Sūtra*, chap. 9, when a king asked his retainers to bring saindhava, a wise retainer could understand which saindhava the king referred to without receiving further explanation. Thus, saindhava indicates direct communication. 206

samādhi. Skt. 三 昧 (*sammai*). Concentration. Serene, settled, collected state of mind. 30, 93, 117, 143, 145, 147, 150, 166

   eyes of. 131

samādhi without conflict. 無 諍 三 昧 (*mujō zammai*). See *stepping over the head of Vairochana*. 202

sambhoga-kāya. See *buddha body*.

sambō. See *three treasures*.

sammai. See *samādhi*.

sammyō. See *three cognitions*.

sanchō. See *leaping over*.

sand. 64, 110, 149

   of the Ganges. 147

sandals. 艸 鞋 (*sōai*) Represent nonintellectual understanding. 111, 183, 188

Sandōkai. See *Shitou Xiqian*.

sangai. See *three worlds*.

sangai isshin. See *triple-world-one-mind*.

sangai yui-isshin. 三 界 唯 一 心 . Literally, triple-world-one-mind-only. See *triple-world-one-mind*.

sangaku. See *three learnings*.

sangha. 僧 伽 (*sōgya*); 僧 (*sō*). Community of those who are practicing Buddhism. One of the three treasures.

sangō. See *three actions*.

sanji. See *three periods*.

sanjin. See *three bodies*.

sanjō. See *Three Vehicles*.

sanjū bō. See *thirty blows*.

sanjūni sō. See *thirty-two marks*.

sanjūshichi bodai bumpō. See *thirty-seven bodhipākshikas*.

sankyū. 參 究 . To thoroughly study, examine, or investigate.

sanseken. See *three thousand realms*.

Sanshō. See *Anthology of Enlightenment Poems by the Ancestor of Sanshō*.

Sanshō Doei-shū. See *Anthology of Enlightenment Poems by the Ancestor of Sanshō*.

santetsu. 參 徹 . Complete study and penetration.

santoku. See *three virtues*.

sanze. See *three worlds*.

sanzen. See *three thousand realms*.

sanzen sekai. See *trichiliocosm*.

San ze san, sui ze sui. See *Mountains are mountains, waters are waters*.

sanzō. See *tripitaka*.

sanzu happi. See *three heads and eight arms*.

Sekkō. See *Minister She's love for a dragon.*

self. 1. 我 (*ga*). Ego as an independent entity. Buddhism denies the existence of "self" in this sense. See *five skandhas.* 2. 自己 (*jiko*). A person. 3. 自己 (*jiko*). A person who has realized selflessness which is not separate from the universe. See *original self.* われ (*ware*) can be used for any of these meanings. 17, 32, 33, 46, 47, 70, 77, 78, 89, 97, 102, 106, 110, 157, 162, 163, 164, 165, 166, 179, 182, 183, 186, 200, 206, 209

  abiding. 17, 69

  ignorant. 213

  true. 17, 164

  unchanging. 70

  -views. 36

self-fulfilling samādhi. 自受用三昧 (*jijuyū zammai*). The buddha's realizing and utilizing the joy of samādhi, sometimes contrasted with the aspect of 他受用三昧 (*tajuyū zammai*), the joyful samādhi shared with other beings. 143, 145, 146, 148, 149

selflessness. 17, 21

self-views. See *self,* 1.

sendaba. See *saindhava.*

sendai. See *icchāntika.*

Sengcan. See *Jianzhi Sengcan.*

sengen. See *one thousand eyes.*

Senika. 先尼 (Senni). A Brahman scholar described in the *Mahāparinirvāna Sūtra,* chap. 39, who asserted permanency of soul, but was argued down by Shākyamuni Buddha.

senior Fu of Taiyuan. 太原孚上座 (Taigen Fu Jōza). Ca. ninth–tenth centuries A.D. Dharma heir of Xuefeng Yicun. Lived at Baoen Monastery 報恩寺, Taiyuan (Shanxi 山西), China. 65, 122, 123

senior Fu's realization. According to FLMS, chap. 7: Senior Fu of Taiyuan was lecturing on the *Mahāparinirvāna Sūtra,* when a traveling monk, tenzo of Jiashan, laughed. Later he asked the monk why he had laughed. After some dialogue the monk said, "You explained that the dharma body is immeasurable but you do not really understand the dharma body." Fu asked him to explain. Following the monk's advice he sat upright in concentration and entered realization.

seniors. 46, 50, 75

Senni. See *Senika.*

Sensu Tokujō. See *Chuanzi Decheng.*

sentient beings. 衆生 (*shujō*); 生 (*shō*). Living beings including human beings. It also refers to unawakened people in contrast to buddhas, as in the term "sentient beings and buddhas." 7, 17, 35, 39, 44, 45, 46, 56, 69, 75, 77, 79, 106, 143, 144, 155, 210

Seppō Gison. See *Xuefeng Yicun.*

serpents. 34

Seson. See *World-honored One.*

Sessen. See *Snow Mountain.*

Setchō Chikan. Tiantong Rujing's teacher.

Setchō Jūken. See *Xuedou Zhongxian.*

Setchō Oshō Hyakusoku Juko. See *Xuedou Zhongxian.*

setsu. See *intimate.*

Setsuan Tokkō. See *Zhuoan Deguang.*

Setsugū. See *Snow Palace.*

shippei. See *arched bamboo staff.*

shippō. See *seven treasures.*

shiryō. See *nonthinking.*

shisho. See *document of heritage.*

shi shōgon. See *four right efforts.*

shishū. See *Four Continents.*

Shishuang Chuyuan. See *Linji School.*

shissui. See *six officers.*

Shitou Xiqian. 石頭希遷 (Sekitō Kisen). 700–790. Ordained by Huineng, after whose death he studied with Qingyuan Xingsi. As he did zazen continually in a hut built on a rock at Nan Monastery 南寺, Mt. Heng 衡山(Hunan 湖南), China, he was called Priest Rock Head (Shitou). Author of "Understanding of One and Many" 參同契 (Sandōkai) and "Song of the Grass Hut" 草菴歌 (Sōan-ka). His posthumous name is Great Master Wuji 無際大師 (Musai Daishi). 78, 80, 81, 125, 208, 209

shō. 升. A little. One *shō* is approximately half a gallon at present; in the thirteenth century it was less.

shō. 生. See *birth; sentient beings.*

shō. 正. See *five ranks.*

shō. 證. See *enlightenment.*

shoaku makusa. See *to refrain from all unwholesome actions and to respectfully practice wholesome actions.*

shōbō. See *three periods.*

shōbōgenzō/Shōbōgenzō. See *treasury of the true dharma eye; Treasury of the True Dharma Eye.*

Shōbōgenzō Keiteki. 244–5(n.1)

Shōbōgenzō Zuimon-ki. See *Treasury of the True Dharma Eye: Record of Things Heard.*

shobutsu. See *all buddhas.*

shobutsu no daidō. See *buddha way.*

Shōdō-ka. See *Yongjia Xuanjue.*

shōheki. See *wall.*

shohō. See *all things.*

shohō jissō. See *true suchness of all things.*

shoichinen. See *first thought.*

shōji. See *birth and death.*

shōjin. See *vigorous effort.*

shōjō. See *Hīnayāna.*

shōjō no shū. See *practice on realization.*

shōken. See *encountering.*

Shōko. See *Chenggu.*

shōmon. See *shrāvaka.*

Shōnawashu. See *Shānavāsa.*

shore. 70, 85, 131

Shōshū Fukaku Daishi. See *Dazu Huike.*

shōtai fui. See *Sacred truth doesn't do anything.*

shōtō immo ji. See *just this moment.*

Shouchu. See *Dongshan Shouchu.*

Shouduan. See *Haihui Shouduan.*

shoulder robe. See *kashāya.*

Suimi Mugaku. Touzi Datong's teacher.

Sui Region. See *Zhimen Guangzuo.*

suishu. See *reaching out with your arms.*

Sumeru. Skt. 須彌 (*Shumi*); 迷盧 (*Meiro*). According to Indian mythology there are nine mountains and eight oceans in the world (on earth) around four continents, with Mt. Sumeru at the center. 87, 100

summer. 13, 19, 138

summer practice period. 59, 60

summit. 108, 125

sun. 寸 Japanese measurement which corresponds to Chinese *cun.* One *cun* was 3.072 cm. during the Song Dynasty. 87, 113, 115, 129, 188, 208, 218

sun-face. 218

Sun-face Buddha/Moon-face Buddha. 日面佛月面佛 (*Nichimen Butsu, Gachimen Butsu*). According to the *Buddhas' Names Sūtra,* Sun-face Buddha lives for 1,800 years while Moon-face Buddha lives for one day and night. Cf. *Blue Cliff Record,* case 3:
    Great master Mazu was sick. The temple director said, "How have you been?"
    The great master said, "Sun-face Buddha, Moon-face Buddha." 131, 182

sun-face moon-face. 日面月面 (*nichimen gachimen*). Immeasurable time and short moments. See *Sun-face Buddha/Moon-face Buddha.*

sun (Japanese measurement). 193, 194

sunlight, swift passage of. 31

Sushan Kuangren. 疎山匡仁 (Sozan Kyōnin). Ca. ninth century A.D. Dharma heir of Dongshan Liangjie. Taught at Mt. Su, Fu Region 撫州 (Jiangxi 江西), China.

sūtra. Skt. 經 (*kyō*). Literally, warp as in weaving, later meaning principle of the teaching. Now refers to Indian Buddhist scriptures which take the form of a discourse by Buddha as heard and verified by one of his disciples. See also *tripitaka; twelve divisions.* 32, 38, 39, 51, 55, 63, 104, 135, 147, 148, 156, 183, 186, 218, 249(n.19)

Sūtra of Complete Enlightenment. A Mahāyāna scripture of which the Chinese version is *Yuanjue-jing* 圓覺經 (Engaku-kyō). One chapter. Expounds the practice of meditation and the principle of a complete, immediate awakening.

Suvarna Prabhāsottama Sūtra. Golden Beam Sūtra, or Most Excellent Golden Beam King Sūtra. In East Asia this Mahāyāna scripture was often recited and enshrined for the protection of the nation.

Suzuki, Shunryū. 25

swallow. 吞却 (*donkyaku*). Entirely experiencing. 130, 131

swamps. 107

sword. 112

tadei taisui. See *splattered with mud and wet with water.*

Taibo. See *Five Mountains.* 144

Taigen Fu Jōza. See *senior Fu of Taiyuan.*

Taihei Egon. See *Taiping Huiqin.*

taiho. See *walking backward and backward walking.*

taike. See *great house.*

tail. 94, 109

Taiping Huiqin. 太平慧懃 (Taihei Egon). 1059–1117. Dharma heir of Wuzu Fayan, Linji School. Abbot of Xingguo Monastery 興國寺, Mt. Taiping (Mt. Yang 仰山), Yuan Region 袁州 (Jiangxi 江西), China. Also called Zen Master Fujian 佛鑒禪師 (Bukkan Zenji). 112

instant of. 216

logical. 100

outside. 36

prior. 162

thought of enlightenment. 菩 提 心 (*bodai shin*). The wish and quest for enlightenment that establish the determination to practice. 31, 32, 63, 87, 90, 91, 144, 150, 165, 166

thousand eyes. See *one thousand eyes.*

Threaded-Pearl Capping Verses of the Zen School. Chanzong Songgu Lianzhu Tongji 禪 宗 頌 古 聯 珠 通 集 (Zenshū Juko Renju Tsūshū). A collection of verse commentaries on a wide range of kōans. Edited by Faying 法 應 (Hōō). Published in 1179. Supplemented by Puhui 普 會 (Fue) in 1317.

three actions. 三 業 (*sangō*). Body, speech, and mind. 145

three baskets. See *tripitaka.*

three bodies. 三 身 (*sanjin*). See *buddha body.*

three chiliocosms. See *trichiliocosm.*

three classes. See *ten stages and three classes of bodhisattvas.*

three cognitions. 三 明 (*sammyō*). Three types of supernormal power: Knowledge of previous births, The heavenly eye, which sees the future, Knowledge gained through the extinction of desires. 137

three eyes. The first three of the five eyes.

three heads and eight arms. 三 頭 八 臂 (*sanzu happi*). An asura, a fierce and wrathful deity or fighting spirit. See also *six realms.* 76, 77, 78, 79

three jin of hemp. 麻 三 斤 (*ma sangin*). Cf. *Blue Cliff Record,* case 12: A monk asked Dongshan Shouchu, "What is Buddha?" Dongshan said, "Three *jin* of hemp." (In Tang and Song Dynasties one *jin* 斤 [*kin*] was approximately 600 grams.) 64, 65

three learnings. 三 學 (*sangaku*). Precepts, concentration, and wisdom. 150

three lower realms. Worlds of animals, hungry ghosts, and hell-beings. 145

three periods. 三 時 (*sanji*). The three stages of Buddhist teaching after Shākyamuni Buddha passed away: The period of the true dharma 正 法 (*shōbō*), when teaching, practice, and enlightenment exist; The period of the imitative dharma 像 法 (*zōhō*), when teaching and practice remain; The period of the decline of the dharma 末 法 (*mappō*), when there remains only teaching. Not found in sūtras but believed by some Chinese and Japanese Buddhists. In Japan there was a theory that A.D. 1052 was the first year of the period of the dharma's decay.

   last age of decline. 156

   periods of truth, imitation, and decline. 156

three thousand realms. 三 千 (*sanzen*). According to Tiantai doctrine, a momentary thought contains ten realms—hell, hungry ghosts, animals, fighting spirits, humans, devas, shrāvakas, pratyekabuddhas, bodhisattvas, and buddhas. Each of these realms again contains ten realms. Each of the one hundred realms includes ten essential qualities— form, nature, embodiment, powers, function, primary cause, environmental cause, effect, karmic reward, inevitability of all of these. Each of the one thousand manifestations appears in each of the three worlds (*sanseken*)—that of the five skandhas, that of place or country, that of sentient beings. 32

three treasures. 三 寶 (*sambō*). Buddha, dharma, sangha. All Buddhists take refuge in these. 64, 91

Three Vehicles. 三 乘 (*sanjō*). Types of teaching in response to the capacities of people: Shrāvaka

triple-world-one-mind/triple-world-mind-only. 三界一心 (*sangai isshin*); 三界唯一心 (*sangai yui isshin*). All things in the three realms of desire, form, and no-form appear from mind, and nothing exists outside mind. A teaching of *Avatamsaka Sūtra*.

true body. See *buddha body.*

true dharma. See *three periods.* 7, 22, 116

true dharma eye. 18

true dharma nature. 4

true dragon. See *dragon.*

true human body. See *buddha body.*

true, imitation, and declined periods. See *three periods.*

true man. 194

true nature. 99

true person. 54, 138, 200

True Scripture for Penetrating the Subtle. See *Wenzi.*

true source. 5

true suchness. 實相 (*jissō*). 117

true suchness of all things. 諸法實相 (*shohō jissō*). Things as they are, which are not outside of ultimate truth. Cf. *Lotus Sūtra*, "Skillful Means": Only a buddha and a buddha can finally master the true suchness of all things.

true teaching. 117

trunk. 177

trust. 42, 89

   correct. 42

   right. 148, 158, 159

truth. See *dharma.* 45, 79, 99, 102, 164, 253(n.8)

   complete. 219

   ground of. 37

   single. 22

   universal. 22

   varying your. 56

tsū. See *penetration.*

Tsūgen Shinkyō. See *Wenzi.*

tsūsu. See *six officers.*

turning bodies. 198

turning body and mind. 轉身轉心 (*tenshin tenshin*). To have freedom of body and mind where a barrier is no longer an obstacle. 118

turning dharma. See *Dharma turns you, and also you turn dharma.*

turning dharma wheel. 轉法輪 (*tembōrin*). See *dharma wheel.*

turning point. 轉處 (*tensho*). The "ultimate" realm from which one goes further beyond. 208, 209

turning the body and flapping the brain. 翻身回腦 (*honshin kainō*). Turning deluded body and mind around and entering enlightenment. 94

turning things, being turned by things. 56

turning your head. 廻頭 (*kaitō*). Looking back or inward.

twelve divisions. 十二分教 (*jūni bunkyō*). Classifications of the Buddhist scriptures: Sūtras, or discourses in prose, Discourses in prose and verse, Verse, Causes and conditions of